BURKE AND HARE

ANATOMY
AND
PHYSIOLOGY.

DR KNOX, F.R.S.E. (*Successor to* **DR BARCLAY**, *Fellow of the Royal College of Surgeons and Conservator of its Museum*) will commence his ANNUAL COURSE of LECTURES ON THE **ANATOMY** AND **PHYSIOLOGY** of the Human Body, on Tuesday, the 4th November, at Eleven A.M. His evening COURSE of LECTURES, on the same Subject, will commence on the 11th November, at Six P.M.

Each of these Courses will as usual comprise a full Demonstration on fresh Anatomical Subjects, of the Structure of the Human Body, and a History of the Uses of its various Parts; and the Organs and Structures generally, will be described with a constant reference to Practical Medicine and Surgery.

FEE for the First Course, £3, 5s.; Second Course, £2, 4s.; Perpetual, £5, 9s.

N.B. – *These Courses of Lectures qualify for Examination before the various Colleges and Boards.*

PRACTICAL ANATOMY
AND
OPERATIVE SURGERY.

DR KNOX'S ROOMS FOR **PRACTICAL ANATOMY** AND **OPERATIVE SURGERY**, will open on Monday, the 6th of October, and continue open until the End of July 1829.

Two DEMONSTRATIONS will be delivered daily to the Gentlemen attending the Rooms for PRACTICAL ANATOMY. These Demonstrations will be arranged so as to comprise complete Courses of the DESCRIPTIVE ANATOMY of the Human Body, with its application to PATHOLOGY and OPERATIVE SURGERY. The Dissections and Operations to be under the immediate superintendance of DR KNOX. Arrangements have been made to secure as usual an ample supply of Anatomical Subjects.

FEE for the First Course, £3, 5s.; Second Course, £2, 4s.; Perpetual, £5, 9s.

N.B. – *An Additional Fee of Three Guineas includes Subjects.*

** *Certificates of Attendance on these Courses qualify for Examination before the Royal Colleges of Surgeons, the Army and Navy Medical Boards, &c.*

EDINBURGH, 10. SURGEONS' SQUARE,

25th September 1828

BURKE AND HARE

THE YEAR OF THE GHOULS

BRIAN BAILEY

MAINSTREAM
PUBLISHING

EDINBURGH AND LONDON

First published in Great Britain 2002 by
MAINSTREAM PUBLISHING (EDINBURGH) LTD
7 Albany Street
Edinburgh EH1 3UG

ISBN 1 84018 575 9

A catalogue record for this book is available from the British Library

Typeset in Garamond

Printed in Great Britain by
Mackays of Chatham plc, Chatham, Kent

CONTENTS

ACKNOWLEDGEMENTS

M y grateful thanks are due to Pam McNicol of the Edinburgh City Archives and to Andrew Bethune of the Edinburgh Room, Edinburgh Central Library, for their help in answering particular queries.

Marcia Hackney of Newark Library, Nottinghamshire, helped me immensely by obtaining several obscure publications and tracing the whereabouts of others.

I am also indebted to Dr Ruth Richardson for allowing me to make use of an important revelation in her *Death, Dissection and the Destitute*.

My wife's help and support have, as always, been invaluable throughout the course of my research and writing.

PREFACE

'It is impossible to shut one's eyes to the fact that this husband [Burke] was a professional resurrectionist.'

Henry Cockburn, defending counsel at the trial of Helen McDougal, 1828.

'Burke, William (1792–1829). Irish criminal. Failure in a variety of trades led to his adoption of body-snatching as a livelihood.'

Everyman's Encyclopaedia, J.M. Dent, 1950 edn.

Man in public house: 'You've 'eard of Burke an' 'Are, ain't you, Nobby?'
Second man: 'No. Comics, was they?'
First man: 'Comics, 'e sez! Did y'ear 'im? 'E sez was Burke an' 'Are comics? Oh yes, they was bleedin' comics all right! Dug up dead bodies, didn't they!'

Conversation overheard by author, *c.* 1962.

'Soon Burke and Hare began digging up corpses from cemeteries and selling them to medical schools for dissection.'

Encyclopaedia Britannica, 15th edn., 1984.

'Burke, William (1792–1829). Irish murderer. A notorious body-snatcher operating in Edinburgh . . .'

Oxford English Reference Dictionary,
Oxford University Press, 1996 edn.

Well, that all appears not only unanimous but very conclusive, does it not? Who could doubt such authoritative assertions? Indeed, the tone of the man overheard in the pub implied that, surely, everybody knows that, and I heard a respected TV commentator, only recently, refer to 'Burke and Hare, the famous body-snatchers'.

The fact is, however, that all these random authorities, and many others like them, are wrong! There is not a single shred of evidence to support the idea that either Burke or Hare ever had anything to do with stealing corpses from the grave, or anywhere else. Indeed, in prison after his trial Burke denied that he was a body-snatcher so emphatically as to suggest that he would have been thoroughly ashamed to stoop to such skulduggery. He declared that 'neither he nor Hare, so far as he knows', ever supplied subjects for dissection 'by raising dead bodies from the grave'. During the year 1828, however, when they were committing their appalling crimes, they were quite happy for people to think they were body-snatchers.

The almost universal belief that Burke and Hare were body-snatchers is far from being the only misunderstanding about them. The truth is that there is very little established fact at all about the pair and their activities. A great deal of what we think we know about them is based solely on Burke's confessions – hardly the most reliable evidence. Virtually all we know with absolute certainty is that a suspicious death was reported by a lodger in William Burke's house; that the body was traced to the premises of the anatomist Dr Robert Knox; that Burke was convicted of this one murder, largely on the equally unreliable evidence of his erstwhile partner in crime, William Hare; and that Burke made statements before his execution, confessing to fifteen other murders.

Burke and Hare were in the record books for over a century and a half as Britain's most prolific murderers, and they still remain one of the most prolific serial-killing partnerships in any country at any time. One recent writer, Owen Dudley Edwards, has referred to them repeatedly as 'mass murderers', but the calculated killing of numerous individually selected victims, one by one, needs to be distinguished in terms from the very different and indiscriminate act of mass murder by a terrorist planting a bomb or a maniac going berserk with a firearm and killing many people at the same time. Nevertheless, the crimes of Burke and Hare far outnumbered those of the notorious 'Jack the Ripper', sixty years later, and they have been displaced from the records in terms of numbers only by the Manchester GP Harold Shipman, whose crimes perpetuated the chillingly long and close links between murder and the medical profession.

It seems surprising that the infamous Burke and Hare affair has not generated anything like the degree of interest and investigation that has been shown in recent years in Jack the Ripper. For, although there is not the perennially enticing mystery of 'who done it', the case is gruesome enough and still shrouded in much other mystery, with official silence, missing documents and several questions of identity to keep the armchair sleuth occupied for a long time.

My purpose in this book is to present a comprehensive review of both the case itself and previous commentaries on it – to examine new evidence and correct the self-perpetuating errors about this most famous and gruesome case in Scotland's history of crime; to strip the case down to its bare bones, so to speak, and examine the minute anatomy of the Burke and Hare murders, which, God knows, are almost beyond belief. But we need to begin by examining the social conditions which made their crimes possible, for there was never a better illustration of the famous maxim that 'every society gets the criminals it deserves'.

Brian Bailey
June 2002

1. SHAMBLES

Late Georgian Britain was tormented by an unpalatable choice of evils. Behind society's elegant façade of high fashion, neo-classical architecture and cultural refinement (it was the age of Gainsborough and Sheridan, Sarah Siddons and Jane Austen, Lord Byron and Sir Walter Scott) lay a festering social canker, like a half-buried and unexploded bomb. The dilemma for the authorities was how best to deal with it. Taking decisive action to excise the malignant growth would involve great offence to the majority of the population, with potentially dangerous consequences, bearing in mind recent events across the Channel. But equally, doing nothing and allowing things to go on as they were would inevitably lead to a breakdown of law and order, which were already in a parlous state. The roots of the problem lay in the past, as long ago as the Renaissance and the advent of medicine as a modern science. But the progress of the disease had been accelerated by two more recent events, the Industrial Revolution and the Napoleonic wars.

The growth of industry was accompanied by mass movements of workers from rural to urban centres and by rapid increases in population. In the course of the eighteenth century the population of Britain almost doubled, resulting in urban overcrowding, poverty, insanitary conditions, ill health and industrial injuries. Infant mortality was appallingly high. Tuberculosis, typhus and smallpox were major killers. Hernias and other occupational hazards were common among the working population. One of the urgent needs of a civilised nation was for more doctors and surgeons. Skilled medical attention could no longer be regarded as a prerogative of the upper classes, partly because the rich depended on having fit and healthy working people to create and maintain their wealth. The Napoleonic wars created an even greater demand for doctors and surgeons to deal with wounded soldiers on the battlefields of Europe.

Surgeons had to be trained by qualified teachers of anatomy and surgery. The study of anatomy was by this time recognised as a vital part of the training of skilled medical men. There was no shortage of young men wanting to become surgeons. Students from home and abroad were flocking to British medical schools, which had taken over the lead from pioneering continental universities such as Padua in Italy and Leiden in the Netherlands. The medical school at Edinburgh had become established as the leading school in Britain and one of the finest in Europe. Alexander Monteith, who had founded the Edinburgh school at the end of the seventeenth century, had promised the town council that he could make 'better improvements in anatomy in a short time than have been made by Leyden in thirty years'. And Alexander Monro, who played a major role in establishing Edinburgh's reputation, had himself studied at Leiden.

The surgeons of Edinburgh had been granted 'ane condampnit man' every year since 1505, when the town council had first granted a charter to the Incorporation of Surgeons and Barbers. The medical school's increasing fame and popularity led it to petition the council to grant the right to dissect – in addition to executed criminals – unclaimed corpses, suicides and foundlings who died in infancy. But the city fathers were reluctant to increase the supply by grants which would cause enormous public outrage and civil disorder. When the corpse of a gypsy, executed for murder, vanished from its grave in Greyfriars churchyard in 1678, local people were convinced that it had been stolen 'to make an anatomical dissection of', and a contemporary commented that it was 'criminal to take at their own hande, since the magistrates would not have refused it, and I hear the chirurgeons afferme, the town of Edinburgh is obliged to give them a malefactor's body once a year for that effect'.

The Professor of Medicine at Aberdeen in 1636, William Gordon, had petitioned the Privy Council not only for the bodies of executed criminals, but for those of the poor who died in hospitals, and the local authorities were directed, with startlingly blunt class distinction, to deliver to him

> . . . twa bodies of men, being notable malefactors, executte in
> thair bounds, especiallie being rebells and outlawis; and failzeing
> of them, the bodies of the poorer sort, dieing in hospitalls; or
> abortive bairns, foundlings; or of those of no qualitie, who hes
> died of thare diseases, and hes few friends or acquaintance that
> can tak exception.[1]

The requirement for corpses could certainly not be met legally from the gallows alone. Some later anatomy teachers were apt to suggest that no person ought to be let loose on the unsuspecting public as a qualified surgeon before he had dissected at least three corpses. In practice, the dearth of available bodies necessitated a number of students gathering round a dissecting table to share the same cadaver. The supply in Edinburgh, as at other medical schools in Scotland and England, became increasingly inadequate for the efficient teaching of growing numbers of medical students. The doctors' dilemma was an urgent matter which the medical profession in general and teachers of anatomy in particular continually pressed the government to resolve, but the government remained stubbornly unresponsive, largely because of pressure from the Church; the law in Christian Europe had for centuries permitted only the bodies of executed criminals to be used for lectures on anatomy.

In Scotland, religious opposition to dissection had grown soonest and loudest. Calvinist doctrines had ensured that Scottish education and culture leaned towards the practical sciences rather than the arts, and kept national creativity outside religious debate. That is, until the reality of body-snatching entered the public consciousness and upset the status quo with a vengeance, causing widespread riots, especially in the university towns of Edinburgh, Glasgow and Aberdeen, where there were medical schools. Anatomists were perceived as men who were depriving the poor of their chance of an afterlife, for it was always the poor who were laid out on their cold tables. The mass of the people believed absolutely in the material resurrection of the flesh on Judgement Day, and did not the burial service in the Book of Common Prayer confirm them in this faith? '. . . we therefore commit his body to the ground; earth to earth, ashes to ashes, dust to dust; in sure and certain hope of the Resurrection to eternal life, through our Lord Jesus Christ; who shall change our vile body, that it may be like unto this glorious body . . .' Mutilation of the corpse would surely preclude this consummation. How could it come to pass if their corporeal beings were to reach their ignominious terminal by being rent asunder on marble slabs? Grave-robbery was no more than a misdemeanour in English law, but in Scotland it was a heinous offence.

Sir Walter Scott was aware of this problem as well as the danger of appearing to punish the poor for their poverty. He wrote to Maria Edgeworth in February 1829, after the Burke and Hare revelations:

Certainly I thought, like you, that the public alarm was but an exaggeration of vulgar rumour; but the tragedy is too true, and I look in vain for a remedy of the evils, though it [is] easy to see [where] this black and unnatural business has found its accursed origin. The principal source certainly lies in the feelings of attachment which the Scotch have for their deceased friends. They are curious in the choice of their place of sepulchre – and a common shepherd is often, at whatever ruinous expense to his family, transported many miles to some favourite place of burial which has been occupied by his fathers. It follows, of course, that any interference with their remains is considered with most utter horror and indignation. To such of their superiors as they love from clanship or habits of dependence, they attach the same feeling of attachment. I experienced it when I had a great domestic loss; for I learned afterwards that the cemetery was guarded, out of good will, by the servants and dependents who had been attached to her during life; and were I to be laid beside my lost companion just now, I have no doubt it would be long before my humble friends would discontinue the same watch over my remains, and that it would incur mortal risk to approach them with the purpose of violation. This is a kind and virtuous principle, which every one so far partakes, that, although an unprejudiced person would have no objection to the idea of his own remains undergoing dissection, if their being exposed to scientific research could be of the least service to humanity, yet we all shudder at the notion of any one who had been dear to us, especially a wife or sister, being subjected to a scalpel among a gazing and unfeeling crowd of students. One would fight and die to prevent it. This current of feeling is encouraged by the law which, as distinguishing murderers and other atrocious criminals, orders that their bodies shall be given for public dissection. This makes it almost impossible to assign publickly the bodies of those who die in the hospitals to the same fate; for it would be inflicting on poverty the penalty which, wisely or unwisely, the law of the country has denounced against guilt of the highest degree; and it would assuredly deprive all who have a remaining spark of feeling or shame, of the benefit of those institutions of charity of which they are the best objects. This natural prejudice seems too deeply rooted to be eradicated. If not very liberal, it is surely natural, and so deeply-seated that many of the best feelings must be destroyed ere it can be eradicated.

What then remains? The only chance I see is to permit importation from other countries. If a subject can be had in Paris for ten or twenty francs, it will surely pay the importer who brings it to Scotland, and if the medical men find it convenient to use more oeconomy they will teach anatomy for all surgical purposes equally well, though they may not make such advances in physiology. Something must be done, for there is an end of the *Cantabit vacuus*, the last prerogative of beggary, which entitled him to laugh at the risk of robbery. The veriest wretch in the highway may be better booty than a person of consideration, since the last may have but a few shillings in his pocket, and the beggar, being once dead, is worth £10 to his murderer.[2]

The medical schools, however, could scarcely hope to maintain their popularity with students if they could not produce the raw materials for demonstration of anatomy and practice in surgery. So what could not be done within the law soon found a way of continuing outside it. Medical students, and sometimes their teachers, took it upon themselves to obtain fresh 'subjects' by fair means or foul. Men of distinction in the profession of surgery, such as John Hunter and Robert Liston, are known to have raised corpses from graves in pursuit of their science. Body-snatching became a peculiarly British practice. Other civilised countries in Europe were groping their way towards satisfactory solutions to the problem of training surgeons, and their medical schools were not hampered by unresponsive governments. In Germany, anatomists were permitted to receive the bodies of suicides and prostitutes as well as executed criminals. In the Netherlands, Austria and Italy, governments made proper provision by allowing bodies unclaimed by friends or relatives to be used. Portugal had a very high rate of infant mortality, and anatomists could obtain an ample supply of bodies quite legally. Resurrection men were unheard of in these countries. As for France, bodies were so readily available that the dissecting rooms of Paris's La Pitié Hôpital had around a dozen a day, and those who wanted to sell corpses to the medical schools could get no more than five francs. For a time 'Madame Guillotine' had produced a plentiful supply – upper-class ones, too – supplemented by unclaimed corpses, the dead washed up by the Seine, and those found dead in the streets. The English surgeon John Green Crosse described three dissecting-rooms at La Pitié in 1815. There were ninety tables in all, and there were twenty-three cadavers in one room alone, between about eighty students.

In Britain, however, doctors and medical students increased a growing sense of fear and outrage among the public at large. In their anxiety to dig up corpses and get away without being caught, the amateur body-snatchers' methods were crude and offensive. Having extracted a corpse from its coffin, they would leave the evidence of their nocturnal activity scattered around the open grave to be discovered by the light of day. Stealing a corpse from its grave was no more than a misdemeanour at first, because the law deemed a dead body to be no one's property. But stealing clothes or a coffin was a felony. So body-snatchers customarily took the corpse out of the coffin and stripped it naked before removing it from the churchyard, so as to be convicted, if caught, only of the lesser offence. Piles of earth, broken coffin lids, and shrouds or burial clothes would be seen at once by anyone entering the churchyard at daybreak and the alarm would be raised.

Riots and threats against anatomists became common as such outrages occurred with increasing frequency. Dr Monro's windows were broken by a mob in Edinburgh. The College of Surgeons, anxious to protect its reputation, protested against violation of churchyards and had a clause inserted in the indenture of apprentices forbidding them to rob graves. Nevertheless, since the study of anatomy was their *raison d'être* in Edinburgh, obtaining corpses took priority over strict observance of the rules. In March 1742, when the corpse of a man, Alexander Baxter, who had been buried in the West Kirkyard, was found lying in an empty house adjoining the premises of a surgeon, Martin Eccles, a mob gathered quickly and caused much damage to Eccles's house and other surgeons' premises. The crowd seized the Portsburgh drum and went beating to arms 'down the Cowgate to the foot of Niddery's wynd, till the drum was taken away from them by a party of the city-guard'. The magistrates, 'attended by the officers of the train'd bands, constables, &c atacked and dispersed the mob; and most of them having run out at the Netherbow, that and the other gates of the city were shut, by which they were in a great measure quelled'.[3] In order to maintain public order, Eccles and some of his students were arrested and charged with grave-robbing, but the charges were dropped in due course for lack of proof. The frustrated mob grasped at a rumour a few days later that one of the West Kirk beadles, George Haldane, was involved in body-snatching. The mob burnt his house down during a riot which lasted all night and the whole of the following day.[4]

A few weeks afterwards, the city guard at Potterow Port stopped a man who was carrying a sack and found in it the body of a child, identified later as Gaston Johnson, who had been buried at Pentland kirkyard a week before. The man, a gardener named John Samuel, was publicly whipped through the streets and banished from Scotland for seven years.[5]

The anatomists' need for bodies also created a motive for murder. The precedent, as far as we know, was set by two women, Helen Torrence and Jean Waldie, and the scene of their crime was none other than Edinburgh. Torrence was a needlewoman who lived in a tenement below Waldie and her husband, John Fair, a stabler's servant. Waldie (women at that time continued to be known by their maiden names after marriage) was a housewife and sick-nurse. She had been sitting up with a child whom she confidently expected to die of his illness, and had promised some local surgeon's apprentices that she would 'at coffining, slip something else into the coffin, and secrete the body; but said afterwards, that they were disappointed in this, the parent refusing to consent'.[6]

Some time later, Janet Johnston, wife of a sedan-chair porter, John Dallas, called on Helen Torrence to collect a shirt Torrence had made for Johnston's son. Waldie was with Torrence drinking ale, and Johnston needed little persuasion to join them. When Johnston was well settled in with her pint pot, Waldie said she was unwell and went upstairs to her own place, but then stole out, went to the Dallas's house in Stonielaw's Close, and kidnapped their young son John, whom his mother had left alone. By the time Waldie got him back to her apartment, the boy was dead. Meanwhile, Janet Johnston had left, and Torrence and Waldie got the medical students to come and fetch the body they had promised. The students offered them two shillings for it, but the women got them up to an additional ten pence. Torrence carried the dead child through the streets to their premises and was paid another six pence for this service.

The crime was discovered when young John Dallas's corpse was found dumped in the street with all-too-obvious signs of its having been in the surgeons' hands. Torrence and Waldie were brought to trial and blamed each other for the crime. Waldie claimed that the boy must have been accidentally smothered while concealed under her coats. When their defence was rejected and both were convicted of murder, Torrence claimed that she was pregnant, but this was soon disproved, and the women were hanged in Edinburgh's Grassmarket on 18 March 1752. It was less than a year after a new Act decreeing that *all* executed murderers were to be either publicly dissected or hung in chains. The preamble to the Act for Preventing the horrid Crime of Murder (25 Geo. II) asserted that 'It is become necessary that some further Terror and peculiar Mark of Infamy be added to the Punishment.'

Meanwhile, the demand for bodies so far outstripped the capabilities of medical students to keep pace with it that an import trade started from Ireland and France, where corpses were cheap and plentiful. They could be bought from Irish body-snatchers for ten shillings each in the early days of the trade. Cargoes of bodies were landed at Britain's leading ports, disguised in crates marked 'fish' or 'apples' or 'glue'. Provided that their sea-crossing was brief and their distribution to the medical schools prompt and efficient, they reached their destinations undetected and still fresh enough to be of use.

Many cases are recorded, however, of imported corpses being discovered by their stench of putrefaction, when ships had been delayed by bad weather from entering port, or bodies had rotted during over-long voyages. Glasgow was the main clearing-house for bodies imported from Ireland, and on one occasion a dreadful stench from a shed at the Broomielaw led to the discovery of putrefying corpses which had been addressed to a merchant in Jamaica Street by Irish medical students, and documented as a cargo of cotton and linen rags.

A box brought to the King's Arms at Lancaster on the coach from Liverpool, in October 1826, was opened because passengers had complained of the smell. Addressed to 'Archibald Young, Esq., 59 South Bridge-street, Edinburgh', it was found to contain the putrid corpses of a middle-aged woman and an infant boy. The box, which measured 22 x 15 x 12 in, could be traced back only as far as Manchester, but it had undoubtedly come from Ireland. The coroner's verdict was 'Found in a box, Lancaster'.[7]

An opportunity had clearly presented itself to the underworld of Britain for opportunists to move in and supply teachers of anatomy with subjects for dissection, relieving medical students of the burden of responsibility for quarrying their own raw materials. At first, men with an eye for the main chance carried out this work as casual labourers, raising corpses when chances occurred and, as itinerant salesmen, disposing of them wherever they could. But as the demand for subjects continued to increase, a corps of specialists in body-snatching grew and turned the robbing of graves into a profession, encouraged – and sometimes actually employed – by the leading teachers of anatomy, who were out of business themselves if they had no corpses. Professional body-snatchers were engaged in what has been called 'the foulest trade in human history'.

Grave-robbery was not, of course, a new invention of Georgian Britain. It occurred in ancient Egypt and the Roman Empire, and has, some claim, to be regarded as one of the oldest offences against humanity. Necrolatry played some part in the European witch-craze of the sixteenth and seventeenth centuries. Witches were believed to exhume the corpses of children and executed criminals to use parts as ingredients in magic potions. Readers hardly need reminding of the delectable ingredients of the witches' brew in *Macbeth*. And werewolves, according to the Jacobean dramatist John Webster, 'steal forth to churchyards in the dead of night, and dig dead bodies up'.[8] The great Vesalius himself had obtained his first skeleton by stealing the body of a hanged man from outside the city walls of Louvain, and was subsequently sentenced to death for body-snatching by the Inquisition, though the sentence was commuted.

But body-snatching had never before been a commercial business, driven by market forces, and it dawned only slowly on the British public as a whole that isolated incidents, here and there, were but the tip of an iceberg. Few people at the turn of the nineteenth century suspected that doctors were in league with body-snatchers on a scale that was a disgrace to a supposedly civilised country.

Private individuals, meanwhile, were taking extreme measures to protect their newly buried loved ones from the resurrection men. They sometimes hired guards to watch new graves throughout the night. Spring-guns were occasionally set near graves. In Edinburgh, a man had a crude land-mine buried in his daughter's grave. Another common and effective method of protection was to have a huge stone slab lowered onto the lid of the coffin. This could be left until the corpse was out of danger of exhumation, being no longer fresh enough for the doctors' purposes, then lifted and made available for the next bereaved family that required it.

The specialist suppliers — variously known as body-snatchers, resurrection men, grabs and sack-'em-up men — soon developed a degree of finesse in their work that was beyond the amateurs, who only wanted fresh corpses as easily as they could get them and had no interest in protecting a trade. Professional body-snatchers did not leave open graves and shattered coffins to provoke local communities into defensive action. They took care to cover their tracks by tidying up and replacing soil and turf so that, nothing being suspected, they need have no fear of visiting the same churchyards again. Two men working by the light of an oil-lamp, with another to keep watch, could quickly and quietly uncover a coffin buried only a few hours earlier, perhaps, in shallow and uncompacted soil, remove the lid, extract and strip the corpse, stuff it in a sack and restore the grave, leaving the churchyard virtually as they had found it except for the missing resident.

As revelations of grave-robbing grew, and the public became ever more outraged as it realised the extent of the foul trade, two particular methods of protection were favoured, especially in Scotland. One was to appoint armed watches to guard churchyards at night. Men, usually local volunteers, would spend the hours of darkness in specially built watch-huts, keeping a lookout for any disturbance. The weakness of this system was that the men would get drunk, fall asleep, or shoot nervously at some perfectly innocent citizen passing through the churchyard.

Another method, invented in Scotland a little later, was the iron 'mortsafe'. The mortsafe was a strong and heavy iron grille which was lowered by block-and-tackle into a grave to form an impenetrable cage round the coffin until all danger of disinterment was past. A correspondent to the *Quarterly Review* in 1820 wrote, 'The iron cage or safe is a Scotch invention which we have lately seen at Glasgow, where it has been in use between two and three years . . . The price paid for this apparatus is a shilling a day.'[9]

The Edinburgh *Weekly Chronicle* had devoted a leader column to the existing system of supplying teachers of anatomy with subjects, pointing out that it was indispensable in the present state of the law. But the fury of the public could not be abated, and the zealousness with which the Scots guarded against body-snatching and pursued and punished resurrection men, when they were caught, led to a serious situation for the medical schools.

One obvious consequence was to drive the trade across the border, and resurrection men in England – even as far away as London – did good business supplying corpses to Edinburgh and Glasgow. A diary kept by one London body-snatcher, generally believed to have been Joshua Naples, is preserved in the library of the Royal College of Surgeons, and the entry for Wednesday, 15 January 1812, is fairly typical of its contents:

> Went to St Thomas's. Came back, packd up 2 large and 1 small for Edinburgh. At home all Night.

The diary or log-book consists of 16 leaves (i.e. 32 pages, not 16 pages, as some writers have it). The pages are carefully ruled and mostly written in a flowing and legible hand, and cover the period from November 1811 to December 1812. The identification of this diarist as Joshua Naples is based chiefly on the fact that he is known to have been literate. The son of a stationer and bookseller, he served under Nelson and worked as a grave-digger after his discharge from the navy, then became a professional body-snatcher, working with a gang operating from Southwark and led by Ben Crouch. Naples was later given a job in the dissecting-room at St Thomas's Hospital, but eventually died of drink.

It is very likely that this same man gave evidence to the Select Committee on Anatomy set up by the House of Commons in 1828. Three professional body-snatchers were granted immunity from prosecution and protected from identification by the use of the initials AB, CD and FG. (One naturally wonders why the third was not EF, but speculation about that is pointless.) CD is thought to have been Naples. He was asked by the committee to state the number of subjects he and his colleagues had supplied to the anatomy schools in 1809 and 1810:

> A: The number in England was, according to my book, 305 adults, 44 small subjects under three feet; but the same year, there were 37 for Edinburgh and 18 we had on hand that were never used at all.
>
> Q: Now go to 1810 and 1811?
>
> A: 312.
>
> Q: Adults for that year?
>
> A: Yes, and 20 in the summer, 47 small.
>
> Q: 1811 to 1812?
>
> A: 360 in the whole, 56 small ones, these are the Edinburgh ones and all.
>
> Q: Go to 1812 and 1813.
>
> A: The following summer there were 234 adults, 32 small ones.
>
> Q: At what price, on the average, were these subjects delivered?
>
> A: Four guineas adults, small ones were sold at so much an inch.[10]

The apparent confusion between the committee ('1809 and 1810') and the witness ('the same year') is explained by the fact that there was little demand for bodies during the summer months before the days of refrigeration, and a year for the body-snatcher was the winter period from the autumn of one year to the spring of the next, when most demonstrations of anatomy took place.

There are many other recorded instances of body-snatchers in England eagerly supplying the market in Edinburgh. One of the most remarkable occurred in October 1826 when dockers at St George's Dock, Liverpool, complained about the dreadful stench from three casks they had put aboard a smack bound for Leith. The casks were opened and found to contain eleven naked corpses, six male and five female, pickled in brine. The shipping note read, 'Please ship on board the *Latona* three casks of Bitter Salts, from Mr Brown, Agent, Liverpool, to Mr G.H. Ironson, Edinburgh'. The carter who had delivered the casks to the dock was traced and said that he had been hired by a Scotsman to collect them from a cellar at 12 Hope Street. This address turned out to be the house of a clergyman, Rev James McGowan. He had let the cellar to a man named Henderson, who said he was a cooper.

Police went down to the cellar and found themselves in a veritable charnel house. There were twenty-two corpses consisting of nine men, five women and eight children, both male and female. Some of them had been lifted from the parish churchyard, where three empty graves had been found. Some were in an advanced state of decomposition. A young Scot named James Donaldson was later identified by local witnesses as one of a number of men who came to the cellar frequently with a hand-cart bearing casks. He was charged with having conspired 'with divers other persons, lately, at Liverpool, and unlawfully, wilfully, and indecently disinterred, taken and carried away, divers dead bodies, which had lately before that time been interred'. One witness testified during the trial that a tierce of brine in the cellar had been found to contain the bodies of babies, and this evidence made the foreman of the jury feel so ill that he had to leave the court to recover. Donaldson was sentenced to twelve months in the Kirkdale House of Correction and fined £50, and two other men were identified later as members of the Hope Street gang and similarly charged and sentenced. One of them was identified by the carter as the man who had hired him to transport the casks to the dock, but 'Mr Henderson', who had rented the cellar from Rev McGowan, was never traced.[11]

Nevertheless, in spite of all this apparent activity to supply subjects to Edinburgh, the medical school there, the *Westminster Review* reported, 'is now subsisting entirely on its past reputation, and in the course of a few years it will be entirely at an end, unless the system be changed'. The difficulty of procuring subjects, the article continued, had led many students to leave the place in disgust, as they were unable to pursue their studies properly. The Liverpool Literary and Philosophical Society added its voice to the call for new legislation in 1825, and pointed out that increasing prosecutions and more severe sentences for body-snatching had, among other things, 'compelled students to leave London and Edinburgh for Dublin and Paris, where the difficulties of acquiring anatomical knowledge are not so great'.[12]

This was the situation when Burke and Hare appeared on the scene. It was admirably summarised by the Royal College of Surgeons of England in a petition sent later to the Home Secretary, one of a continuous flow of appeals from the medical profession to have the study of anatomy placed on a legal footing. After observing that it was the college's duty, under the terms of its charter, to examine those who intended to practise surgery to ensure that they had acquired a sufficient knowledge of human anatomy, the petition went on:

> In the present state of the common law . . . the Individual who dissects a human body, or even has it in his possession for any other purpose than that of burial, is guilty of a misdemeanour unless it be the body of a Malefactor hanged for Murder.
>
> Bodies used for dissection in the anatomy schools have necessarily been procured by illegal means, by the invasion of consecrated ground and the disturbance of graves, in a way disgusting to society at large and especially offensive to the friends and relatives of the deceased . . .
>
> The Council . . . have laboured under much embarrassment from the inconsistencies and contradictions of the law itself, which at the same time that it declares the Student to be guilty of a misdemeanour if he attempt to obtain anatomical knowledge, renders him also, when afterwards engaged in practice, liable to a civil action on account of any mistake which his ignorance of Anatomy may lead him to commit.[13]

Or, as Sir Astley Cooper, President of the Royal College of Surgeons, put it more bluntly, an ignorant surgeon 'must mangle the living if he has not operated on the dead'. 'You must employ medical men,' Sir Astley told the committee:

> . . . whether they be ignorant or informed; but if you have none

but ignorant medical men, it is you who suffer from it; and the fact is, that the want of subjects will soon lead to your becoming the unhappy victims of operations founded and performed in ignorance.[14]

The predicament in which the anatomy teachers found themselves (not only in London and Edinburgh, but also in Bristol and Liverpool, Glasgow and Aberdeen, Manchester and Sheffield, Cambridge and Leeds and other cities which had their own medical schools in the first quarter of the nineteenth century) forced them to encourage body-snatchers and in effect become their partners in crime. Sir Astley Cooper himself became known as 'King of the Resurrectionists' because he was one of the best clients of the London body-snatchers. He boasted that there was 'no person, let his situation be what it may, whom, if I were disposed to dissect, I could not obtain'.

Nevertheless, the doctors purported to be horrified by their enforced association with men whom they freely represented in their public pronouncements as the scum of the earth. The hypocritical moral position of the medical men, who had once been body-snatchers themselves, was that they had done it in the interests of science and the public good, whereas the professionals did it for money!

Of course, it was hardly to be expected that men who made their livings by theft would be scrupulously honest in their business dealings. One Edinburgh body-snatcher obtained an advance of £2 10 shillings from an anatomy lecturer for a corpse he had promised, then delivered a box filled with rubbish. Another sold a corpse to the lecturer John Lizars, then stole it back from his dissecting-room and sold it to Lizars' rival Knox, getting £25 for the one corpse. But the assumption that the doctors were entirely altruistic and the grave-robbers totally depraved was an easy trap to fall into. One author went so far as to say that the Anatomy Act, which became law in 1832, 'permitted cultured, brave and honourable members of the medical profession to escape the slimy tentacles of the resurrectionists'.[15]

At any rate, by 1827, the stage was well set for an enterprising double-act of criminal depravity, which made its dramatic entrance in one of the kingdom's most handsome cities.

NOTES

[1] G.A.G. Mitchell, 'The Medical History of Aberdeen and its Universities'. Lecture printed in *Aberdeen University Review*, Spring 1958, p. 234.

[2] H.J.C. Grierson (ed.), *Letters of Sir Walter Scott*, Vol XI, 1828–31, (London, Constable, 1936), pp. 124–26.

[3] *Scots Magazine*, March 1742, p. 140.

[4] Ibid, pp. 140–41.

[5] *Scots Magazine*, July 1742, pp. 336–37.

[6] *Scots Magazine*, February 1752, p. 98.

[7] *Lancaster Gazette*, 7 October 1826.

[8] John Webster, *The Duchess of Malfi*, Act V, Scene II.

[9] *The Quarterly Review*, Vol 23, 1820.

[10] Evidence given to the Select Committee on Anatomy, 1828.

[11] *Liverpool Mercury*, 13 and 20 October 1826; 3 and 10 November 1826; 26 January 1827.

[12] *The Humble Petition of the Liverpool Literary and Philosophical Society to the Honourable the Commons of Great Britain and Ireland, in Parliament Assembled*, May 1825.

[13] *Petition of the Royal College of Surgeons in London to the Viscount Melbourne, His Majesty's Principal Secretary of State for the Home Department*, 10 December 1831. Home Office papers in Public Record Office, HO 44/24.

[14] Evidence given to the Select Committee on Anatomy, 1828.

[15] James Moores Ball, *The Body-Snatchers*, (New York, Dorset Press, 1989 ed), p. 187. (Originally published in 1928 as *The Sack-'Em-Up-Men*.)

2. UNION

Scotland's capital had become one of the finest cities in northern Europe, with an elegant New Town designed by James Craig and developed northward from 1770 to 1870 from the medieval fortress perched acropolis-like on Castle Rock. New streets on a grid pattern, with squares and crescents, gardens and open spaces, boasted the fashionable neo-classical architecture of Robert Adam and William Playfair. Princes Street and George Street, Queen Street and Charlotte Square prestigiously linked the Scottish city with the royal family, and King George IV, donning the kilt, had already paid a popular visit. Sir Walter Scott, then living in Castle Street, had helped to organise the celebrations and David Wilkie, RA, had recorded the great event on canvas.

Within half a century of the New Town's development, its residents had included, besides Scott, the philosopher David Hume and the political economist Adam Smith, worthy representatives of the Age of Reason. Thomas Carlyle and Thomas De Quincey lived there, as well as John Wilson, the university's Professor of Moral Philosophy, more widely known by his pen-name in *Blackwood's Edinburgh Magazine* of 'Christopher North'. Among the students at the university in 1827 was the eighteen-year-old Charles Darwin, a doctor's son who had come here to study medicine. The city was enjoying a new reputation as one of the leading cultural centres of Europe, basking in an unrivalled 'Golden Age'.

But what of the Old Town, which remained unaltered to the south of the castle? Like so many other towns and cities of Georgian Britain, Edinburgh was a place of stark contrasts. From Calton Hill you could gaze across at the 'Athens of the North' in one direction and at 'Auld Reekie' in another. Edinburgh had a dual personality, and, though Stevenson was not yet born, we may perhaps be forgiven for calling the New and Old Towns the city's Jekyll and Hyde faces. While the local gentry of the New Town was proud to parade itself in this new cosmopolitan metropolis, which was attracting visitors such as Shelley and Turner, Mendelssohn and Paganini, the Old was the grisly haunt of body-snatchers.

Defoe described the place half a century or so before the New Town was begun. The city, he wrote:

> . . . lies under such scandalous inconveniences as are, by its enemies, made a subject of scorn and reproach; as if the people were not as willing to live sweet and clean as other nations, but delighted in stench and nastiness; whereas, were any other people to live under the same unhappiness, I mean as well of a rocky and mountainous situation, thronged buildings, from seven to ten or twelve story high, a scarcity of water, and that little they have difficult to be had, and to the uppermost lodgings, to fetch; we should find a London or a Bristol as dirty as Edinburgh, and, perhaps, less able to make their dwelling tolerable, at least in so narrow a compass; for, though many cities have more people in them, yet, I believe, this may be said with truth, that in no city in the world do so many people live in so little room as at Edinburgh.[1]

Tall tenement buildings, known as 'lands', crowded together in narrow stinking wynds and closes beneath a permanent pall of smoke from the congested multitude of chimneys. Filthy winding staircases, called 'turnpike stairs', led from squalid yards and alleys to apartments where washing hung out of the windows during daylight hours, and human and other refuse was tipped out of them at night. 'Stinking' had been the adjective commonly used by writers and visitors to describe old Edinburgh for centuries. Neither the grey houses nor the grey streets had drains. Slum dwellers obliterated all consciousness of their miserable plight by means of heavy drinking. Pallid and emaciated inhabitants of the poorer quarters shuffled along dingy alleyways dodging the excrement of dogs and the vomit of drunks, keeping a wary ear open for the brief incantation 'Gardy loo!', signalling the ritual dousing of piss and garbage from above.

The chief problem was, as with many other British towns at the time, the rapid rise in population. Although Edinburgh was not one of the new manufacturing towns, like Manchester and Birmingham, its population had been increasing since the failure of the Young Pretender's rebellion of 1745, and within the first thirty years of the nineteenth century it had more than doubled.

One of the improvement works Edinburgh was engaged in was the digging of the Union Canal to link the city with the Forth and Clyde Canal near Falkirk. This brought thousands of men seeking employment on the project. Among them was a large contingent of Irish labourers, part of a continuous stream of poverty-stricken immigrants seeking unskilled work in the industrial towns of Britain. They constituted the cheapest labour in western Europe. They formed close communities which quickly acquired reputations for heavy drinking, especially on Saturday nights, and for being the 'lowest, dampest, dirtiest, most unhealthy and ruinous' rabble wherever they settled.[2] The squalor of the Irish ghettos was notorious throughout the country, in Edinburgh as in London, Leeds and Liverpool. Friedrich Engels famously described conditions in the area of Manchester known as Little Ireland. The people arrived here as:

> . . . primitive peasants, uprooted by pressure of want from a poor and inefficient rural society untouched by industrialism and with a long tradition of oppression and violence. Ill-equipped for more sophisticated work, desperate to seize whatever means of life a strange and unfriendly environment offered, they were bound to depress living standards and harshen the struggle for survival among the lowest strata of the population.[3]

In the slums of large urban centres, they had become notorious for their practice of taking in sub-tenants, thus increasing what were often already unhealthily overcrowded lodgings. Often they dispensed with beds and slept on straw which had also been used by cows or pigs. If a labourer was possessed of a bed, 'he would take as a lodger, as a tenant of half his bed, another labourer at a weekly rent'.[4] The Irish were also notorious for their 'wakes', when they allowed corpses to lie about for several days while money was collected to pay for their funerals. A corpse might be laid out for ten days or more in a tiny room where others slept, notwithstanding the stench of putrefaction.

Irish immigration was a permanent matter of concern to the Scottish authorities. It was stated that this increasing labour force 'lowered greatly the moral tone of the lower classes, and greatly increased the necessity for the enforcement of sanitary and police precautions where they have settled in large numbers . . . It is painful to contemplate what may be the ultimate effects of this Irish immigration on the morals and habits of the people . . .'[5]

Sir Walter Scott commented on this problem too:

> The great number of the lower Irish which have come over here since the peace, is, like all important occurrences, attended with its own share of good and evil. It must relieve Ireland in part of the excess of population, which is one of its greatest evils, and it accommodates Scotland with a race of hardy and indefatigable labourers, without which it would be impossible to carry on the very expensive improvements which have been executed. Our canals, our railroads, our various public works, are all wrought by Irish. I have often employed them myself at burning clay, and similar operations, and have found them labourers quiet and tractable, light-spirited, too, and happy to a degree beyond belief, and in no degree quarrelsome, keep whisky from them and them from whisky. But most unhappily for all parties they work at far too low a rate – at a rate, in short, which can but just procure salt and potatoes; they become reckless, of course, of all the comforts and decencies of life, which they have no means of procuring. Extreme poverty brings ignorance and vice, and these are the mothers of crime. If Ireland were to submit to some kind of poor-rate – I do not mean that of England, but something that should secure to the indigent their natural share of the fruits of the earth, and enable them at least to feed while others are feasting – it would, apparently, raise the character of the lower orders, and deprive them of that recklessness of futurity which leads them to think only of the present. Indeed, when intoxication of the lower ranks is mentioned as a vice, we must allow the temptation is well-nigh irresistible; meat, clothes, fire, all that men can and do want, are supplied by a drop of whisky; and no one should be surprised that the relief (too often the only one within the wretches' power) is eagerly grasped at.[6]

Among these immigrant Irish navvies was one William Hare, a former farm labourer in his native land. Born at Newry, he was illiterate and uncouth – a lean, quarrelsome, violent and amoral character with the scars from old wounds about his head and brow. Professor John Wilson later saw him in prison and described him as the most brutal man he had ever seen.

His dull, dead, blackish eyes, wide apart, one rather higher up than the other; his large, thick, or rather coarse-lipped mouth; his high, broad cheekbones, and sunken cheeks, each of which when he laughed – which he did often – collapsed into a perpendicular hollow, shooting up ghastlily from chin to cheek bone – all steeped in a sullenness and squalor not born of the jail, but native to the almost deformed face of the leering miscreant – inspired not fear, for the aspect was scarcely ferocious, but disgust and abhorrence, so utterly loathsome was the whole look of the reptile.[7]

Owen Dudley Edwards, who refers pointedly to 'a great divide between professional historians and amateur criminologists',[8] rightly pours scorn on Peter Mackenzie's speculation in *Old Reminiscences of Glasgow and the West of Scotland* that Burke and Hare had previously carried on a trade in murder in Ireland. But he speculates himself that Hare might have been in the Irish militia, deserting and fleeing to Scotland after receiving a brutalising punishment of several hundred lashes with the cat-o'-nine-tails.[9] There is no shred of evidence that I am aware of to support this idea.

When his employment on the Union Canal had ended, Hare worked as a labourer and met a man named Logue who ran a cheap lodging house at the bottom of Tanner's Close, one of the squalid alleys off the West Port near its junction with the Grassmarket. These alleys led between the walls of a dense conglomeration of slum tenements northward to King's Stables, below the castle mound. To the customary filth and dankness of these slum passages was added the distinction, in this case, of a permanent stench of animal putrefaction from tanneries at the back of the 'lands', which gave the close its name. Logue's tenement had eight beds, and he charged threepence a night. This did not limit his customers to eight at a time, however. Sometimes they slept three to a bed.

Hare became one of Logue's lodgers and evidently took a fancy to his common-law wife, Margaret Laird. An Irish Catholic like himself, she had worked on the canal, too, digging in a navvy's jacket alongside the men, and was a hard-featured and debauched virago. She was nicknamed, for some reason that escapes me, 'Lucky', and she had a young child. No doubt it was Hare's friendship with her that got him thrown out of the house by Logue, but in 1826 Logue died and Hare, having heard the news, returned to Tanner's Close to pursue his interest in the widow. She, it is said, was already being comforted by a young lodger, but Hare seems to have insinuated himself not only into her bed but also into possession of the house. By some date in 1827, Hare had elevated himself to the status of landlord, and was relieved of the need for regular employment, although he appears to have worked intermittently as a labourer or street vendor. He spent much of his time drinking and fighting in public with 'Lucky', who was 'often brutally intoxicated and seldom without a pair of black eyes'.[10]

Hare's estate consisted of three rooms on one floor of a building of random stone walls with some waste ground behind it. The two larger rooms were equipped with the eight beds between them. Anyone passing by in Tanner's Close could see through the windows into both of these rooms, but the third room was a smaller closet at the back, with a window looking only onto a wall and a shed or stall which appears to have served as a stable and a pig-sty. Hare had acquired a horse and cart, and he occasionally ventured out with them hawking fish and scrap.

To this insalubrious doss-house came William Burke, a fellow-Irishman from Ulster, born near Strabane in County Tyrone in 1792, the son of a labourer, Niel Burke. Burke's published confession in the Edinburgh *Evening Courant* gave his birthplace as 'Orrey, Co Tyrone', and the *Dictionary of National Biography* and most subsequent writers gave it as Orrery. But there is no such place as either Orrey or Orrery, and, as Owen Dudley Edwards has pointed out, the name is almost certainly an erroneous transcription of Urney, three miles south-west of Strabane. (By a curious coincidence, one of the ruling elders of the parish of Urney was a man named Knox.) William Burke had also come to Scotland in 1818 to work on the Union Canal, leaving his wife, Margaret, and two children in Ireland. His wife refused to join him in Scotland, and he never saw her or his children again. The Union Canal took four years to construct, and for some years afterwards, Burke worked as an itinerant farm labourer and a pedlar of old clothes around Peebles and Leith. At Leith, Burke had learned from his landlord or a fellow-lodger how to mend shoes.

While still working as a navvy, he had met an illiterate woman known as Helen or 'Nelly' Dougal or McDougal. She was a native Scot, born at Redding, near Falkirk, where Burke had lived while employed on the canal, but the surname was only that of the man she was living with at the time, by whom she had two children. She may have worked as a prostitute among the canal navvies. She absconded with Burke, and by 1827 the pair were in Edinburgh, repairing old boots and shoes and hawking them among the city's poor. They were lodging with an

Irishman, Mickey Culzean, proprietor of an establishment whimsically known as 'The Beggar's Hotel' in Portsburgh.

In November of that year Burke and Nelly had met Maggie Laird in the street and gone for a drink with her. It appears that Burke was already acquainted with Laird. When he mentioned that he was intending to move away and seek work as a cobbler, Maggie said that there was a room in Hare's house which might suit him. He and Nelly could live there and carry on his trade in Edinburgh. This was the first time the two men met, but they quickly became firm friends. It was also the first time the two women had met, but no love was lost between them.

Burke's elder brother Constantine was also living in Edinburgh with his wife Elizabeth (née Graham) and their children, and was employed as a street-cleaner by the city police. There is no mention anywhere, in the records of the subsequent events surrounding Burke and Hare, of either Maggie Laird's or Nelly McDougal's children. The *Evening Courant* alleged later that Margaret Laird had murdered the first child she had with Hare, but there is no evidence to support this or any speculation about the fate of McDougal's two children by previous consorts.

William Burke was, to all outward appearances, a more pleasant and sociable character than his new friend Hare. His parents were respectable Catholics, and he had been given at least a basic education. When he was nineteen, he had followed Constantine into the army, and served for seven years as a batman in the Donegal Militia. He was married to Margaret Coleman at Ballina, County Mayo, while a serving soldier. John Wilson described him as he appeared at the age of thirty-six in his prison cell:

> A neat little man of about five feet five, well proportioned, especially in his legs and thighs – round-bodied, but narrow-chested – arms rather thin – small wrists, and a moderate-sized hand; no mass of muscle anywhere about his limbs or frame, but vigorously necked, with hard forehead and cheek bones; a very active, but not a powerful man, and intended by nature for a dancing master. Indeed he danced well, excelling in the Irish jig, and when working about Peebles and Innerleithen he was very fond of that recreation. In that neighbourhood he was reckoned a good specimen of the Irish character – not quarrelsome, expert with the spade, and a pleasant enough

companion over a jug of toddy. Nothing repulsive about him, to ordinary observers at least, and certainly not deficient in intelligence.[11]

Nevertheless, Professor Wilson found him 'impenitent as a snake, remorseless as a tiger'. Wilson noted Burke's 'hard, cruel eyes' and his voice, 'rather soft and calm, but steeped in hypocrisy and deceit; his collected and guarded demeanour, full of danger and guile – all, all betrayed, as he lay in his shackles, the cool, calculating, callous, and unrelenting villain'.[12] But this, of course, was a case of being wise after the event.

James Maclean, a fellow-Irishman living nearby in the West Port, told Charles Kirkpatrick Sharpe, the antiquary and friend of Sir Walter Scott, that Burke was a peaceable man and steady at his work when sober, and 'even when drunk, rather jocose and prone to banter, but by no means riotous or quarrelsome, without considerable provocation'. But Helen McDougal was of 'dull morose disposition', and the two 'led a most unhappy life, everlastingly quarrelling, and on these occasions she was often severely beaten by him'.[13] Nevertheless, the two were genuinely attached to each other. When Burke was exhorted by a local priest to return to his wife in Ireland, he refused and was excommunicated.

The various portrait sketches purporting to be of Burke, made by press artists in court or in gaol, have only two things in common – the round face and the penetrating eyes. Some drawings show him with long sideburns, others without. One gives him more of a pug-nose than the rest. Another represents him as balding at the temples, while others give him a good head of hair. One shows him wearing a cravat in the dock, but others give him only a thin scarf or neckerchief.

Burke and Nelly had scarcely settled into their new accommodation, in November 1827, before another of Hare's lodgers, an old soldier named Donald, died, apparently of dropsy. For Hare, this was a disaster, for the old man had owed him £4 in rent, and his quarterly army pension, due shortly, would have covered the debt. Preparations were made for the old man's burial by the parish, and a day or two after his death, the body was placed in a coffin ready for the hired mourners known in Scotland as 'saulies'.

In the meantime, however, Hare (according to Burke) had hatched a plan for recovering his bad debt, and as he needed help in carrying it out, he approached Burke. The slums fringing High Street and Canongate were well-known resorts of the 'resurrectionists', and it was impossible to be part of the low life of Edinburgh at that time and not know that fresh corpses could be sold as anatomical subjects. As there were no friends or relatives to claim Donald's body, why not sell it to the doctors? If Burke would help him, he could have a share of the proceeds.

According to one of Burke's confessions, Hare 'started the coffin lid with a chisel'. In the other confession, Burke said that Hare 'unscrewed the nails'. Either way, the two men lifted out the corpse and hid it in one of the beds, then filled the coffin with tanner's bark collected from the yard at the back and refixed the lid. The coffin was then taken away at the expense of the parish and with brief solemnity interred in a paupers' grave in the kirkyard of St Cuthbert's, known as the West Kirk, a quarter of a mile away.

The Wester Portsburgh district where Burke and Hare lived was close to several hospitals and burial grounds, well guarded at night against body-snatchers, and beyond the Infirmary, in the High School Yards between Cowgate and Roxburgh Terrace, was Surgeons' Square, where university and extramural anatomy lecturers had their premises. Either Burke or Hare had heard of Professor Monro, third of a famous dynasty which had held the university chair of anatomy since 1720. Burke and Hare walked the half-mile from Tanner's Close to the College yard, where they encountered a young man whom they asked to direct them to Dr Monro, or any of his men. The man, probably a medical student, enquired what they wanted Dr Monro for, and when they nervously confided in him that they had a body to dispose of, the young man directed them to the premises of Dr Robert Knox, at 10 Surgeons' Square. Knox's biographer, Henry Lonsdale, gives the date of this event as the evening of 29 November, but it cannot have been the day on which Donald died as given by William Roughead in his book on the trial. Burke himself said it was 'about Christmas, 1827', but he added that it was 'a day or two after the pensioner's death' when Hare suggested selling the body to the doctors.

Burke and Hare, at any rate, were met by three students, subsequently known to them as Fergusson, Miller and Jones. The two novice dealers were hesitant to come to the point, but eventually admitted that they had a body for sale, and were told to bring it when it was dark. They were not asked whose body it was nor how they had obtained it. They went back to Tanner's Close, stuffed the corpse into a sack, and returned to Surgeons' Square later that night. They were greeted by the same three students, who told them to bring the body upstairs to the lecture room. Here, they took the body from the sack and laid it on the dissecting table. It was still dressed in the shirt in which Donald should have been buried. The students told Burke and Hare to take away the shirt, which they did. Dr Knox's assistants, used to receiving corpses from body-snatchers, would have been well versed in the law regarding clothes and other property. A corpse dug up from a churchyard was deemed to belong to no one. But clothing – even a shroud – was property, and its theft was punishable as a felony under Georgian criminal law. So experienced body-snatchers and anatomists alike took good care not to be caught with any item in their possession which could make them liable to prosecution for the greater offence. Dead bodies were always sold naked. As Burke and Hare were removing Donald's shirt, Dr Knox himself entered the room, looked at the naked corpse and suggested a price of £7 10 shillings. This being readily agreed by Burke and Hare, Knox told Jones to settle with them. As they saw Burke and Hare out, one of the students said *'they would be glad to see them again when they had any other body to dispose of'*.[14] Hare took £4 5 shillings of the proceeds, and gave Burke £3 5 shillings.

Before we proceed further with events, we should ask ourselves if the story of the old pensioner Donald is entirely true. It is based solely on the subsequent confessions of Burke. If we do not believe it, it opens up the possibility, among other things, that Burke and Hare murdered more than the sixteen victims usually accepted as their total tally. But it is not only Burke's statements that we need to be wary of. Dr Knox's biographer, Henry Lonsdale, stated that Burke and Hare 'furnished thirteen victims in all to Knox's rooms during their eleven months' operations'.[15] Owen Dudley Edwards refers repeatedly to Burke 'murdering seventeen people'. But to the best of our knowledge, Burke and Hare between them murdered sixteen people, one of whom Burke was not involved with. Burke himself committed or took part in fifteen murders.

The first (and perhaps seemingly obvious) question – though no one seems to have asked it before – is, how had Donald managed to accumulate a debt of £4 in rent? If Hare was charging him three pence a night for his bed, £4 would represent almost a year's rent. Are we to take it that the evil Hare, out of the goodness of his heart, had been letting the matter slide, when Donald received his pension quarterly? Secondly, if Donald had really owed Hare £4, it appears uncharacteristically generous of Hare to take only five shillings profit and allow Burke nearly half the proceeds. Perhaps there was never any debt at all. Did Hare invent the debt in order to make his idea of selling the body appear reasonable to

Burke, whom he needed as an accomplice? Or did they devise the story of the debt together in order to make the idea of selling the body seem somehow less callous afterwards? Or, worse still, did they really murder Donald, along with the rest, and if so, how many others, of whom we know nothing, might they have killed?

Perhaps the best reason for accepting Burke's version of events is the detailed description he gave of their first sale and their encouraging reception in Surgeons' Square. It has the ring of truth about it. The man who diverted them from Monro to Knox must have been one of Knox's own students, and was as eager as the doctor's agents that night – Fergusson, Miller and Jones – that there should be an ample supply of subjects available.

Possibly Donald's debt to Hare had mounted up because Hare had sold him an old shirt, and Maggie Laird had provided him with food and drink while he was ill. We shall never know, but there are no overwhelming reasons to doubt that Burke's story was true in substance if not in detail. What seems much more likely is that it was Burke, rather than Hare, who was the author of the plot. This would account for Burke's generous share of the money they received. If it was Burke who had suggested to Hare that they could sell the body, and that he, Burke, would take the lead in doing so (he being clearly the superior in matters of public relations), Hare would presumably have been more than satisfied to recover the money he was owed and have five shillings profit out of the deal.

At any rate, by the time the sale was completed, a seed had been planted in the minds of the pair, which apparently lay dormant through the winter months but was to germinate early in the spring of 1828 and grow with mind-boggling vigour in the course of that year.

NOTES

[1] Daniel Defoe, *A Tour through the Whole Island of Great Britain*, (London, Penguin edn., 1971), p. 577.

[2] 'Report on the state of the Irish poor in Great Britain, 1836', quoted in H.C. Darby (ed.), *A New Historical Geography of England after 1600*, (Cambridge University Press, 1976), p. 172.

[3] Quoted in Kellow Chesney, *The Victorian Underworld*, (London, Penguin Books), 1982, p. 69.

[4] M. Dorothy George, *London Life in the Eighteenth Century*, (London, Penguin Books, 1985), p. 129.

[5] Quoted in Sir Llewellyn Woodward, *The Age of Reform 1815–70*, (Oxford

University Press, 1997), p. 601.

[6] Letter to Maria Edgeworth in Grierson, pp. 126–27.

[7] *Blackwood's Edinburgh Magazine*, March 1829.

[8] Owen Dudley Edwards, *Burke & Hare* (Edinburgh, Polygon Books, 1980), p. 289.

[9] Ibid, p. 37.

[10] Robert Buchanan et al, *Trial of William Burke and Helen McDougal before the High Court of Justiciary at Edinburgh on Wednesday, December 24, 1828* (Edinburgh, 1829), p. xiv.

[11] *Blackwood's Edinburgh Magazine*, March 1829.

[12] Ibid.

[13] Robert Buchanan et al, *Trial of William Burke and Helen McDougal*, pp. xiii–xiv.

[14] Burke's official confession in prison, 3 January 1829; my italics.

[15] Henry Lonsdale, *A Sketch of the Life and Writings of Robert Knox the Anatomist*, (London, Macmillan, 1870), p. 103.

3. CONTRACT

There were body-snatchers who were not technically grave-robbers or 'resurrection men'. Two London operators, Cornelius Bryant and Israel Chapman, became specialists, for instance, in doing deals with undertakers or masters of workhouses to obtain bodies before they were buried, and they even stole bodies from houses before funerals could take place. A man named Joliffe, living at Bethnal Green, attempted to bring a charge in 1826 against two men who, he said, had stolen the body of his wife, who had died only that night, while he was asleep in the next room. But the magistrate ruled that the men had not broken any law unless they had also taken away an article of clothing or some other property – which, of course, they had not.

There was no question, however, of Burke and Hare having stolen old Donald's body, or his shirt, since they were already in Hare's possession. As far as we know, neither Burke nor Hare had committed any serious criminal act at this point. They had used sleight of hand to turn a situation to their own advantage. It was dishonest, but not felonious.

The two men must have spent the winter months brooding over the ease with which they had made £7 10 shillings. As Burke mended shoes, Hare collected his rents and they spent their profits on drink they could hardly dismiss from their minds that fatal invitation to call at 10 Surgeons' Square again when they had another body to dispose of. They must have been tempted at some point to join the body-snatching fraternity, but hesitated partly, perhaps, through cowardice, and partly because of the dawning realisation that there was an easier way of obtaining dead bodies, circumventing the risky business of nocturnal digging in guarded or booby-trapped kirkyards.

At some date in the winter of 1828, probably early February, it seems that another lodger of Hare's named Joseph, who had been a miller, fell ill and became delirious. Hare and his wife were anxious that the fever should not deter other lodgers. If rumour got abroad that an infectious disease such as cholera or typhus was present in Hare's house, it would ruin his business. Burke and Hare were suddenly presented with motive and opportunity. We do not know how old Joseph was, but it is probable that he was getting on in years and was unlikely to recover from the illness. Burke remarked in one of his statements that Joseph had been quite well off at one time and was related by marriage to someone of status in the Carron Ironworks. If he was now lodging alone in Hare's house for threepence a night, it is perhaps a reasonable assumption that by this time he was an elderly widower with no close relations. After weighing up the risks for a while, no doubt, Burke and Hare made up their minds to ease the poor fellow on his way to oblivion. After making him practically unconscious with whisky, one of them pressed a pillow over Joseph's face while the other lay across his body to prevent him from thrashing about and making a noise.

The job was quickly done and the two men lost no time, when it was dark enough, in carrying the body to Surgeons' Square, where they were greeted at No. 10 by Dr Knox's students and asked to lay out the corpse for inspection as before. This time they were paid £10 and no questions were asked: money for a dram! The pair may even have been persuaded that they were performing a public service. One English resurrectionist put up a spirited defence when brought before a magistrate, complaining that the police would be better engaged in looking after thieves and house-breakers than apprehending respectable men who lived by supplying the faculty with subjects for dissection.

At any rate, whatever Burke and Hare may have done before, they had now committed murder and been well paid for it. There is no reason to suppose that they had ever heard of Torrence and Waldie. They needed no precedent to make them aware of the opportunities offered to men of cunning by the present state of the law. Burke said in his prison confession that he had not 'the smallest suspicion of any other person in this, or in any other country, except Hare and himself, being concerned in killing persons and offering their bodies for dissection; and he never knew or heard of such a thing having been done before'. But now they had crossed the Rubicon and there was no going back. They appeared to have got away with murder and they did not waste much time in trying their luck again.

A man of about forty from Cheshire, whose name they did not know, came to Hare's house for a few nights. Burke referred to him merely as an Englishman, saying that he was tall and dark and had been selling spunks (matches or tinder) in Edinburgh. He fell ill with jaundice and, like old Joseph, presented a threat to Hare's lodging-house business. Burke and Hare were unable to resist the temptation of furthering the cause of medical science by selling his corpse to Dr Knox for a further £10. This was like manna from heaven for the Irishmen. The local body-snatchers had all the risk and trouble of excavating graves by night; sometimes having to bribe undertakers and watchmen; sometimes having to transport corpses over considerable distances from remote churchyards, always with the risk of discovery; sometimes being shot at. Burke and Hare had hit upon a way of circumventing all these inconveniences. But they could not expect Hare's lodgers to keep falling ill. Impatient for more easy money, and emboldened by their previous experiences and the encouragement of the doctor and his assistants, they took a greater risk next time.

Abigail Simpson, who lived at Gilmerton, a few miles south-east of Edinburgh, was an old woman whose former employer allowed her a weekly pension of eighteen pence and a can of kitchen fee (dripping). She regularly walked into Edinburgh to collect it and generally hung around selling salt and camstane (kaolin or pipe-clay used by women to whiten their doorsteps, etc.) to supplement her meagre income. On 11 February 1828 (according to Burke's confessions) she came to Tanner's Close with Hare, and began drinking with him until she was so drunk that she could not go home. She told Hare that she had a daughter, and Hare merrily said that he was a single man and would marry the daughter and take care of them both. Next morning she was ill, but still drank more despite vomiting. She was lying on her back in bed, dressed in 'a drab mantle, a white-grounded cotton shawl and small blue spots on it', insensible from all the ale and whisky she had consumed. Hare suggested to Burke (or so Burke said) that they should smother her and sell her body to the doctors. Drinking heavily with their intended victims was to become a fixed routine in their method. Alcohol served a dual purpose – it made the victims weak and relatively insensible and gave the killers Dutch courage.

Burke laid himself across the old woman to prevent her from struggling, while Hare clapped his hands over her mouth and nostrils. When she was dead, the two men undressed her and put the body in a chest. Hare said he would throw the clothes into the canal. Then they informed Dr Knox's assistants that they had another subject. Mr Miller sent a porter to meet them during the evening at a rendezvous below the Castle Rock. Burke and Hare carried the chest to this spot and then accompanied the porter who carried it to Knox's premises. The corpse was cold and stiff when Dr Knox came in to look at it while they were there. 'Dr Knox approved of its being so fresh,' Burke said later, 'but did not ask any questions.' They were paid £10.

Burke's account of this murder raises several interesting questions. Burke made two confessions after his conviction for murder. One was made in Calton Jail on 3 January 1829 in the presence of the Sheriff, the Procurator-Fiscal and the Sheriff's Clerk. The other was made to some person unknown, later in the month, and published in the Edinburgh *Evening Courant* after Burke's execution. In both of them, Burke said that the murder of Abigail Simpson was the first he and Hare committed, and in the *Courant* confession he was specific about the date and time – the morning of 12 February 1828. He said that he 'did not know the days nor the months the different murders were committed, nor all their names', but added that all the murders were committed between 12 February and 1 November 1828. He did mention certain months and seasons in the course of his two confessions, but why did he recall the earlier date with such certainty? The twelfth of February that year was a Tuesday. Was it some anniversary – his birthday, perhaps – that made it stick in his mind? In dealing with the subsequent murders, his memory was less precise in terms of dates and less consistent in terms of the order of victims, and in spite of his two statements, made nearly three weeks apart, there are strong reasons for doubting that Abigail Simpson was the first victim of the fiendish partners. On 1 December 1828, Hare also gave information to the Sheriff. His statement has been lost, but among those who saw it was Sir Walter Scott, who noted that, while Hare's confession agreed with Burke's as to the number and description of the victims, they differed in the order in which the murders were committed. Hare, apparently, said that Joseph the miller was the first victim, and this seems much more likely for several reasons.

The order of the whole series of murders cannot be established with certainty. We do not have Hare's testimony and Burke's confessions are contradictory. But there are some clues in the wording of the confessions and the prices Burke said they got which make the order in which I give them seem more probable, I think, than the sequences given by other writers on the subject, such as William Roughead and Hugh Douglas.

In selling the body of Donald, the old army pensioner, the two inexperienced men had approached the matter with natural nervousness and caution and, according to Burke's confessions, did not try anything like it again for more than two months. It seems highly unlikely that they would take the risk of luring an old woman who was known on the streets of Edinburgh into Hare's house and killing her. Someone might see them together, and they were not so familiar with Dr Knox and his men at that stage that they could be confident that medical men would not ask any questions about the unburied corpse of a drunken woman. There would be much less likelihood of suspicion if they took another of Hare's old lodgers who was dying of some disease and whom no one would miss. This would also help to explain the cessation of activity during the winter months after selling Donald's body. Burke and Hare did not immediately summon up the courage to set out on a murder spree by taking victims off the streets. They spent the winter quietly waiting for another opportunity to present itself in Hare's lodging house.

It is difficult to overstate the brutality of their method of execution. Most of their victims, even though drunk, must have been conscious that they were being murdered for several moments, but were rendered incapable of any physical resistance. The most basic human instinct of clinging to life was suppressed, and they must have been seized by panic as their lungs seemed likely to burst in the struggle for air.

In Burke's *Courant* confession, the nameless Englishman was the second of their victims and he, too, fell seriously ill in Hare's house. These two old derelicts could be disposed of in relative secrecy. Only Burke and Hare themselves, and possibly their women, would have known anything about it. Abigail Simpson was the unfortunate target, we may surely assume, of two furtive and skulking devils emboldened by the smoothness of their previous transactions with Knox and his men, as well as the implied encouragement to bring as many bodies as they could, and their greed for more easy money.

Burke remarked in his *Courant* confession that he and Hare 'often said to one another that no person could find them out, no one being present at the murders but themselves two; and that they might be as well hanged for a sheep as a lamb'. They certainly took a huge step of mind-boggling recklessness or stupidity with their next victim, who fell into their hands (as mentioned in *both* of Burke's statements) in April.

Early one morning, generally believed to have been Wednesday, 9 April, Burke was drinking rum and bitters in William Swanston's shop in the Canongate when two young prostitutes came in. They were Janet Brown and Mary Paterson, aka Mitchell, both in their late teens and well known on the city streets. Mary, in particular, was a good-looking girl who had turned to prostitution in desperation, having been orphaned in childhood. She had curling-papers in her hair. Both girls had spent the previous night in the Canongate watch-house, having been arrested for a disturbance of the peace. On their release at six o'clock, they had gone, for some unexplained reason, to their former lodging at the house of a Mrs Lawrie, although they were now lodging with a Mrs Isabella Burnet or Worthington in Leith Wynd. No doubt both landladies were brothel-keepers.

Burke approached the girls in Swanston's and bought them drinks, then invited them to his lodgings for breakfast. Mary, the more bold and impulsive of the two, took little persuading and after a time Burke overcame Janet's reluctance with flattery and extravagant promises. The three left Swanston's shop with two bottles of whisky. But instead of walking them to Tanner's Close, Burke took them to his brother Constantine's place in nearby Gibb's Close off the Canongate, telling them he was lodging there. He was no doubt anxious to avoid being seen by anyone who might recognise the girls, either in the streets or in Hare's place.

A bed hung with tattered curtains and a truckle-bed were among the scant furnishings of a single room reached via a dark passage and a narrow staircase. Con Burke and his wife were still in bed, but Mrs Burke got up and prepared breakfast for the visitors, and they washed down their eggs, bread and smoked haddock with tea and whisky. By the time Con Burke left for work, Mary Paterson was almost senseless. Janet, however, was still wide awake, and Burke persuaded her to go out with him for a breath of air. He took her to a nearby tavern where he plied her with pies and beer, then took her back to Gibb's Close. They were just sitting down at the table to consume more whisky when the curtains round the bed flew open and the livid features of Nelly McDougal appeared.

Nelly had called in while Burke was out, to find the young and attractive Paterson slumped across the table and Burke out, as Elizabeth Burke must have told her, with another girl. A furious row ensued, with Nelly shrieking abuse at Janet Brown and threatening violence. Elizabeth Burke left hurriedly, though not before explaining to Janet, somewhat needlessly perhaps, that the screaming woman was Mr Burke's wife. Janet said she had not known that Burke was a married man. Nelly's wrath then turned on her husband, and Burke threw a glass tumbler at her, cutting her forehead above one eye. He pushed her out of the room and locked the door. Nelly had accused Janet of seducing her husband, but Burke was the seducer, with lust in his loins taking temporary priority over murder in his mind. Janet, however, was not to be coaxed into bed by Burke's Irish charm, and insisted on leaving. This was doubtless because of Nelly McDougal's fearsome presence on the other side of the door. Burke escorted Janet safely past his wife into the street, and she went back to Mrs Lawrie's house.

Elizabeth Burke, meanwhile, had gone to fetch the Hares. When they arrived, Burke and Hare manoeuvred their three female relatives into waiting outside the room. Then they laid the stupefied Mary Paterson onto one of the beds and had no trouble in snuffing out her short, sad life.

Burke went at once to Surgeons' Square to arrange another delivery. While he was gone, Janet Brown turned up again. She had a servant girl with her, sent urgently by Mrs Lawrie to help Janet bring Mary Paterson back. But Janet, half drunk herself, had taken twenty minutes to find the place again, having to ask directions from neighbours and the spirit-dealer Swanston. Nelly McDougal's rage at Brown had not subsided, and Maggie Laird had been told the tale, for she flew at Janet and had to be restrained by her husband. Hare told Janet that Burke had gone out for a walk with Mary. Janet accepted Hare's offer of a drink while she waited for them to come back, and sent the girl back to tell Mrs Lawrie that she would not be long.

We can only guess how close to death Janet Brown was during those few minutes. She was drinking whisky in the company of Hare and three possible accomplices – his wife, McDougal and Eliza Burke – with her friend Mary lying dead a few feet away, hidden by the bed-curtains, and Burke due back at any moment to pack up Mary's corpse and get it to Dr Knox. But Mrs Lawrie sent the maidservant back for Janet and the two girls then left together. Nelly and Maggie went home to Tanner's Close, and when Burke came back, he and Hare stuffed Mary Paterson's doubled-up corpse into a tea-chest.

However much Burke's sister-in-law may have known or suspected about these goings-on, it is clear that Burke was not keen to leave the tea-chest there until dark, when Con would be home from work. So Burke and Hare carried the box straight to Surgeons' Square in broad daylight. When they got to High School Yards, some schoolboys followed them, chanting 'They're carrying a corpse!' Burke and Hare were admitted to Dr Knox's rooms by 'Mr Ferguson and a tall lad' and paid, according to Burke's *Courant* confession, £8.

There are several contradictory statements about what happened at 10 Surgeons' Square that afternoon, but it is certain that someone immediately recognised the dead girl. Burke's prison statement makes it sound as if it was the 'tall lad', who 'seemed to have known the woman by sight', and he and Fergusson asked where they had got the body. Burke told them that he had bought it from an old woman at the back of the Canongate.

In the *Courant* confession, Burke said, 'One of the students said she was like a girl he had seen in the Canongate as one pea is like to another.' At the end of this dictated statement Burke added in his own hand, 'Mr. fergeson was the only man that ever mentioned any thing about the bodies He inquired where we got that yong woman paterson.'

There are, however, other versions of this transaction. Knox's biographer, his former pupil Henry Lonsdale, says that:

> A pupil of Knox's, who had been in her company only a few nights previously . . . eagerly and sympathisingly sought for an explanation of her sudden death, Burke on his next visit was confronted with his questioner in the presence of two gentlemen, and declared that he bought the corpse from an old hag in the Canongate, and that Paterson had killed herself with drink.[1]

As the corpse smelt strongly of whisky, this explanation was accepted. We have already noted that heavy consumption of whisky played a vital role in the murders committed by Burke and Hare. Their victims, as Charles Kirkpatrick Sharpe wrote:

> . . . were enticed to their tragical end by the present of spirituous liquors, which rendered them passive in the clutches of their butchers. It is too certain, that the use of whisky, in this town at least, is prevalent beyond example – and that the older parts of the city, even in mid-day, exhibit scenes that rival Hogarth's Gin Lane, or the beastly orgies of the ancient Scandinavian savages.[2]

A further witness to these exchanges was David Paterson, who was not related to Mary, but was a young man employed by Dr Knox. He declared later that he came into the room to find Miller in conversation with Burke and Hare, and 'a female subject stretched upon the floor. The beautiful symmetry and freshness of the body attracted my attention.' Shortly afterwards, Paterson heard Fergusson say that 'he was acquainted with the deceased, and named her as Mary Mitchell . . .'[3] A few days later Paterson asked Burke, who had called on another errand, 'where he had procured the last subject', and Burke replied that he had 'purchased it from the friends of the deceased', whereupon Paterson asked where her relatives lived. Burke paused, looking suspiciously at Paterson, before retorting, 'If I am to be catechised by you, where and how I get subjects, I will inform the doctor of it, and if he allows you to do so, I will bring no more to him, mind that.'[4]

Burke and Hare were paid, according to Paterson, £10 for this body, and he was almost certainly right. Why would these useful suppliers be offered, and accept, a lower price than normal for such a fine specimen – especially one so fresh, which was in Knox's premises within four hours of the murder, according to Burke, and still warm? The only explanation, if Burke's memory was correct, is that Mary Paterson was one of their first victims, sold before a tariff had become well established whereby the suppliers got £10 in winter and £8 in summer. This was because there was always a greater demand for subjects during the autumn and winter months. Most teachers of anatomy and surgery held their lecture courses then. In the days before refrigeration, bodies could not be preserved for long enough in the summer for them to remain useful for the necessary period of time, and the stench would have been intolerable on hot summer days. In winter, corpses were stored in cold cellars and the dissection rooms were decidedly chilly.

April was too early for summer rates to be in force, and Burke and Hare evidently got £10 for other corpses delivered *after* Paterson's. Of the £10 they received for the majority of their victims, split fifty-fifty in theory, Hare actually took £6, one pound of Burke's share being appropriated by Maggie Laird ostensibly as a kind of tax on his use of her premises.

In the 'official' confession Burke said that the body was disposed of 'five or six hours after the girl was killed, and it was cold, but not very stiff, but he does not recollect of any remarks being made about the body being warm'. In the *Courant* confession, however, made nearly three weeks later, he recalled that Mary Paterson 'had twopence halfpenny, which she held fast in her hand'. If rigor mortis had not yet set in, this tight grip on her coins would indicate a cadaveric spasm occurring at the moment of death under severe nervous tension. The students asked Burke to cut off the girl's hair, which still had her curling-papers in it. One of them handed him a pair of scissors, and 'she was warm when Burke cut the hair off her head'.

Whether warm or cold, limp or stiff, it is certainly clear that Mary Paterson's corpse made a dramatic impression, for one reason or another, on all who saw it, including Knox himself. One or more of them recognised the girl as someone they had seen around Edinburgh or were more familiar with, and all of them were impressed by the beauty of the naked but lifeless figure. Knox, Burke said, 'brought a Mr — , a painter, to look at her, she was so handsome a figure, and well shaped in body and limbs'. He added that 'she was not dissected at that time, for she was three months in whisky before she was dissected'. Who would have told Burke this? It surely can only have been Paterson. Knox's biographer wrote that the body of Mary Paterson 'could not fail to attract attention by its voluptuous form and beauty; students crowded around the table on which she lay, and artists came to study a model worthy of Phidias and the best Greek art'. Knox, he added, 'wishing for the best illustration of female form and muscular development for his lectures, had Paterson's body put in spirit for a time, so that when he came to treat of the myological division of his course, a further and daily publicity was given to Paterson's remains . . .'[5]

Davie Paterson, the janitor, also stated that it was the common opinion among Knox's students and assistants that it was a finely proportioned body, 'so much so, indeed, that many of the students took sketches of it . . .'[6] Necrophilia, it seems, superseded medical science for a time on Dr Knox's premises. There is a surviving pencil drawing by J. Oliphant which certainly appears to endorse opinions of Paterson's shapely form, but there is a touch of the macabre in the fact that this 'pin-up' was drawn from a corpse.

Meanwhile, Janet Brown and the two solicitous madams, Lawrie and Worthington, continued to enquire about Paterson's whereabouts. Janet Brown asked Constantine Burke about her friend when she met him in the street one day. 'How the hell can I tell about you sort of folk?' he said. 'You are here today and away tomorrow.' He added that he could not answer for everything that took place in his house while he was out at work.

Burke and Hare had, by this time, resumed normal business. The two fiends took to lurking in the dark and dingy streets and wynds of the Old Town like predatory animals ready to pounce on and devour the weakest and most vulnerable prey. Destitute, feeble and homeless creatures who depended on the kindness of strangers for a drink and a roof over their heads for a night fell easily into their foul ambushes. Their next victim, probably, was a destitute old woman who came to Hare's place looking for a night's lodging. Burke thought it was in May. He did not know the woman's name. She was drinking heavily and soon became quite drunk. Burke declared to the Sheriff in his official confession that he suffocated her himself while Hare was out, and that evening they disposed of the body, in the customary manner, for £10. But in his *Courant* confession, Burke told a different story. According to this version, the drunken woman fell asleep after being lured into the house by Hare's wife, and 'when Hare came home to his dinner, he put part of the bed-tick on her mouth and nose, and when he came home at night she was dead'. Burke was mending shoes at the time, he said. They took her clothes off and put the body into a tea-chest for delivery to Dr Knox. When he told this story, Burke had had nearly three weeks sitting in the condemned cell to think about it, and he had every reason to implicate Hare as deeply as possible in the whole series of murders.

Another of Hare's temporary lodgers was a woman named Mary Haldane. The clerk writing down Burke's confession in prison noted that Burke 'knows nothing farther of her'. But again, in the *Courant* confession, Burke, putting her much further down the list in order, said that she was a stout old woman, with only one large tooth in her mouth, who had two daughters, one of whom had been in Calton jail until sentenced the previous summer to fourteen years' transportation. 'Mrs' Haldane, who was unmarried, fell asleep in a drunken stupor on some straw in Hare's stable, and the two suffocated her there and then, keeping the body hidden in the stable that night and taking it to Surgeons' Square the next day.

By this time, Burke and Hare, responsible for six profitable murders, had settled into a routine, scouting for suitable victims and disposing of them in their familiar manner. They had not used a pillow or cushion to smother their victims since the first, Joseph the miller, but relied on their bare hands, one of them clapping one hand over the mouth and holding the nostrils closed with the other, while his partner lay across the body to prevent struggling. The method had the supreme advantage that it left no marks on the body, and 'when they kept the mouth and nose shut a very few minutes', as Burke described it in his *Courant* confession:

> . . . they could make no resistance, but would convulse and make
> a rumbling noise in their bellies for some time; after they ceased
> crying and making resistance, they left them to die of
> themselves; but their bodies would often move afterwards, and
> for some time they would have long breathings before life went
> away.

NOTES

[1] Lonsdale, pp. 101–2.

[2] Robert Buchanan et al, *Trial of William Burke and Helen McDougal.* Sharpe was the anonymous editor of this transcript of the trial from the shorthand notes of John Macnee.

[3] 'Echo of Surgeons' Square', *Letter to the Lord Advocate, Disclosing the Accomplices, Secrets, and Other Facts Relative to the Late Murders* etc. (Menzies, Edinburgh, 1829). See Appendix V.

[4] Ibid.

[5] Lonsdale, pp. 101–2.

[6] 'Echo of Surgeons' Square', *Letter to the Lord Advocate.*

4. PRACTICE

Burke and Hare called their victims 'shots', body-snatchers' slang, and it appears likely that they allowed and perhaps encouraged people (their neighbours and possibly their consorts) to believe that they were body-snatchers, to account for their evident increase in wealth, since rumour had got about even beyond the shadowy confines of the underworld that body-snatching was a lucrative business, however ghastly. It would also explain their business with tea-chests and the like.

Although one naturally tends to associate all the duo's criminal activity with the darkness and stealth favoured by professional body-snatchers, who stayed at home on moonlit nights, it is remarkable that Burke and Hare committed almost the whole series of their murders during daylight hours. The reason was partly to do with the premises they occupied. Murder could not be committed in Hare's house at night, when the place might be full of lodgers sleeping two or three to a bed. During the day these vagrants and derelicts would be out working or begging in the streets, and the evil pair and their women had the place to themselves. The murders in Hare's premises were carried out either in Burke's room, which was hidden from outside, unlike the interiors of the two larger rooms, or in the stable.

There were no coroners' inquests in Scotland. A sudden death was of no interest to the authorities unless some evidence of suspicious circumstances was presented to the Procurator-Fiscal. Delivery of a body in broad daylight would be less likely to arouse suspicion than one carried furtively through the streets under cover of darkness.

'Christopher North' characterised the sequence of victims of Burke and Hare as 'First ae drunk auld wife, and then anither drunk auld wife – and then a third drunk auld wife – and then a drunk auld or sick man or twa . . .'[1] The truth, however, is a great deal more startling and varied than this summary suggests. But before resuming the gruesome litany of the murders, it will be useful to consider the men who offered Burke and

Hare a ready – not to say voracious – market for their wares, and unwittingly incited multiple homicide. Who *were* these irresponsible reptiles whose actions cost the lives of so many?

The three medical students who were present at 10 Surgeons' Square when the Irish salesmen made their first cold call were William Fergusson, Alexander Miller and Thomas Wharton Jones. These young men were to become eminent surgeons. Jones was only narrowly beaten by von Helmholtz to being recognised as the inventor of the ophthalmoscope. Fergusson, born only a few miles from Edinburgh at Prestonpans, became Professor of Surgery at London's King's College, a post he held for thirty years. He invented many surgical instruments and was elected a Fellow of the Royal Society in 1843 and President of the Royal College of Surgeons in 1870. He was also President of the General Medical Council and a surgeon to Queen Victoria, by whom he was duly knighted. At the time we are concerned with, however, the three, all about nineteen years old, were keen students and assistants of Dr Robert Knox.

Born in Edinburgh, Knox was thirty-six years old. His mother's forbears were German, but he claimed descent on his father's side from the famous Protestant reformer, who had lived in a house in the High Street only yards from what was now Surgeons' Square. Knox was conservator of the museum of Edinburgh's College of Surgeons and had in 1826 succeeded John Barclay as proprietor of the school of anatomy set up independently of the university's medical school, which was presided over by Professor Monro. Third of a declining dynasty and a disappointment to his employers and students alike, Monro saw his students deserting him for the lectures of first Barclay and then Knox, as well as other extra-mural teachers. Knox had himself failed his first university examination in anatomy because of the teaching inadequacies of Monro *tertius*, and had transferred his allegiance to Barclay, eventually becoming his partner and then his successor.

John Barclay taught anatomy for nearly thirty years. He bought the three-storey house at 10 Surgeons' Square and had his anatomy theatre on the top floor, continually enlarging it as his classes grew. Barclay considered Knox to be 'a person of precision, method, and expertness, a growing naturalist, and an excellent human and comparative anatomist'.[2] Knox became an assistant surgeon in the army and tended the wounded at Waterloo, then spent some time in South Africa and France before returning to Edinburgh to join his teacher. There were other extra-mural teachers of anatomy and surgery in the square. John

Gordon lectured next door at No. 9 and David Craigie at No. 3. William Cullen taught in the house built by John Bell at the other side of the square at the eastern end of Surgeons' Hall. But none of them attracted so many students as either Barclay or, after his retirement in 1825, Robert Knox. The lectures of both Barclay and Knox were so popular that, their anatomical theatre being limited in seating capacity, they had to give matinée performances. In the winter season of 1827–28, when Burke and Hare joined the motley crew of Knox's suppliers of subjects, Knox had 247 registered medical students, compared with the 138 of his nearest rival, John Lizars. Monro at the university had 88 and John Aitken, another lecturer in Surgeons' Square, only 47.[3] At one point in Knox's career, his students constituted the largest anatomy class in Britain.

Knox presented a stiff upright figure, balding prematurely, with powerful shoulders and long arms. He had lost his left eye, which had atrophied as a result of smallpox in his infancy, leaving an empty socket. His students naturally nicknamed him 'Old Cyclops'. When his concentration was at its most intense during his lectures, the muscles in his face were restless. 'These involuntary twitchings,' his biographer observed, 'were far from agreeable, especially those which affected his under-lip, the crossing of which from side to side produced a kind of smacking noise.'[4] He was flamboyant in his dress, with gold chains, diamond rings and embroidered waistcoats, all of which served to distract attention from his ravaged features. 'Knox,' said his biographer, 'in the highest style of fashion, with spotless linen, frill, and lace, and jewellery redolent of a duchess's boudoir, standing in a classroom amid osseous forms, *cadavera*, and decaying mortalities, was a sight to behold, and one assuredly never to be forgotten.'[5]

He was arrogant and contemptuous of his professional colleagues, whom he regularly slandered with jealous lies. He is reported to have begun one lecture by describing an operation in which his famous rival Robert Liston had lost a patient. Without mentioning Liston by name, Knox sarcastically referred to 'this professional celebrity, a gentleman who, I believe, regards himself as the first surgeon in Europe'. After ridiculing Liston's judgement in this case, Knox concluded, 'It is surely unnecessary for me to add that a knowledge of anatomy, physiology, pathology and surgery, is neither connected with nor dependent upon brute force, ignorance and presumption.'[6]

He also attacked Dr Robert Christison and Dr James Syme in public, as belonging to a clique in the Royal Society, and referred to Professor

Richard Partridge, of King's College, London, who had failed to acknowledge Knox's work in a published paper as 'true to his class . . . [and] bound to strike out of his paper any view not of London growth'.[7] 'In the lecture-room,' wrote the historian of the Edinburgh medical school, 'the ridicule which he cast on the opinions, and too often on the men, of the time, did not on the whole help him.'[8] Even Knox's loyal friend and biographer, who religiously avoided anything in his text that was to Knox's discredit, had to admit that, 'Instead of a tongue that speaketh no evil, and the soft word that turneth away wrath, he showed an almost habitual disregard for prudent reticence.'[9]

Fierce professional rivalry was a feature of the period, however, and Knox was not the only eminent medical man in Edinburgh to resort to vilification of his colleagues. Dr James Gregory, Professor of the Practice of Medicine at the university, had written of the famous surgeon John Bell, generally regarded as one of the greatest of his time, 'Any man, if himself or his family were sick, should as soon think of calling in a mad dog as Mr John Bell, or any who held the principles he professes.'[10]

John Lizars, a colleague at different times of both Robert Liston and John Bell, once condemned an operation carried out by James Syme, implying that Syme had endangered his patient's life and ruined his health through lack of care. Syme, who had been a competitor for the post Lizars held as Professor of Surgery at the Royal College of Surgeons of Edinburgh, sued for a thousand guineas in damages for a false and malicious statement, though there is no record that he got it.

One of Knox's subsequently eminent pupils, John Hughes Bennett, a pioneer in the use of the microscope in clinical pathology, turned out to have absorbed more than expertise in anatomy from his teacher. He became President of the Royal Medical Society, a Fellow of the Royal Society of Edinburgh and the Edinburgh College of Physicians, and Professor of the Institutes of Medicine, but when he lectured, he became 'too often condemnatory of others, and hence did not fail to stir up antagonism . . . his critical and sarcastic remarks on the works of others did not make him a favourite among his professional brethren'.[11]

Knox's own acid tongue, together with the general opinion that he had married beneath him, left him with very few friends, either social or professional. He lived at Newington, a fashionable suburb to the south-east of Edinburgh, but we know so little about his elusive wife that even her name, Mary, is known only from inference. Lonsdale ignores Knox's marriage altogether and barely mentions his wife, who, like five of his six children, preceded him to the grave. Despite his shortcomings, however, Knox was a man of considerable intellect and a brilliant teacher. Among others taught by him, as well as those mentioned above, were Sir Richard Owen,[12] who became Director of the Natural History Museum at Kensington, and John Goodsir, Professor of Anatomy at Edinburgh University from 1846. Knox published learned papers on comparative and human anatomy and translated the works of foreign anatomists. 'From 1826 to 1835,' one of his biographers wrote, 'there was but one temple worthy of the name in Edinburgh, in which aspiring youths might worship in the spirit of Galen . . . and that temple was "Old Surgeons' Hall", where Robert Knox presided as high priest, oracle and philosopher.'[13] (Knox moved his classes from Barclay's house to the old Surgeons' Hall in 1832, when it was vacated by the College of Surgeons.) To maintain his reputation, Knox needed to ensure that he had an adequate supply of fresh corpses. He had never been a body-snatcher himself, like Liston and other contemporaries, but he was prepared to pay professional resurrectionists to keep him supplied, and he paid good prices promptly, so that they were keen to do business with him rather than other surgeons who might haggle over prices and be dilatory in paying up.

And so Burke and Hare, purely by chance, had joined the small army of suppliers scattered about Britain and Ireland from whom Dr Knox purchased his subjects for demonstration. The two Irishmen were not known to him by name. He rarely saw them, for their frequent calls became a nuisance and he asked them to deal with his porter, David Paterson, who lived close to them in the West Port. His senior students also acted as negotiators with the two men known to them only as 'John' and 'William'.

Henry Lonsdale explained the circumstances in which the anatomists of Edinburgh frequently procured subjects for their classes:

> It is needful to revert to the mode of procuring 'subjects' from lodging-houses, to show the grounds for believing, as all Knox's men did, that Burke and Hare trafficked in the dead of unclaimed strangers. If the artisan or tramp, the sma' pedlar, the gaberlunzie, and other waifs and strays, decrepid and aged, classed as unknown vagabonds, died in a lodging-house where ten or more persons slept, the removal of the corpse became an urgent necessity . . . Those who knew the Old Town of Edinburgh, its wretched 'wynds', its hovels, or rather styes, its whisky shops and dens of iniquity, could have no difficulty in

comprehending the frequency of casualties amid such a frightfully debased population. Life was everywhere surrounded by the contingencies of death. The filth and horrors of Paris, as described by Eugène Sue, had their counterpart in the Cowgate, Canongate, and Grassmarket. Housed in the sunless and fetid alleys, or the worse tainted *cul de sacs* or 'closes', sheltering by dilapidated gables and sheds for cattle, or half smothered amid burrowed ruins and cellarage tenanted with rats and vermin, men, women, and children huddled together in brutal fashion. Of what consideration was life to mortals in the veriest rags and tatters, in the midst of stench, and feeding on the garbage of the gutters, or the poison of the dram-shops? Was death not rather a consummation devoutly to be wished? Human beings so lost to shame and natural feeling would have sold the corpse of their neighbours, and as readily that of their nearest relative, for a few bottles of whisky . . . Now, all bodies obtained in this way were, of course, but recently dead; the same remark was applicable, but not so forcibly, to some exhumed bodies removed immediately after the regular interment.[14]

Soon after Burke and Hare had delivered the corpse of Mrs Haldane to Knox's premises, an old cinder woman, whose name, Burke thought, was Effie, came to Hare's house. She sometimes sold small pieces of leather to Burke for his cobbling, offcuts she had obtained from a local coach-works. Burke took her into Hare's stable and plied her with whisky until she was drunk and fell asleep in the straw. Then he and Hare suffocated her and sold her body to Dr Knox for £10.

One day Burke encountered a constable, Andrew Williamson, and another man, dragging a drunken woman, who had been found 'sitting on a stair', to the West Port watch-house. Burke intervened on the woman's behalf and offered to take her off their hands and escort her to her lodgings – an offer, it seems, that the policeman was pleased to accept. Burke was asked in prison by the *Courant* representative if the policeman knew him when he gave the woman into Burke's charge. Burke replied that he had a good character with the police; '*or if they had known that there were four murderers living in one house they would have visited them oftener*' (my italics). The woman, needless to say, was taken not to *her* lodgings but to Burke's, and soon appeared on Knox's dissecting table. Burke said in his *Courant* confession that they got £10 for her, so this murder took place when Knox's winter rates were still being paid, before June.

The unimposing entrance to Hare's lodging-house was becoming more like the ominous portal of Dante's *Inferno*, as if the sign 'Beds to let' had the dread inscription in small print underneath, 'All hope abandon, ye who enter here.' The next ill-fated entrants were an old woman and her grandson from Glasgow. Burke dated these murders to 'about midsummer'. The boy, who was around twelve years old, was a deaf mute. Burke and Hare murdered the woman 'at the dead hour of night', while she slept, having consumed much whisky as usual. They stripped off her clothing and covered her with the bedclothes, then fetched the child, who was sitting with Nelly and Maggie at the fire in the kitchen, into the same room, and killed him too, laying him beside his grandmother.

It is worth bearing in mind that some of these so-called 'old women' or 'drunk auld wives' were maybe not so old as we might imagine. Destitute and ill cared-for folk might appear old, but the grandmother of a twelve-year-old boy, for instance, could be well under fifty herself, and if she was capable of walking from Glasgow to Edinburgh, as one version of the story suggests, she was hardly on her last legs.

There is a story, often repeated, that Burke, instead of suffocating the boy, put him across his knee and broke his back. It originates from *The Court of Cacus* by Alexander Leighton, who, writing more than thirty years after the events, heard various tales at second- or third-hand which may have been enhanced, if not actually invented, by the author's fertile imagination. It seems highly unlikely that Burke and Hare would depart from their tried and trusted method so far as to kill anyone in a violent manner which would require explanation when seen by medical men, and we can safely dismiss this tale as a piece of sensational embroidery.

After leaving the two corpses where they were for an hour, the two men stuffed them into a herring-barrel, which they carried into the stable. In the morning, they lifted the barrel onto Hare's cart, hitched Hare's old horse to it, and set off for Surgeons' Square. They had progressed no farther than the Meal Market, however, a mere few yards from Tanner's Close, before the nag came to a halt and refused to budge, despite the blows and curses of its owner. This commotion soon drew a small crowd of spectators, so Burke quickly found a porter with a hurley (a two-wheeled barrow) and employed him to wheel the herring-barrel the rest of the way. Hare accompanied the porter while Burke went on ahead to prepare for the barrel's reception. The students he met there had some difficulty in extracting the two pallid corpses from the barrel, as they were 'so stiff and cold'. (This indicates that rigor mortis had set in and it must have been during the afternoon when the delivery was made.) Burke and Hare were paid at the agreed summer rate of £8 for each of the bodies. They went home and Hare shot the horse in the tanner's yard. The wretched animal had two large holes in its shoulder which had been stuffed with cotton by the animal's previous owner and covered over with a piece of skin to hide the wounds when he sold the horse to Hare.

On 24 June (Burke rather curiously remembered that it was the anniversary of the Battle of Bannockburn), Burke and Nelly left Edinburgh for a few days to visit Nelly's father near Falkirk. They left Hare in want of funds; he had pawned his clothes. But when Burke and Nelly came back, Hare had 'plenty of money'. Burke asked him if he had been doing any business. At first Hare denied it, but Burke did not believe him and 'went to Dr Knox, who told him that Hare had brought a subject'. It turned out that Hare had taken home a woman he had found drunk in the street, murdered her, and sold the corpse to Knox for £8, but was reluctant to share the proceeds.

The solid partnership was developing a few cracks. Burke alleged that Maggie Laird had, at some point, tried to persuade him to murder Nelly McDougal, on the grounds that she was 'a Scotch woman' and could not be trusted. The idea was that Burke and Nelly should go to the country for a few weeks and Burke, having done the deed, would then write to tell Hare that Nelly had died and been buried. This was in order to be able to show the letter to the neighbours and allay suspicion. But Burke would have none of it. We cannot be certain that this suggestion was made prior to the visit to Falkirk, but it seems very likely and, added to Hare's secretive bit of private enterprise while they were absent, it was enough to make Burke and Nelly move to other lodgings.

Only two streets away from Tanner's Close lived a cousin of Burke's, who was married to John Broggan, a carter. Broggan and his wife, who was pregnant, rented a basement room behind a shop in a five-storey tenement. There was some waste ground behind it, and Broggan's apartment could be reached via a narrow passage from the West Port or down some steps from the waste ground. The 'house', as such places were commonly called in Edinburgh at the time, adjoined one occupied by a Mrs Ann Connoway and her husband John, and the passage to Broggan's entrance separated the Connoways from another house occupied by a Mrs Janet Law and her husband Robert, who worked at one of the local tanneries. Burke and Nelly moved in with the Broggans, and Burke soon took his revenge for Hare's deceit. The separate dens of Burke and Hare were about to become twin abodes of evil.

NOTES

[1] *Blackwood's Edinburgh Magazine*, March 1829.

[2] Lonsdale, p. 44.

[3] John Struthers, *Historical Sketch of the Edinburgh Anatomical School*, (Edinburgh, Maclachlen and Stewart, 1867), p. 92.

[4] Lonsdale, p. 125.

[5] Ibid, p. 126.

[6] Alexander Leighton, *The Court of Cacus*, (Edinburgh, Houlston & Wright, 1861), pp. 20–21(n).

[7] Lonsdale, p. 334.

[8] Struthers, p. 82.

[9] Lonsdale, p. 269.

[10] Struthers, p. 41.

[11] *Dictionary of National Biography*

[12] Owen was also, like his master, subject to jealousy and intolerance. Charles Darwin was among the victims of his hostility.

[13] Lonsdale, p. 162.

[14] Ibid, pp. 99–101.

5. JAMIE

Margaret Haldane was a daughter of the elderly prostitute Mary Haldane whom Burke and Hare had murdered in Hare's stable. According to Burke's official confession, Margaret came to Broggan's house, but he could not remember why. Burke killed her himself. He laid her face down on the bed and 'pressed her down, and she was soon suffocated'. She was easily disposed of, as she had got so drunk that Burke thought she 'was not sensible of her death, as she made no resistance whatever'. He committed the murder in the morning, took the body to Knox's premises in a tea-chest during the afternoon and got £8 for it. Hare was not present, and 'neither Broggan nor his son knew the least thing about that or any other case of the same kind'. But Burke's mention of *Margaret* Haldane presents us with a slight puzzle, for in the *Courant* confession Burke said that it was *Peggy* Haldane he had killed.

We might easily assume, since 'Peggy' is a common diminutive of 'Margaret', that they were one and the same person. But in the early nineteenth century, 'Peggy' was a popular name in its own right. Furthermore, Burke declared that Margaret's sister was married to a tinsmith in the High Street, named Clark. And in the *Courant* confession, he said that Mrs Haldane, 'who had a daughter transported last summer from the Calton jail for fourteen years', also had another daughter 'married to – in the High Street'. But the woman that Burke said he had killed was, according to his story, a lodger of Hare's, and she and her mother were 'both of idle habits, and much given to drinking'. If we can safely assume, then, that the one Burke admitted to killing in Broggan's house was neither Clark's wife nor the one transported, Mrs Haldane must have had three daughters, not two.

Is it possible that Burke confused the names of Margaret and Peggy because he had murdered them *both*? If so, we must revise the number of murders generally attributed to Burke and Hare. Alexander Leighton gathered information many years afterwards that led him to assert that Mrs Haldane did indeed have three daughters, but that the one murdered was done to death in Tanner's Close, when she came there searching for her mother. According to this version, she had been told by David Rymer, a grocer and publican in West Port, that her mother had been seen going into Hare's house. But is Burke likely to have confessed (twice) to carrying out a murder by himself in Broggan's house if it were not true? If there is any truth in the hearsay that Leighton picked up, it would seem to confirm that two of Mrs Haldane's daughters were murdered as well as herself. And if Burke had 'forgotten' why one of them turned up at Broggan's, it was probably because he was reluctant to admit that he had taken her there for sexual intercourse while Broggan and his family, not to mention Nelly, were out.

Roughead and Douglas both place the murder of Margaret Haldane immediately after that of her mother, because Burke mentioned them together in his *Courant* confession. Douglas said it 'seems unlikely that these two murders would be separated in time . . .'[1] But, on the contrary, it does seem very likely that they were. Burke's statements make it clear that, having moved out of Hare's premises, he killed the daughter himself to get his own back on Hare. The two Haldanes are not placed together in the 'official' confession, which Burke later said was the only one that could be relied on. Hugh Douglas considered that the order of the murders 'hardly seems relevant to us today'.[2] But consideration of the unfortunate people who came into fatal contact with Burke and Hare is the only recognition that they lived and died, and served humanity, albeit unwillingly, in death. Unlike the soldiers who have died in battle, they do not have permanent memorials in their honour, but although the manner of their deaths was appalling and far from heroic, they too served their country in a noble purpose. An attempt to determine the circumstances of their deaths is the least we can do for them. (See table at the end of this chapter.)

Despite the strained relations between the two murderers and their women, the partnership was too successful to be dissolved. Burke and Hare realised that they could work better as a team than as separate individuals, and soon resumed normal business.

Mrs Ostler was a washer-woman who came to Broggan's house to wash some clothes. Hare was there with Burke, and they got the woman drunk and suffocated her in their well-practised modus operandi. She had ninepence-halfpenny in her hand, which she grasped so firmly that they had difficulty prising it out when she was dead. 'Mrs Broggan,'

Burke said, 'was out at the time.' They put the body in a box which they then concealed in a coal-house in the passage until the afternoon, when they took it to Surgeons' Square and got £8. Burke said that this murder took place in September or October. The earlier month seems more likely, for by October, one supposes, Dr Knox's winter rates should have been in force. 'Arrangements have been made,' said the announcement of his new season of lectures, 'to secure as usual an ample supply of Anatomical Subjects.'

The new season was underway by the time Ann McDougal came to Edinburgh on a short visit. She was a young married woman, a cousin of Nelly's former partner. She had come to see Nelly, probably at her invitation, following the visit to Falkirk. She stayed in Edinburgh for a few days, but then Hare came round to Broggan's, and he and Burke began dosing her with whisky until she became drunk and fell asleep during the afternoon. Burke claimed he felt some delicacy about being the first to lay hands on her, she being a friend. So Hare stopped her breath while Burke held her down. They undressed the body and put it in a 'fine trunk' provided for the purpose by Davie Paterson, Knox's assistant, he having been notified that 'John' and 'William' had another 'thing' for sale.

When Broggan came home from work, he saw the trunk and began asking questions about it, but Burke and Hare gave him some whisky and each of them gave him one pound ten shillings to pay the rent he owed. He then quietened down. They gave him the money, Burke said, 'that he might not come against them for the murder of Ann McDougal, that he saw in the trunk, that was murdered in his house'. Does this mean that Burke and Hare were either so drunk themselves, or so stupidly complacent by this time, that they left the trunk open with a corpse in it for anyone to see?

As soon as it was convenient, at any rate, Burke and Hare carried the trunk to Surgeons' Square and were paid £10 for Ann McDougal's corpse. Shortly afterwards, John Broggan and his wife absconded with the rent money, leaving Burke and Nelly responsible for both the flat and young John Broggan. Soon afterwards, Burke and Hare chanced upon another young victim.

James Wilson was a mentally subnormal young man, well known to people in the streets of Edinburgh as 'Daft Jamie'. Eighteen years old, his father had died when he was twelve. Jamie had left home after a thrashing from his mother when he had accidentally toppled a cupboard full of her household crockery. He still saw his mother regularly and she washed his clothes, but he would not return to live in the house. He slept in doorways except when someone took pity and offered him a bed for the night. He wandered about the streets with bare feet, which were deformed, causing him to limp, and was partly paralysed on his right side. Although tall and said to be strong for his age and condition, he would tearfully refuse to fight when younger boys mocked and goaded him, saying that it was only bad boys who fought. He would not wear the shoes and better clothes that well-wishers occasionally offered him to protect him from the elements, on the grounds that if people thought he was sufficiently dressed, they would no longer give him anything. Among his few possessions were a brass snuff-box and a copper spoon with seven holes, which Jamie called the days of the week, identifying the large one in the middle as Sunday. One of his favourite pastimes was asking riddles, but he would get upset when those to whom he posed them knew or could guess the answers. 'What month do ladies talk least?' he would ask, and delight in giving his baffled companion the answer, 'February, because there are fewer days in it.' Or, 'Why is a jailer like a musician?' 'Because he maun tak' care o' his key.'

Jamie's best friend was Robert Kirkwood, known as 'Bobby'. Once Bobby tricked Jamie out of a dram of whisky, and when others asked Jamie what he was going to do about it, he replied, 'What could ye say to puir Bobby? He's daft, ye ken.'

One morning in October, William Burke was having an early drink in Rymer's shop when he saw Maggie Laird in the street taking Jamie Wilson towards her house. A few minutes later she came into Rymer's, bought a pennyworth of butter, and asked Burke for a dram. While she was drinking it, she stamped lightly on Burke's foot. This is the first positive evidence of Maggie Laird's complicity in the murders. He, understanding the signal, followed her back to Tanner's Close. Hare was there with Jamie and had given him whisky. When Burke arrived, the two men lured Jamie into the small room which had formerly been Burke's, sat him on the bed and pressed him to have more whisky. Jamie was reluctant to drink more, and was 'very anxious making inquiries for his mother, and was told she would be there immediately'. Maggie Laird left the room and locked the door, leaving the three men inside, and slipped the key under the door. She had, Burke said, 'led poor Jamie in as a dumb lamb to the slaughter . . .'

After a time Jamie lay down on the bed, although he was not drunk. Hare, according to Burke's story, reclined behind or beside him with his head resting on one hand, watching. Burke was close by. Suddenly Hare, growing impatient, 'threw his body on the top of Jamie, pressed his hand on his mouth, and held his nose with the other'. Jamie, however, was weak in his mind, not in his body, and he put up a fierce fight, struggling so desperately that he and Hare fell off the bed. Hare did not let go, and Burke then got himself across Jamie's arms and legs, and the two fiends gripped tight until Jamie ceased to struggle and his body went limp. He was soon dead. 'He never got up nor cried any,' Burke said. It was not yet noon. They stripped the body naked, Hare going through the pockets and finding the snuff-box and spoon. He kept the box himself and gave the spoon to Burke. They put Jamie's corpse into a chest which Hare kept clothes in, and carried it that afternoon to Surgeons' Square, where they received £10.

There is an alternative version of these events, however, which the Edinburgh *Weekly Chronicle* printed after the trial, claiming that it was based 'upon the foul authority of Hare'. According to this, it was Burke who took Jamie to Hare's house after meeting him in the Grassmarket, where Jamie was looking for his mother. After being induced to drink 'a quantity of spirits', Jamie fell asleep on the floor and Burke then leapt on him and tried to strangle him, but had to howl for Hare's assistance when Jamie fought manfully. Burke threatened to stick a knife into Jamie if Hare did not help him. Hare then lent a hand by holding Jamie down.

This version seems much less likely than Burke's account, since neither man would have wanted to leave signs of violence on the body, and they had shown plenty of patience before in waiting for their victims to be in a suitable condition for their tried and tested method. But on the other hand, the act of murdering a well-known figure like Daft Jamie indicates a startling recklessness which might mean that, by this time, Burke and Hare thought they could get away with anything and were ready to throw all sane precautions to the winds. Subsequent events lend some substance to this probability.

Burke and Hare normally took care to destroy their victims' clothing, but this time Burke took Jamie's clothes and gave them to his brother Constantine's children, who were 'almost naked, and when he untied the bundle they were like to quarrel about them'. Burke on this occasion refused to pay Maggie Laird the usual pound out of his share of the proceeds. After all, he was no longer a tenant there. But Maggie was so put out that she refused to speak to Burke for three weeks.

When news of Jamie's death broke later on, many sentimental ballads and broadsheets appeared on the streets, with excruciatingly bad verses about Daft Jamie. None of the brutal acts of murder of Burke and Hare caused more widespread horror than their premeditated killing of this happy innocent:

> He's to be pitied, that's such a silly[3] elf,
> Who cannot speak nor wrestle for himself.
> Jamie was such a simpleton,
> He'd not fight with a boy;
> Nor did he ever curse or swear,
> At those who'd him annoy.[4]

Meanwhile, at 10 Surgeons' Square on the morning after the murder, the corpse of what David Paterson described as a 'stout young man' was unpacked and immediately recognised as Daft Jamie by several of Knox's students. According to Paterson, Knox denied that the corpse was that of Jamie, but, later, when word got around that Jamie had been missed from his customary haunts, Knox ordered dissection of the corpse at once, before other corpses that had been there longer. William Fergusson promptly severed Jamie's head and feet.

Was Paterson telling the truth when he made these damaging allegations? By the time he made them, he had allegedly been sacked by Knox, and it is commonly believed that he wanted to avenge himself on his former employer. Nevertheless, it seems rather unlikely that he would have invented this account of the disposal of Jamie's corpse. Jamie was stated in the trial indictment to have been living, at the time, in the house of James Downie, a porter, at Stevenlaw's Close in the High Street. It is hardly surprising that Paterson and others recognised him. William Fergusson lived with his brother John in Charles Street, and Alexander Miller had lodgings in Clerk Street, both in the Old Town. Almost everybody in central Edinburgh must have been familiar with the appearance of this innocent youth, a figure of fun to the insensitive and an object of compassion to others. It is quite probable that Robert Knox, who lived on a different social level, did not know him, but what was he to do when he realised that he had on his slab the unburied corpse of a well-known character who had only recently been seen alive and well? Burke and Hare had by now, between them, sold to Dr Knox sixteen 'subjects' (fifteen of which they had murdered) in the course of a little over ten months. They must have been regarded at Surgeons' Square as very useful contacts, and whatever dawning apprehensions may have crossed the minds of Knox or his students, such regular and reliable suppliers were not to be discouraged by awkward questions or any hesitation in paying the agreed price.

So far from Christopher North's monotonous 'auld wives' tale, their victims had now included Mary Paterson and Jamie Wilson, both teenagers, and the deaf mute child of twelve. If their evil progress had not soon been terminated, it is difficult to believe that they would not soon have begun to prey on children, easily kidnapped off the streets and more easily put to death.

Paterson, meanwhile, now out of a job, was rumoured to be planning to move west in partnership with Burke, to procure more bodies and dispatch them to Hare, who would sell them as usual to Knox. This story seems, at first sight, wildly improbable, partly because Burke had good reason not to trust Hare with money, and partly because Hare was the last man on earth to be left in charge of public relations with educated men. But in any case, before any such plan could be put into operation, events took a different turn.

NOTES

[1] Hugh Douglas, *Burke and Hare*, (London, Robert Hale, 1973), p. 136.

[2] Ibid.

[3] 'Silly' was used in the sense of 'innocent', not 'imbecilic'.

[4] *A Laconic Narrative of the Life and Death of James Wilson, known by the name of Daft Jamie*, W. Smith, 1829.

ALTERNATIVE VERSIONS OF THE ORDER OF MURDERS

BURKE 1 (OFFICIAL)	BURKE 2 (*COURANT*)	ROUGHEAD	DOUGLAS	BAILEY
1. Simpson*	Simpson	Joseph	Joseph	Joseph
2. Joseph*	Englishman	Englishman	Simpson	Englishman
3. Paterson	'Old woman'	Simpson	Englishman	Simpson
4. 'Old woman'	Paterson	'Old woman'	'Old woman'	Paterson
5. Englishman	Grandmother	Paterson	Paterson	'Old woman'
6. Mrs Haldane	Grandson	Effie	Effie	Mrs Haldane
7. Effie	Joseph	Drunk woman	Drunk woman	Effie
8. Grandmother	Lodger (Hare)	Grandmother	Grandmother	Drunk woman
9. Grandson	Effie	Grandson	Grandson	Grandmother
10. Drunk woman	Drunk woman	Lodger (Hare)	Lodger (Hare)	Grandson
11. Lodger (Hare)	Jamie Wilson	Ann McDougal	Mrs Ostler	Lodger (Hare)
12. Marg. Haldane	Ann McDougal	Mrs Ostler	Ann McDougal	Marg. Haldane
13. Mrs Ostler	Mrs Haldane	Mrs Haldane	Mrs Haldane	Mrs Ostler
14. Ann McDougal	Marg. Haldane	Marg. Haldane	Marg. Haldane	Ann McDougal
15. Jamie Wilson	Mrs Ostler	Jamie Wilson	Jamie Wilson	Jamie Wilson
16. Mrs Docherty	Mrs Docherty	Mrs Docherty	Mrs Docherty	Mrs Docherty

* Although no record of Hare's statement to the Sheriff exists, it is believed that he gave Joseph as the first victim and Simpson the second. Other writers on the case have generally followed one of the first four columns.

6. CLIMAX

On the morning of Hallowe'en, Friday, 31 October, regarded in Scotland especially as the most perilous night of the year, when devils and other malevolent beings were abroad, Burke went to Rymer's for his usual early dram. While he was drinking, a poor woman came in begging for charity. Burke recognised her Irish accent and asked where she was from. She told him Inishowen in Donegal, and that her name was Mary Docherty. Well, what a coincidence! Burke, buying her a dram, told her that his mother's name was Docherty, so it was, and that *she* had come from Inishowen. They must be related! The woman told him that she had come from Glasgow to look for her son. She had no money, and had had no breakfast that morning. The ever-solicitous Burke persuaded her to come home with him and have some porridge and another wee dram.

We have two rather contrasting impressions of Burke's 'house' at about this time. One is Christopher North's description:

> Burke's room was one of the neatest and snuggest little places I ever saw – walls well plastered and washed – a good wood-floor – respectable fireplace – and light well-paned window. You reached the room by going along a comfortable, and by no means dark passage, about fifteen feet long – on each side of which was a room, inhabited, the one by Mrs. Law, and the other by Mr. and Mrs. Connoway. Another short passage (with outer and inner door) turned off into the dwelling of Mr. Burke – the only possible way of making it a room by itself – and the character of the whole flat was that of comfort and cheerfulness to a degree seldom seen in the dwellings of the poor. Burke's room, therefore, so far from being remote or solitary, or adapted to murder, was in the very heart of life, and no more like a den than any other room in Edinburgh.[1]

The other description is in Thomas Ireland's contemporary account of *The West Port Murders*:

> In approaching Burke's you enter a respectable-looking *land* from the street, and proceed along a passage and then descend a stair, and turning to the right, a passage leads to the door, which is very near to Connoway's and almost directly opposite to Mrs. Law's; a dark passage within the door leads to the room . . . [which] presented a disgusting picture of squalid wretchedness; rags and straw, mingled with implements of shoemaking, and old shoes and boots in such quantities as Burke's nominal profession of a cobbler could never account for. A pot full of boiled potatoes was a prominent object. The bed was a coarse wooden frame without posts or curtains, and filled with old straw and rags.[2]

Perhaps Professor Wilson saw it after it had been cleared of all its contents by the police.

Burke and Mrs Docherty, at any rate, were seen entering by both Mrs Connoway and Mrs Law, who were sitting together by Mrs Connoway's fireside with the door open. Four others were present in Burke's house – Nelly McDougal, and a Mr James Gray and his wife Ann, with their infant child, who were lodging there. Burke and Nelly had not been slow to sub-let the premises they now occupied. Ann Gray's maiden name was McDougal and her father was none other than the man Nelly had lived with, bearing him two children before she left to live with Burke.

Having introduced Mrs Docherty to everyone and settled her down with food and drink, Burke left, ostensibly to buy enough drink for the Hallowe'en party they were to have that night. But in Rymer's shop he found Hare, and told him that he had 'a good shot for the doctors'. Hare went to Burke's house to have a look, saw the 'old woman' washing her striped shift, and left after a few minutes.

The woman's married name was Campbell, but she was commonly known as Docherty and repeatedly referred to as an 'old woman'. We may again doubt if she was old. The only person who was at all specific later with regard to the woman's age was a Mrs Stewart with whom Mrs Docherty had stayed for one night when she came to town looking for her son Michael. Mrs Stewart thought she was 'between forty and fifty', and in 'as good health as any woman could be, to all appearance'.

William Noble, Rymer's shop-boy, described her as 'middle-aged'. Professor Christison, who later carried out a post-mortem examination, testified that except for a 'very slight incipient disorder of the liver', all her internal organs were 'unusually sound' and there were no signs of any disease.

During the afternoon, Burke told the Grays that he wanted the bed that night for Mrs Docherty, who was a relation of his, and that he would pay for them to lodge somewhere else. He fixed them up at Hare's place. Mrs Connoway turned up briefly and was introduced to the stranger, who was sitting by the fire 'supping porridge and milk'. Nelly McDougal told her that Mrs Docherty was a Highland woman, a friend of her husband's.

At about four o'clock, young Broggan, the former tenant's son, who called Nelly McDougal 'aunt', came in and saw Burke and Nelly, Hare and Maggie, the Grays and two 'strange women', one of whom was Mrs Docherty and the other Mrs Connoway. The Grays left shortly afterwards and went to Tanner's Close with Maggie, who must have come straight back, because Mrs Law saw her there between six and seven. Soon after dark Nelly McDougal called at Mrs Connoway's and asked her to keep an eye on her door until she came back, as it did not lock. John Broggan left at about seven o'clock. At about nine, the Grays came back briefly to get their child's clothes, and saw Burke and Hare drinking, their two women dancing, and Mrs Docherty singing.

Some time later, Mr Connoway remarked to his wife that he thought someone had gone into Burke's. His wife took a light to have a look, but found only Mrs Docherty there, somewhat the worse for drink. Mrs Docherty followed her out, saying she was going to meet someone in St Mary's Wynd who had promised to 'fetch her word about her son'. Mrs Connoway dissuaded her from going out in that condition, as she would get lost or be picked up by the police. Instead Mrs Docherty went into the Connoways' house and stayed with them for about an hour and a half. She told them that her own name was Docherty and her married name Campbell, and she would not hear of it when Mrs Connoway told her Burke's name, insisting it was Docherty like her own because he had told her so himself.

While Mrs Docherty was with the Connoways, Hare, Maggie and Nelly turned up with a bottle. They all started drinking again and Hare, Nelly and Mrs Docherty started dancing. The others soon left, but Mrs Docherty would not go until Burke came home. Mrs Connoway was anxious for her to leave, as it was getting late and she had to be up by four in the morning to get her husband's breakfast before he went to work. But Mrs Docherty bade her not to be cruel to strangers, and only left when Burke came home between ten and eleven o'clock. Mrs Connoway then locked her door and went to bed.

At ten o'clock, Burke had knocked at the door of David Paterson, who lived in the Wester Portsburgh nearby, but was told by his sister that he was out. Amid all the comings and goings of the late afternoon and evening, the notable absentee was Burke. We have no account of his whereabouts between about four o'clock, when young Broggan saw him, and ten o'clock when he knocked at Paterson's door. No one appears to have asked him what he was doing during those six hours. Meanwhile, Hare and Maggie had gone home for their supper and Nelly McDougal joined them, but they were not there long, all three leaving again before Mrs Gray went to bed at around eleven. About half an hour later, neighbours heard a disturbance in Burke's house – not, it appears, an infrequent occurrence. Mrs Connoway thought she heard fighting. Mrs Law heard scuffling and fighting, and recognised Burke's voice in the noise that went on for some time before she fell asleep.

Hugh Alston, a grocer who lived in a flat above the shop which fronted the building, came home with his wife at about half-past eleven and heard a noisy quarrel between two men as well as a woman's voice crying 'for God sake get the police, there's murder here'. The noise came from Burke's house, and Mr Alston went to find a policeman, but without success. When he came back the noise had subsided and the woman had stopped crying out.

Around midnight, David Paterson came home to find Burke rapping at his door. He told Paterson he wanted to see him at his house, so Paterson followed him there, noticing that Burke walked 'a little drunkish ways'. Burke and Hare were there with their women. Burke told Paterson that he had 'procured something for the doctor', and pointed to the straw at one end of the bed. Burke was evidently hoping for some money on account, but Paterson told him that only Dr Knox could deal with that. Paterson then left.

At two o'clock in the morning of Saturday, 1 November, John Broggan came back to find Hare and his wife in bed and Burke and Nelly standing and talking by the window. At about eight, Nelly McDougal went to Mrs Law's and asked to borrow her bellows to get a fire started. She asked Mrs Law if she had heard Burke and Hare fighting. Mrs Law enquired about the 'little woman'. Nelly replied that she had been 'using too much freedom with William', so she had 'kicked the damned bitch's backside out of the door'. Soon afterwards, Mrs Law was with Mrs Connoway when they heard Hare in the passage calling for Mrs Law, but they did not answer. At about nine, Burke went to see Paterson, who had sent his sister Elizabeth to fetch him. She had been directed to Burke's door by Mrs Connoway. Paterson told Burke that if he had anything to say or do with Dr Knox, to go and settle direct with him. Burke said he would and left. Shortly afterwards, Burke went to Hare's looking for Gray, to 'give him a dram of spirits', and met Gray outside with his child in his arms. Burke asked him to come back to his house for breakfast. Gray and his wife returned to Burke's, where they found Burke and Nelly, Mrs Law and Mrs Connoway, and young Broggan. Mrs Gray and Mrs Connoway asked Nelly about the old woman, and got similar replies to the one Mrs Law had received, that she had been turned out of the house for being too familiar with Burke.

Burke suddenly started splashing whisky about the room. He threw some from his cup towards the ceiling, and sprinkled more about the bed and the straw on the floor, and over his own chest. This was seen by Mrs Connoway, Mrs Law, Mrs Gray and Broggan. Burke said he wanted the bottle 'toom' (empty) to get more. Mrs Gray, who was smoking a pipe, looked around the straw at the foot of the bed for her child's stockings, and Burke, with an oath, told her to 'keep out there'. Around midday, when the neighbours had left, Burke told young Broggan to sit on a chair in the corner near the straw until he came back, and not let anyone near it. But after Burke went out, Broggan left too.

Early in the afternoon, Paterson saw either Burke or Hare – he could not remember which – standing with Dr Knox and Jones in Knox's premises in Surgeons' Square, telling them that he had a subject. Knox told Paterson that if they brought a package he was to take it from them.

There were more comings and goings at Burke's house in the afternoon, but later on, 'in the darkening', Mrs Gray was in the house with her husband and child when, suspicious of Burke's strange behaviour, she lifted some of the straw at the foot of the bed and uncovered first an arm, then the naked body of a woman whom she and her husband immediately recognised as Mary Docherty. There was a little blood on the face. Mr Gray went out at once and met Nelly McDougal on the stairs. He asked her about the body. (Mrs Gray overheard the conversation outside and testified that her husband told McDougal that 'he had found a corpse in the house'.) Nelly fell on her knees and begged him to 'hold his tongue and she would give him a few shillings, and if he would be quiet, it might be worth £10 a week to him'. Mrs Gray then spoke to Nelly herself and got a similar offer. Mrs Gray said, 'God forbid that my husband should be worth that for dead bodies,' and asked McDougal what she meant by bringing her family into disgrace by it. Nelly said, 'My God, I cannot help it,' and Mrs Gray replied, 'You surely can help it, or you would not stay in the house.' Mr and Mrs Gray left with Nelly hot on their heels and met Maggie Laird in the street. Maggie tried to persuade them all to go back in the house and not attract attention by quarrelling in the street. But the Grays went to a public house for a while before Mr Gray went off to inform the police. Mrs Gray had told Mrs Connoway that a dead body had been found in the house, and later took her in, while everyone else was out, to show her the corpse, but Mrs Connoway was afraid to look and went back home.

Burke, meanwhile, had been to Rymer's shop and bought a tea-chest, which he said he would send Maggie Laird for, and she duly turned up to collect it. At about six o'clock, Burke knocked at the door of a porter, John McCulloch, in Allison's Close, off the Cowgate. He asked the man to come with him, as he had a job for him. McCulloch followed Burke to his house and was shown a tea-chest. Hare was there, too. McCulloch saw Burke put the body, together with some straw, into the box. He saw some hair hanging out and stuffed it in before the lid was put down, which required some pressure.

The box was then roped and McCulloch was given instructions to carry it along the Cowgate to the head of the High School Wynd, where Burke would meet him. The porter was in the wynd when Burke and Hare and their women caught up with him and led him to 10 Surgeons' Square. McCulloch took the box into the house, where Paterson was waiting, and put it down in the cellar. He was then asked by Burke to come with them all to Newington. It was about seven o'clock. The five all trooped off to Newington with Paterson and Jones, waiting outside while Paterson and Jones went into Dr Knox's house and told him about the delivery. Knox gave Paterson £5 to divide between the two suppliers, with instructions to call at Surgeons' Square on Monday, by which time Knox would have seen the subject and would give them the rest of their money. In a public house, Paterson gave £2 10 shillings each to Burke and Hare, and they gave the porter five shillings. When Burke came home, he met Mr Connoway, who told him that local gossip had it that Burke had murdered the woman. Burke laughed and said he did not care what all Scotland said about him.

At approximately the same time as the tea-chest was being deposited at Surgeons' Square, James Gray arrived at the police office and reported his suspicions to Sergeant John Fisher, who went with him and an officer named Findlay to Burke's house. They met Burke and Nelly coming up the stairs from the apartment, and Fisher asked them to go back inside. The place was empty and there was no body. Fisher, learning that the Grays had been evicted the night before, suspected that they were causing a scene out of spite. He asked Burke what had happened to the woman who had been there the day before, and Burke said that she had left about seven o'clock that morning. Hare and several others, he added, had seen her go. Fisher looked round and found bloodstains on the bed and the straw. He asked Nelly McDougal how they came to be there, and she said that a woman having her period had been there a fortnight ago and the bed had not been washed since. McDougal told Fisher that this woman lived in the Pleasance and could be found.

Nelly added that she had since seen Mrs Docherty, who had apologised for her behaviour the night before. Fisher asked her what time she had left the house. McDougal's answer was that she had gone at seven o'clock on the Friday night. This discrepancy between Burke and Nelly led Sergeant Fisher to take them both to the police office, where they were interviewed by Lieutenant Paterson, who, later that evening, went to Burke's house with Sergeant Fisher and Mr Black, a police surgeon. They saw the signs of fresh blood and took away a striped nightgown which was lying on the bed.

At about seven o'clock on Sunday morning, Lieutenant Paterson and Sergeant Fisher called on David Paterson, at his home, and he went with them to Dr Knox's premises, where he unlocked the cellar and showed them the tea-chest, still tied with rope. The box was opened and the naked corpse of an elderly woman was found doubled up inside it. The face had a livid colour and there was blood round the mouth. Mr Gray was sent for, and he identified the body as that of the woman he had seen alive in Burke's house on Friday and dead under the straw on Saturday. The body was removed to the police office, where Mrs Law also identified it. The corpse was examined by Alexander Black, who considered that the woman had probably died by violence, but he could not say so with certainty. When it was shown to Burke and McDougal, they denied ever having seen the woman, dead or alive. The Hares and Broggan were then arrested at Tanner's Close and taken to the police office where they, too, denied all knowledge of the woman.

Meanwhile, the press had got hold of the bare facts, and rumour began to spread through the city. The uncertainty surrounding the first revelations of events is well illustrated by the *Evening Courant*'s account of 3 November:

> An old woman of the name of Campbell, from Ireland, came to Edinburgh some days ago, in search of a son, whom she found, and who afterwards went out of town, in search of work. She took up her lodgings on Friday, in the house of a man named Burt or Burke, in the West Port. It appears that there was a merry making in Burke's that night; at least the noise of music and dancing was heard, and it is believed the glass circulated pretty freely among the party. The old woman, it is said, with reluctance joined in the mirth, and also partook of the liquor, and was to sleep on straw alongside of Burke's bed. During the night shrieks were heard; but the neighbours paid no attention, as such sounds were not unusual in the house. In the morning, however, a female, on going into Burke's, observed the old woman lying as if dead, some of the straw being above her. She did not say any thing, or raise any alarm; but, in the evening, circumstances transpired which led to a belief that all was not right, for, by this time the body had been removed out of the house, and, it was suspected, had been sold to a public lecturer. Information was conveyed to the police, and the whole party taken into custody. After a search, the body was found yesterday morning in the lecture room of a respectable practitioner, who, the instant he was informed of the circumstance, not only gave it up, but afforded every information in his power. The body is now in the police-office, and will be examined by medical gentlemen in the course of the day. There are some very strong and singular circumstances connected with the case, which have given rise to the suspicions.[3]

Professor Christison and Mr Newbigging, a local surgeon, carried out a post-mortem examination and concluded that there was justification for a suspicion of death by suffocation, such as strangling, smothering or throttling, but that this could not be proved by medical science. Christison, later Sir Robert, was then a young Professor of Medical Jurisprudence at Edinburgh University. He became one of the leading early figures in forensic medicine, partly on the strength of his meticulous examination and presentation of the evidence in the case of Mrs Docherty. He soon had a reputation as an unimpeachable witness.

Many years later he became President of the British Medical Association and was one of Queen Victoria's physicians.

Burke, Hare and the two women were charged with murder and brought before Mr George Tait, the Sheriff-substitute, later that day. The prisoners then made statements in the presence of Mr Tait and the Procurator-Fiscal, Archibald Scott. Burke told a ludicrous tale about a hooded stranger in a greatcoat who came on the Friday evening asking where he could get a pair of shoes mended, and Burke took him home. While he was mending the shoes, the man remarked about the place being quiet and asked Burke if he could leave a box there for a short time. Burke agreed, and the man went out and came back shortly with a box, which he put down near the bed, untying the rope round it. Burke, who had his back to the man, heard him handling straw. When he had paid for his shoes and left, Burke found a dead body among the straw. He did not notice whether it was a man or a woman! He left it there until the stranger came back for it the following day, bringing a porter with him. He said he would give Burke two guineas for his trouble in keeping the body for him. He proposed to take it to one of the doctors in Surgeons' Square, and Burke put him in touch with Paterson. He was then shown the dead body of a woman in the police office, and he thought it was the body under the bed, but it had 'no likeness to Mary Docherty, who is not nearly so tall'. Mrs Docherty had left his house at three o'clock on Saturday afternoon he said, seen by Nelly McDougal, Margaret Laird and Mrs Connoway, and had not come back. He admitted that he had splashed whisky about to prevent any smell from the dead body, and said that blood on the pillow-slip resulted from his having struck Nelly McDougal on the nose. Blood on the sheet was due to the fact that Nelly was menstruating at the time. Burke was then asked if the man who brought the body, and afterwards came back with the porter, was William Hare. Burke said it was!

Nelly McDougal said that Mary Docherty had left at two o'clock on Friday afternoon. The corpse in the police office was not hers, as it had grey hair, whereas Mrs Docherty's was dark. McDougal had no knowledge, she said, of a body being in her house, until she was arrested. She had neither spoken to Gray about it, nor offered him money to keep quiet. Her explanation of the blood on the sheet and pillow-slip agreed precisely with Burke's.

A week later, on 10 November, Burke and McDougal made further statements. Burke now said that Mrs Docherty was in his house on the Friday, not Saturday, and during their Hallowe'en drinking, he and Hare had fallen out and started fighting. Their wives tried to separate them, and when the fighting stopped, they realised that Mrs Docherty was missing. They searched and found her lying dead under the straw. Burke and Hare then decided to strip the body and sell it to the surgeons, and later stuffed the stiff corpse into a box, which may have caused some bruising. They roped it up with a clothes line and got the porter McCulloch to carry it to Surgeons' Square. Burke said that he had not done any harm to the woman, and his opinion was that she had been 'suffocated by laying herself down among the straw in a state of intoxication'. Young Broggan, Burke added, had no knowledge of any of this business. McDougal's second statement was brief and consistent with her first, adding only that she had thrust Mrs Docherty out of the door by the shoulders after she had become troublesome, and never saw her afterwards.

We have no exact knowledge of either Hare's or Maggie Laird's original statements, but the *Courant* reported that Hare had accused the lad Broggan of striking Mrs Docherty in the passage and killing her.[4] The authorities were satisfied, however, that John Broggan was entirely innocent, and he was released. Burke, McDougal, Hare and Laird were kept in custody in the Calton jail throughout November, while further enquiries were being made and legal tactics considered.

The Lord Advocate, Sir William Rae, was faced with a dilemma. The prosecuting authorities had a corpse, an apparent motive, several witnesses, and four suspects in prison. But unfortunately, the medical men were unable to say with certainty that the woman had been murdered, and bearing in mind the reluctance of Scottish juries to convict on circumstantial evidence when the sentence would be death, they could not count on a successful outcome. Moreover, even if it were established beyond doubt that the woman *had* been murdered, it would be impossible to prove who had committed it.

Sir William decided at last that the only way in which any of the four could be brought to justice was for one to testify against the others. He came to the conclusion that the principal party in the affair was William Burke. Although it would be possible for McDougal to testify against Burke, since she was not married to him, she was simply saying nothing. And Margaret Laird could not testify against her husband, Hare. So Hare was the only choice, and the Lord Advocate authorised an approach to be made to him. He may well have been encouraged in this tactic by Hare's readiness to implicate the innocent boy, Broggan, in the murder.

On 1 December, Hare was offered immunity from prosecution if he would disclose the facts about Mrs Docherty's murder and any other such crimes committed by Burke. Hare needed little persuading to turn King's Evidence, and he must have sung like a canary, detailing the series of murders and laying all the blame, naturally, on his erstwhile friend. As Hare could not testify against his wife, Margaret Laird was also guaranteed her freedom.

Rae had already written to the Home Secretary, Sir Robert Peel, to inform him that an Irishman was to be tried on *two* counts of murder only, 'as we are most anxious to conceal from the public the extent to which such crimes have been carried, and of which fortunately little idea is at present entertained'.

Outrage quickly grew among the population as the gang's activities were revealed in the newspapers, which printed sensational and inaccurate stories to boost their circulations, and the flames of anger were fanned by popular broadsheets sold in the streets. All missing persons were suddenly assumed to be victims of the murderous partners, and streetwise children went round chanting a new rhyme of monosyllabic words and names:

> Up the close and doon the stair,
> But and ben[5] wi' Burke and Hare.
> Burke's the butcher, Hare's the thief,
> Knox the boy who buys the beef.

Among those who learned of the arrest of Burke and Hare was Janet Brown. She went to the police, told them about the disappearance of her friend Mary Paterson and identified the prisoners in whose company she had last seen her. And a local baker claimed to have seen one of Constantine Burke's sons wearing a pair of trousers which he, the baker, had given to Daft Jamie.

The Lord Advocate was now confident that a successful case could be brought against Burke for the murders of Mary Paterson, James Wilson and Mrs Docherty, and against Nelly McDougal in the case of Mrs Docherty. Within a few days of Hare's treachery, Burke and McDougal were committed for trial.

NOTES

[1] *Blackwood's Edinburgh Magazine*, March 1829.

[2] Thomas Ireland (publisher), *West Port Murders*, (Edinburgh, 1829), pp. 121–22.

[3] *Edinburgh Evening Courant*, 3 November 1828.

[4] Ibid, 6 November 1828.

[5] 'But and ben' – a two-roomed house; also used as an adverb meaning 'back and forth'.

7. TRIAL

With characteristic Presbyterian indifference to the most important holy day in the Christian calendar, the trial of William Burke and Helen McDougal commenced at ten o'clock on the morning of Christmas Eve, before the High Court of Justiciary in Parliament Square. Burke and McDougal had been brought from the Calton jail the night before to the cells below the court, in the imposing building where the Scottish Parliament had sat until the union with England in 1707, and where the king, George IV, wearing the kilt and the Royal Stuart tartan, had been entertained at a magnificent banquet in 1822. The Parliament Hall was lined with statues and portraits of eminent Scots beneath a heavy hammerbeam roof of Scottish oak, and was divided into two parts by a screen, the High Court occupying one end and the Sheriff's Court the other.

The huge, loyal crowd which had cheered the king along the New Town's Princes Street six years earlier now reverted to a vast incensed mob in the Old Town's Lawnmarket, High Street and Cowgate, clamouring to get into the courtroom. Local police were reinforced by a contingent of 300 drafted in to help preserve the public peace and keep the approaches to the court clear. Troops of cavalry and infantry were on standby in case of disturbances which the police could not contain. By nine o'clock the court was full to overflowing, and the first public act of the Lord Justice-Clerk, the Right Honourable David Boyle, was to order the opening of a window, which let a cold winter draught through the stuffy crowded room. Throughout the trial many of the lawyers wrapped their gowns round their heads, giving them the appearance of an assembly of monks.

Lord Boyle was supported on the bench by Lords Pitmilly, Meadowbank and Mackenzie. The prosecution team was led by the Lord Advocate, Sir William Rae. The leading defence counsel were Sir James Moncrieff, the Dean of Faculty, for Burke, and Mr Henry

Cockburn for McDougal. It was claimed as a tribute to Scottish justice that such distinguished counsel gratuitously represented the destitute prisoners, but there were hints in the press that fees were paid from some anonymous source. Even so, 'Had they been tried in England, not all the wealth of the Indies would at that date have rendered it possible for counsel to do more than cross-examine witnesses on their behalf.'[1]

A list of fifty-five witnesses had been drawn up by the prosecution, chief of whom would be William Hare. The others included Dr Knox, his students Fergusson, Jones and Miller and his former assistant Paterson, as well as Janet Brown and Burke's brother Constantine, whose sons Richard and William were also listed. Items produced in evidence would include clothing belonging to all three victims as well as a linen sheet and pillow-case, a plan of certain houses in Wester Portsburgh, and a brass snuff-box and spoon.

The lengthy indictments accused Burke of murdering Mary Paterson or Mitchell, James Wilson, and 'Madgy or Margery, or Mary McGonegal or Duffie, or Campbell, or Docherty'. Helen McDougal was accused only of the last crime. Counsel for the defendants (or 'pannels' in Scottish law) immediately objected to the trial proceeding on this accumulation of separate charges, which would be prejudicial to both prisoners.

Mr Patrick Robertson, for Burke, stated that, so far as he could discover from the records of the court, 'this is the first case in which it was ever attempted, on the part of the prosecutor, to charge, in one libel, three murders, committed at different times'. He argued that it was inconsistent with the principles of Scottish law to force a pannel to defend himself against three unconnected charges of murder at once, and that the minds of the jury members would inevitably be prejudiced against Burke in one case by evidence produced in connection with the others, and against McDougal by evidence in connection with alleged crimes she was not charged with. He pointed out that in English courts it was not customary to combine two felonies in the same indictment. Although the prisoners were to be tried under the law of Scotland, it surely could not be wrong to ascertain 'how those persons would be dealt with in the other end of the island'.[2] Mr Robertson thought their Lordships would 'not be inclined to form a precedent, which, in the *first* place, would be injurious to the law of the country; and, in the *next* place, would be injurious to the unhappy persons now brought to this bar'.[3]

The Lord Advocate replied that his intention in including McDougal in the same indictment as Burke was, so far from doing anything to prejudice a prisoner on trial, exactly the opposite. It would be in her interests to be so placed, rather than have all the evidence in the case against Burke repeated in the case against her afterwards. But he did not insist on it. If she and her counsel wanted a separate trial, so be it.

As to the charges against Burke, Sir William believed strongly that the alleged murders were so close in time, in place and in motive, that they should be tried together. 'I am told by my learned friend, that this is the first case that has occurred where three murders have appeared in one libel, and it is with pain that I acknowledge the truth of the statement. It is with sorrow I admit that there is not only no precedent of such a thing in the annals of this Court, but in the annals of any civilized country whatever.'[4] Nevertheless, the crimes were 'all of one name and species, all of one class and description, and stamp a character upon the pannel, which a jury and the Court are bound and entitled to look to', and he, the Lord Advocate, 'ought to be allowed to proceed to trial against Burke, on the three different charges for murder contained in this indictment'.[5]

The Dean of Faculty then rose to press the arguments put by Mr Robertson. He conceded that there was nothing illegal in the framing of the indictment, but insisted that it was a matter for the Court's discretion. The three charges were separate charges of the murder of 'different persons, totally unconnected with one another, living in different places, and in different circumstances; and the last of these acts is said to have been committed in conjunction with a third person, who is not stated to have any connexion with the other acts'. If the prosecutor were able to prove *one* of these murders, it would infallibly lead to the death of the defendant, so where was the necessity for charging him at the same time with other murders? 'I may have an alibi as to one – in another there may be no murder committed – in a third it may have been committed by a different person.' But the jury would be perplexed by the mixture of the whole together and the prisoner 'may be convicted upon the mere impression of guilt from the multiplication of charges, without any sufficient evidence in any one of them'.[6]

These legal arguments about the framing of the indictment were protracted, with much quoting of precedents going back as far as 1696, and it was late in the morning when the Lord Justice-Clerk asked his fellow-judges to give their opinions on them. Lord Pitmilly spoke first. He thought it right that McDougal's case should be separated from the two acts she was not charged with, and considered that, since Burke's counsel had requested it, Burke should be tried on one charge first, and the others afterwards if necessary. Lord Meadowbank agreed, and Lord Mackenzie announced, at considerable length, that he had nothing to add to what had been said.

The Lord Justice-Clerk's decision was that the discretion of the Court could be exercised in allowing Burke to be tried separately on each charge, but the public prosecutor could choose which charge he wished to proceed with first. The Lord Advocate proposed to proceed with the third case, that of Mrs Docherty, and since that was the murder with which McDougal was also charged as 'art and part guilty' along with Burke, she could not be prejudiced by reference to the other murders with which she was not charged, and so he would try them both together.

The prisoners were asked if they were guilty or not guilty of the third charge in the indictment, and both pleaded not guilty. A jury of fifteen men was then chosen by ballot and sworn in, consisting of local merchants, tradesmen and artisans. Among those summoned for jury service that day was a local portrait painter, George Andrew Lutenor, but his name did not come out in the ballot. If he had been chosen, one wonders if his close attention to the evidence in the case might not have been superseded by his fascination with the physiognomy of those taking part in the drama. Lutenor did make drawings of some of the participants, including Maggie Laird with her child in her arms. The chosen members elected John McFie, a merchant of Leith, as their chancellor, or chairman. By the time the trial actually commenced, it was already midday on Christmas Eve.

Sir William Rae began calling his witnesses, and most of them were brief and to the point. James Braidwood, a builder and fireman, had made the house-plans produced in evidence. Mary 'Stewart or Stuart' said that 'Mrs Campbell' had been in good health when she left her lodging-house on the morning of 31 October, and Charles McLauchlan, who also lodged there, confirmed this and said that the woman went by the name of Marjory McGonegal, but was also known as Mrs Campbell or Duffie. He was asked in cross-examination, 'Did she ever call herself Docherty?'

'Not that I know of,' he replied. Both he and Mrs Stewart, however, had identified the body as that of the woman who had lodged with them. William Noble, Rymer's shop-boy, said that he had seen Burke talking to the woman in the shop, and that Burke had later come in for a tea-chest, which was not yet paid for.

Hugh Alston was then questioned by Archibald Alison, one of the Crown prosecution team:

'Do you live in the same land in which William Burke's house is situated?'

'Yes, sir, I live in the first flat upstairs, and Burke lives in the sunk flat below the shop.'

'The shop is between your house and his?'

'Yes, sir, exactly.'

'Now, sir, do you recollect on the night of the 31st October, when you were going home, hearing any noise there?'

'Yes, sir, I did.'

'What hour was it?'

'I could not speak to the exact minute, but it was about half-past eleven.'

'Were you going along the passage at that time which leads up to your house?'

'Yes, sir, I was.'

'You were going along the passage that leads to your house, on the line of the street?'

'Yes, sir.'

'What did you hear, sir?'

'I heard, as it were, two men quarrelling and fighting, making a great noise; there was a woman's voice that attracted my particular attention, the cry of a woman, of murder.'

'What did you do upon that, sir?'

'My wife, who was with me, went up to my house, and I went down and stopped a little upon the stair to see that there was no person upon the stair till I ventured down to the bottom.'

'You know Connoway's door?'

'Yes, I believe that is the door next to the passage.'

'Did you go as far as it?'

'Near to it, within a yard or so of it.'

'Now, tell us as distinctly as you can, the different sounds you heard when in that situation.'

'I heard these two men making a great noise, as if wrangling or quarrelling. I heard no strokes or blows – I heard a woman crying murder, but not in that way as I could consider her in imminent danger herself.'

'Well, sir, what more did you hear?'

'That continued probably for half a minute, or a minute; she still continued to cry murder – it was a very strong voice for a female voice; standing there a minute or two, there was something gave a cry, as if proceeding from a person, or animal, that had been strangled.'

'That of a person, or animal, that had been strangled?'

'Yes, I could hardly distinguish it from that of a human being.'

'Well, sir, at this time did you hear any noise on the floor?'

'I heard these two men's voices, but I could not say that I heard anything else.'

'No blows?'

'No, just a great deal of noise they were making by speaking.'

'Very loud?'

'Yes.'

'Now, after this remarkable sound had ceased, did you hear the female voice still crying murder?'

'Yes; she struck upon something, I do not know what she struck with, but slapped the door as if crying for the police, and cried "murder here".'

'Well, sir, did you remain any length of time there?'

'After this I went for the police; I was often afraid of fire, and I went for a policeman, but could not find one.'

'Did you return to the stair then?'

'Yes. I did not go far down; I went down a little way.'

'Did you hear anything when you returned the second time?'

'I heard the men speaking, and the woman ceased to cry murder; I thought everything was over. They seemed to have removed to a greater distance, and the noise had ceased.'

'Now, in the course of the time you were listening, did you hear any wrangling or struggling at that time?'

'I might hear feet moving on the floor, but I can't say more.'

'How far might you be from Burke's door when you heard the sound?'

'It could not exceed three yards or so; it might be about three yards, but I do not think it exceeded that.'

'Do you mean the door of the house, or the passage that leads to the house?'

'The door of the passage that leads to the house.'

'Will you be so good as tell us how far Burke's door is from that passage?'

'I never measured it, but I think it would be about fifteen feet. I was three yards from the outer door.'

'There is a turn in the passage?'

'Yes, sir, there is.'

'Was the outer door shut?'

'I was not so far forward as to see that; it appeared to me that it was on that door the woman struck. It was on the door of the passage, not the door of the room.'

'You heard that a body was found?'

'Yes, in the evening of Saturday, about seven or eight o'clock.'

'Did that circumstance of a body being found fix your recollection of what you have mentioned?'

'Yes, I recollected immediately.'

Mr Alston was cross-examined by the Dean of Faculty, who asked where Alston had gone when he went for the police.

'To the mouth of the passage above Burke's passage. I saw one at the top of the street, but he was without my cry; and when I returned, I did not consider it necessary to get one, as the sound had ceased a good deal.'

'Did you go down to the Grassmarket?'

'No.'

'The woman that made the noise on the door, struck on the door, and called murder; did you believe the voice you heard came from her?'

'It was the same identical voice that called murder, that *took* me down the stairs.'

'That was not the voice of the woman, that struck on the door, if she cried at the same time, and said there was murder?'

'Yes, I think she said, "For God sake get the police, there is murder here".'

The Lord Justice-Clerk interrupted to ask Alston if they were to understand that 'the voice that was uttering these cries, of a person or animal strangling, was different from that of the woman calling murder'.

'Yes,' Alston answered, 'it was quite different.'

The Dean of Faculty continued:

'I think I have it down quite distinct; it was on the door, not the outside door, that the woman was striking; how do you know that, when you was three or four yards from that door?'

'I tried the experiment since on the door of the room; a person was shut in, and he struck the side of the room door, and I said that was not the sound, but the outer door.'

The foreman of the jury asked Mr Alston if the cries of murder proceeding from the passage came from Burke's house.

'I have no doubt of that, sir,' was the reply.

Mrs Connoway and Mrs Law both testified at greater length on the goings-on during Hallowe'en night, and John Broggan and Elizabeth Paterson added their recollections. David Paterson described events connected with the corpse, from Burke knocking on his door at midnight to the police opening the tea-chest in Knox's cellar. He was cross-examined by the Dean of Faculty:

'Paterson, you have seen the man Hare before that came into Court, and you looked at?'

'Yes, my Lord.'

'You know that Dr Knox had dealings with him for dead bodies?'

'Yes, my Lord.'

'Before that time?'

'Yes, my Lord.'

'You know whether he had dealings before with Burke about subjects?'

'Yes, my Lord.'

'Did they seem to act conjunctly?'

'Yes, my Lord.'

'Who appeared to be the principal party?'

'I have seen both in their turn.'

'You have seen both assume the principal part?'

'Yes, my Lord.'

Moncrieff wanted to know if Paterson had shared out equally the £5 paid on account so as to prevent the two men quarrelling over the money, and Paterson confirmed this.

'Have you known quarrels between Burke and Hare, respecting such booty?'

'I have seen them drunk on the streets, and have heard disputes and quarrels between them.'

'More than once?'

'Yes, my Lord.'

'Often?'

'Yes, my Lord.'

Mrs Gray was called next, and after explaining all the details of finding the body under the straw, she was asked if there was much straw on it, and how the body was lying.

'On the right side, sir,' she answered, 'with her face to the wall.'

'Did you leave it there?'

'Yes, just threw the straw upon it. My husband went away before me; he met Mrs Burke on the stair; I went out immediately after.'

'Did you see him meet her?'

'Yes.'

'What passed at that time?'

'He asked about the body, and she told him to hold his tongue, and she would give him a few shillings; and if he would be quiet, it might be worth £10 a week to him.'

'Did you say anything about the body?'

'I turned back and went into the house.'

'What passed then?'

'I spoke to her about the body, and she bade me hold my tongue.'

'Did you say what body it was?'

'I told her it was the woman's that was well last night, singing and dancing on the floor.'

'Did anything more pass?'

'She bade me hold my tongue – she did not know that I heard her speak to my husband – and she said she would give me five shillings or six shillings if I would hold my tongue.'

'What more?'

'She repeated the words over again; and if I and my husband would be quiet, it would be worth £10 a week to us; and I said, God forbid that I would be worth money with dead people.'

'Did you give information after that to the police?'

'It was my husband.'

'Did you see Burke after that?'

'No, sir.'

During cross-examination, the Dean of Faculty asked Mrs Gray if McDougal had said anything else after offering them money to keep quiet.

'Yes,' was the answer. 'She said, "My God, I cannot help it."'

The Lord Justice-Clerk wanted to know if these words were spoken before or after McDougal had offered them money; Mrs Gray confirmed that it was after that.

'What was your reply?'

'I said, "You surely can help it, or you would not stay in the house."'

'Did she make any reply to that?'

'No, sir.'

Mr Gray was asked about these events, and described how, when he and his wife had found the corpse, he had packed their belongings and was on the way out when he met Mrs Burke.

'That is McDougal, the prisoner at the bar?'

'Yes.'

'What passed?'

'I asked what was that she had got in the house; and she said, what was it? and I said, "I suppose you know very well what it is." She fell on her knees, and said . . .'

'Did she drop in a supplicating attitude?'

'In a supplicating attitude, imploring that I would not inform of what I had seen.'

'Did she offer you any reward for that?'

'She offered me some money, five or six shillings, to put me over till Monday; and there would never be a week after that, but that I might be worth £10 a week.'

'What did you do upon this?'

'I said my conscience would not allow me to do it. After I came back, I heard her in the room, narrating the same words to my wife.'

'What were these words she said to your wife?'

'They were words very nearly to the same purpose as those to myself, though they were not exactly the same.'

'Did she say she could not help it?'

'Yes, she said so.'

'Was there any reply made to that?'

'No, sir.'

'Not upon the stair?'

'No indeed. I did not stop long with her.'

'Now, after this conversation in the house, did your wife and you leave it?'

'We did, sir.'

'And did Mrs Burke, or McDougal, follow you?'

'She followed us, sir; and when we got out into the street, we met Mrs Hare.'

'Now, what happened there?'

'We met Mrs Hare there, and she inquired what we were making a noise about and said, "Can't we go into the house, and decide our matters there, and not make a noise about them here?"'

'And you went into a public house, and stopped there some time?'

'Yes; and I went and gave information at the police-office.'

The porter, McCulloch, told how he had collected a box from Burke's and taken it to 10 Surgeons' Square. Cautious about implicating himself in a crime, he reluctantly admitted that he knew there was a dead body in it.

'Did you see him put nothing in the box?'

'The sheet.'

'Did he take anything like the person of a human body?'

'Yes; I think it was something like the person of a body.'

Lord Meadowbank interrupted, 'You have no doubt that it was a body, in short?'

'No, my Lord.'

McCulloch was followed by Sergeant Fisher, who described his part in the arrest and investigation. After explaining that he had gone to Burke's house at Gray's request, and found no body there, but had met Burke and McDougal coming upstairs, and had asked them to go back inside with him, he replied to Mr Alison's question as to what had happened then.

'I asked Burke what had become of his lodgers, and he said, that there was one of them, pointing to Gray; and that he had turned out him and his wife for their bad conduct.'

'What took place then?'

'I then asked them what had become of the little woman that had been there on the Friday, the day before; and he said that she was away; and I asked, when did she leave the house, and he said, about seven o'clock in the morning.'

'Did he say anything about any other person being present when she went away?'

'He said William Hare saw her go away. Then I asked, was there any other person saw her go away; and he said, in an insolent tone of voice, there were a number more. I then looked round the house to see if I could see any marks on the bed, and I saw the marks of blood on a number of things there; and I asked Mrs Burke, the pannel at the bar, how they came there; and she said that a woman had lain in there, about a fortnight before that time, and the bed had not been washed since.'

'Well, what more?'

'She said, as to the woman, she could find her; she knew her perfectly well, and that she lived in the Pleasance. She alluded to the little woman, that I had asked where she was; and she said, the woman can be found; she lives in the Pleasance; and she said she had seen her that night in the Vennel, and that she had apologised to her for her bad conduct the night previous. I asked her then what time the woman had left the house; and she said, seven o'clock at night. When I found them to vary, I thought the best way was to take them to the Police Office; and I told them that it was all personal spite, but that I must take them to the office, as I was sent down.'

Fisher testified that he had heard them examined by the Superintendent, and that he went back to the house that night with the Superintendent and Dr Black, and found there a striped nightgown which they took away.

'Did you find any blood?'

'There was a quantity of blood amongst the straw under the bed.'

'Did it appear to have recently come there?'

'Yes, it appeared quite fresh.'

'Now, next morning, did you go to Dr Knox's premises in Surgeons' Square?'

'Yes.'

'Was there a person of the name of Paterson with you?'

'Yes.'

'Did you get anything?'

'Yes; we went down to the cellar, and he said "Here is the box, I do not know what is in it," and we opened it, and found the body of a woman in it.'

The Lord Justice-Clerk asked if the body was quite naked.

'Quite naked,' Fisher answered, and then explained, in reply to Mr Alison's questions, how Gray had been sent for and identified the body before it was removed to the police office. The Lord Advocate asked Fisher if the body was shown to the prisoners.

'Yes.'

'What took place then?'

'They all denied it.'

'Denied what?'

'Denied all knowledge of the body.'

The Lord Justice-Clerk interrupted to ask if they denied ever having seen it at all.

'Of ever having seen it,' Fisher replied, 'dead or alive.'

In cross-examination, the Dean of Faculty asked Fisher if Hare denied all knowledge of it.

'Yes; he said he never saw it, dead or alive.'

'His wife the same, I suppose?' said Mr Cockburn.

'Yes.'

Burke and McDougal had sat calmly and attentively throughout the proceedings thus far, sipping water and occasionally exchanging a word or two. Around four o'clock in the afternoon, Burke asked when they would be given dinner, and was told they must wait until six. When this hour came, they were given bread and soup and had to consume it in the dock while the trial continued.

Outside, as darkness fell, large numbers of people hung around in the streets waiting for news, while inside the courtroom there was much excitement and anticipation as Sir William Rae called his star witness, William Hare. Every spectator seems to have been struck by this man's loathsome appearance as the artificial light emphasised his hollow cheeks and sunken eyes. He stepped up to the witness box with a sinister smile on his face and took the oath.

Lord Meadowbank addressed him first. If Hare spoke the truth, the whole truth and nothing but the truth about the transaction now under investigation, he could never afterwards be questioned in a court of justice. His Lordship meant, of course, about these particular matters, but did not say so. If Hare should deviate from the truth, however, or prevaricate in the slightest degree, the inevitable result would be the most 'condign punishment' that could be inflicted. It is open to question whether Hare understood 'condign'. It may have crossed some minds that he was being threatened with the death penalty for contempt of court. Lord Boyle reminded him that he was here only in connection with the death of an elderly woman named Campbell or McGonegal.

'T'ould woman, sir?' Hare asked, and this was confirmed.

Hare told the Court, in answer to Sir William Rae's questions, that he was an Irish Catholic, had been in Scotland ten years and had known Burke about twelve months. He had seen Burke in Rymer's on the morning of 31 October and Burke had told him that there was an old woman in his house he had got off the street and 'he thought she would be a good shot to take to the doctors'.

'What,' asked the Lord Advocate, 'did you understand by the word "shot" for the doctors; did you understand the meaning of it?'

'Yes.'

'What was it?'

'That he was going to murder her.'

After describing the drinking and merry-making of the evening, which led to a fight between himself and Burke, Hare was asked where the old person was at this time.

'She was sitting at the fire, and she got up and desired Burke to sit down, and she said that she did not want to see Burke abused.'

'Did she run out?'

'Yes, she ran out twice to the entry, and cried out for the police.'

'She went out twice to the passage?'

'Yes.'

'What did she call out?'

'It was either murder or police, I could not say which, but it was some of them.'

'Well, how was she brought back again?'

'It was Nelly McDougal that fetched her back.'

'Both times?'

'Yes.'

'Did she then get any push, or fall over on the ground?'

'Yes, she did; when we were struggling, I pushed her over a little stool.'

'And you continued to struggle while she lay there?'

'Yes; she raised herself on her elbow – she was not able to rise, being drunk – and called on Burke to be quiet.'

Sir William asked Hare what Burke did after they had stopped fighting.

'He stood on the floor; he then got stride-legs on the top of the woman on the floor, and she cried out a little, and he kept in her breath.'

'Did he lay himself down upon her?'

'Yes, he pressed down her head with his breast.'

'She gave a kind of cry, did she?'

'Yes.'

'Did she give that more than once?'

'She moaned a little after the first cry.'

'How did he apply his hand towards her?'

'He put one hand under the nose, and the other under her chin, under her mouth.'

'He stopped her breath, do you mean?'

'Yes.'

'Did he continue this for any length of time?'

'I could not exactly say the time – ten or fifteen minutes.'

'Did he say anything to you when this was going on?'

'No, he said nothing.'

'Did he then come off her?'

'Yes, he got up off her.'

'Did she appear dead then?'

'Yes, she appeared dead a wee.'

'Did she appear to be quite dead?'

'She was not moving; I could not say whether she was dead or not.'

'What did he do then?'

'He put his hand across her mouth.'

'Did he keep it there for any length of time?'

'He kept it two or three minutes.'

'Did she appear to be quite dead at that time?'

'She was not moving.'

'What was you doing all this time?'

'I was sitting on the chair.'

Hare said that Burke had stripped the body, doubled it up at the foot of the bed, tying the head to the feet, and covered it with a sheet and straw. Mrs Hare and McDougal had run out into the passage when they heard the first screech. Neither of them had attempted to save the woman. When Burke had covered the body, they had come in again and gone back to bed. Burke left, and in ten minutes came back with Mr Jones.

'Was it not Mr Paterson?'

'It was the doctor's man.'

After Hare had answered questions about the porter coming to collect the box and all of them going to Surgeons' Square and Newington before being paid the £5, Henry Cockburn rose to cross-examine him:

'Mr Hare, how long did you say you have been in Edinburgh?'

'About ten years.'

'What have you been employed at during all that time?'

'Boatman and labourer.'

'You have not been boatman all that time?'

'Yes.'

'Where?'

'On the canal.'

'Have you been employed in any other way?'

'I had a horse and cart, selling fish.'

'Any other way?'

'No.'

'Have you been engaged in supplying bodies to the doctors?'

'Yes.'

'Have you been concerned in supplying the doctors with subjects upon other occasions than that you have mentioned?'

'No – than what I have mentioned.'

The Lord Advocate rose and objected to this line of questioning. Hare was removed from the court while Mr Cockburn attempted to justify his plot to discredit the witness. He said that he intended to ask Hare not only if he had supplied the doctors on other occasions, but if he had ever been concerned in murders besides this one.

Lord Meadowbank incautiously declared that the question should not be put before Mr Cockburn had explained why he wished to put it, and Cockburn then launched into an eloquent defence of his line of questioning, saying that he maintained his right to test the credit of the witness 'on as firm grounds as ever man maintained any proposition'. The witness may be privileged not to answer, he said, but that was no reason not to put the question, because he may choose to answer, and he may answer falsely and thus be contradicted. 'This is so plain, that the idea of protecting a villainous witness, by not letting any question about his own iniquities be even put to him, humbly appears to us to be absolutely monstrous; and I know no authority for it in the law of Scotland.' After arguing the point a little further, Mr Cockburn concluded, 'We are so confident in our opinion of the legality of the question, that we wish it to be put on the record, in order that, if it be rejected, we may find our remedy where we can.'

Mr Archibald Alison, for the Crown, said that the law of Scotland was different from the law of England in this respect, and quoted venerable authorities for the principle that 'no one is to be rendered infamous or disgraced by his own testimony', even though it may aid the defendant.

The Dean of Faculty supported Mr Cockburn's arguments and added that the intention was not to disqualify the witness but merely to test his credibility. The witness could answer the question affirmatively, in which case the fact would speak for itself. He could answer in the negative, which would be lying on oath, or he could refuse to answer at all, in which case the jury would draw their own conclusions.

Lord Meadowbank, excusing himself for his premature judgement, said that his opinion had been confirmed rather than changed by what he had heard. 'I, for one,' he said, 'must throw the law of England altogether out of the question. It is, I believe, in matters of this kind, diametrically opposed to ours.' But he did not believe Scottish law to be inferior or less effectual for the administration of justice. 'The object of our law has always been to get at the truth, and I suspect that it is best to be obtained by preventing witnesses being harassed in the way that would result from such questions as the present being held to be admissible.' He still did not think the question should be put. Lord Mackenzie disagreed, and thought the question could be put so long as the witness was warned that he had no protection in law if he should incriminate himself in matters other than the one being tried, and that he could decline to answer the question if he wished.

The Lord Justice-Clerk ruled that the question *could* be put, and after a few more brief exchanges, Hare was recalled and asked by Mr

Cockburn if he had assisted in taking the body of the old woman to Surgeons' Square. Hare answered 'Yes.'

'Were you ever concerned in carrying any other body to any surgeon?'

'I never was concerned about any but the one that I mentioned.'

The Lord Justice-Clerk then warned Hare that he was not bound to answer questions which might incriminate himself, for if he did, he was not under the Court's protection. 'If you have been concerned in raising dead bodies, it is illegal; and you are not bound to answer that question.'

Mr Cockburn resumed by asking Hare how often he had seen bodies being taken to the doctors. Hare hesitated.

'Do you decline answering that question?'

'Yes.'

'Now, sir, I am going to ask this question, which you need not answer unless you please, was this of the old woman, the first murder that you have been concerned in?'

Hare paused again.

'Do you choose to answer or not to answer?'

'Not to answer.'

'I am going to ask another question, which you need not answer unless you like, was there murder committed in your house in the last October? Do you choose to answer that or not?'

'Not answer that.'

Hare proved to be a man of few words, especially for an Irishman. He confirmed that he understood by Burke's phrase 'a shot for the doctors' that he meant to murder the old woman, but had no idea he was going to do it that night until he saw Burke fall on her after he and Burke had been fighting. He refused to answer questions about previous transactions with Knox, and denied that he had ever received any money from the doctor, though Burke might have given him some. It was Burke, not Paterson, he said, who gave him a share of the £5 paid for the old woman's body.

'Now, sir,' Mr Cockburn continued, 'when Burke was on top of this person, destroying her, where were you?'

'I was sitting on the chair in the same room.'

'How long was he dealing with her?'

'I could not say how long.'

'How long?'

'About ten minutes.'

'And did you sit in the chair?'

'Yes.'

'And did you sit ten minutes on that chair without stirring one hand to help her?'

'Yes.'

Hare said that the two women went out into the passage while the murder was taking place, but he saw it all happen.

'You did not call murder or police?'

'No.'

'Not a word?'

'No.'

'Did you go to the police next day and give information?'

'No.'

'You did not do that, but you took the body to Surgeons' Square?'

'The porter did.'

'You followed him?'

'Yes.'

'And you took money for it?'

'Part.'

'And next day, in the police office, you denied that you knew anything about it?'

'Yes.'

Hare vacated the witness box to make way for his wife, who appeared clutching her child, which had whooping cough. She used the wretched child's attacks to give herself time to think about what she was saying, or recall what her husband had told her to say, for she had, as she told the court twice, 'a very bad memory'. She said little more than to confirm what Hare had already said, in a voice that was sometimes difficult to hear above her child's paroxysms of heaving coughs. After establishing her version of the time, place and those present on the night in question, the Lord Advocate asked her if there had been a quarrel between Burke and her husband. She said there had, and she had tried to stop it. The old woman had cried out 'murder' and then fallen on the ground when she was pushed.

'Now, what more did you see?'

'I saw Burke lying on the top of her, whether on her mouth or on her breast I could not say.'

'Did she make a noise?'

'I could not say; for Mrs McDougal and me flew out of the house, and did not stop in it.'

When she came back, after perhaps a quarter of an hour, she did not see the old woman, and went to bed.

'Seeing nothing of her, what did you suppose?'

'I had a supposition that she had been murdered. I have seen such tricks before.' Surprisingly, no one in court pounced on this last remark.

The witness said McDougal had told her earlier that day that there was a 'shot' in the house, a woman Burke had brought in from some shop. Laird admitted that she had fetched a box from Rymer's at Burke's request, but he had told her he wanted it for old shoes.

Maggie Laird was pressed to say if she and McDougal had talked about the murder, either while they were in the passage or afterwards, and at last she replied, 'We were just talking about her, saying, perhaps it would be the same case with her and I.'

Lord Meadowbank interrupted, 'Is that to say that you might be murdered; is that what you mean?'

'Yes, sir.'

'You know that Mrs Connoway lived next door there, and you know that there was a Mrs Law lived on the opposite side of the passage; did you not think of going there?'

'I dreaded to go there, as I had left my husband three times. The thing had happened two or three times before, and it was not likely that I should tell a thing to affect my husband.'

'I thought you said you left your house three times altogether.'

'I left it for to go away altogether, for I was not contented to stay – not leading a contented life.'

The last witnesses for the prosecution were the medical men, Mr Black and Professor Christison. Neither could say definitely that Mrs Docherty had died from violence, although Mr Black's opinion was that she had, and Professor Christison agreed that there were sufficient grounds for suspicion, but would not go further. There was some discussion as to whether the woman could have suffocated as a result of falling down while intoxicated, as Burke had suggested. The livid hue of the woman's face, her swollen eyes and the small amount of blood issuing from her nose or mouth *could* all be consistent, Professor Christison said, with her having fallen down and suffocated while drunk. The Lord Justice-Clerk asked the Professor if he had opened the victim's stomach. He replied in the affirmative.

'Did you observe anything particular in it?'

'Half-digested porridge.'

'Had it any smell of whisky?'

'No. If it had the smell of whisky, or any narcotic, I should have perceived it.'

'Had the woman been in a dangerous state of intoxication, would there have been the smell of spirits in the stomach?'

'Not necessarily, my Lord.'

This was no great help to the prosecution, but it completed their case. The two pre-trial declarations of each of the defendants were then read out, and as no witnesses were to be called for the defence, counsel began their final addresses to the jury in the early hours of the morning of Christmas Day. There had been no break for rest or refreshment since ten o'clock the previous morning.

During the evening, while the trial was progressing, there had been some disturbances out in the streets. A small crowd of youths had set off to march on Dr Knox's house at Newington. Police had protected the property from them, so they went instead to the university, and succeeded in breaking some of the windows of Professor Monro's lecture-room.

The Lord Advocate summed up the Crown's case in a speech which he began by telling the jury that 'at this late hour, when you must be exhausted with the long trial in which you have been engaged, I shall endeavour not to detain you long'. He then went through all the evidence in minute detail, after saying that the alleged offences were of 'so atrocious a description, that human nature shudders and revolts at it', that such crimes produced terror and dismay, and that he would not allow 'any collateral considerations, connected with the promotion of science', to deter him from his duty to 'bring to light and punishment those deeds of darkness which have so deeply affected the public mind'.

Sir William Rae suggested to the jury that Hare was telling the truth, and said that all the testimony of the various witnesses tended to show that Burke was 'the premeditated author, and leading instrument, in the perpetration of this most hideous act'. He also spoke at considerable length to demonstrate beyond doubt that McDougal was an accessory to the murder. Rae took the opportunity to remind the jury members that he had originally intended to try the pannels on *three* charges of murder, though they must of course confine their attention only to that part of 'the whole system of atrocity' he had brought before them today.

The trial had already been in progress for seventeen continuous hours when, at three o'clock in the morning, the Dean of Faculty commenced his address to the jury on Burke's behalf. He spoke for two hours. Burke and Hare, Moncrieff said, acted together in the trade of procuring subjects for dissection, 'though William Hare, with his usual adherence to truth, chooses to deny this unquestionable fact'. Although that trade may be revolting to the feelings of ordinary people, and tend to prejudice them against him, he reminded the jury, Burke was not on trial for procuring subjects for anatomists. And given that that was his trade, the fact of a dead body being found in his possession was no proof of murder. Even if they were convinced that murder had been committed, they must have proof that it was Burke who had committed it. It could have been Hare who murdered the woman – perhaps that was what the two men were fighting about. What was there to restrain the Hares from lying in order to fix the guilt on the prisoners and extricate themselves from the condition in which they stood? 'What if that cold-blooded, acknowledged villain, should have determined to consummate his villainy by making the prisoners at the bar the last victims to his selfishness and cruelty? What is there to restrain him? Do you think that he is incapable of it?' If the learned prosecutor had possessed clear evidence on which a jury could convict the defendants of wilful murder, the Hares would have been in the dock alongside Burke and McDougal.

Moncrieff asked the jury if a man who had just committed a horrible murder would have gone instantly to fetch a 'surgeon' (he meant Paterson) to look at the body, or, next morning, ask people in for breakfast with his victim lying naked on the floor. He suggested that the Grays were as habitually drunk as the Burkes, the Hares and the Connoways appeared to be, and pointed out that their testimony was confused and contradictory.

Moncrieff dwelt on contradictions in other witnesses' answers. Young Broggan swore that when he had arrived at two or three in the morning, Burke and Hare were in the bed, and he lay down by the fire with the two women. But Hare said that the women were in bed, and Broggan was 'sleeping in the back part of the bed, behind his aunt, as he is pleased to call her'. Maggie Laird said that the women were on the floor, Broggan in the bed with one of the men, and the other in the chair. 'There is contradiction for you! If they were capable of judgement, and in a situation to give evidence, it is impossible that mistake or misconception to this extent could take place.' Whatever may be the truth of the case, he went on, the Hares' story was 'a tissue of inventions; and whatever account is to be given of the manner of the old woman's death, you have not got it from these witnesses'. If a man's life, or liberty, or character, were to hang on the breath of such witnesses as Hare and his wife, 'what security could any man have for his existence in society for a single hour?'

Henry Cockburn rose at five o'clock to speak for McDougal and, like the Dean of Faculty, poured scorn on the testimony of the 'squalid wretch' Hare and his repulsive wife, on whom the prosecution so much depended, but who were really 'the property of the gibbet'. The idea of believing such witnesses in a capital case was shocking. The prosecutor had talked of their being sworn to tell the truth, but 'what is perjury to a murderer; the breaking of an oath to him who has broken into the bloody house of life?' Cockburn urged the jury to distance themselves from 'the cry of the public for a victim', and ignore the notoriety of the case outside the court. 'Let the public rage as it pleases.' Their duty was to decide purely on the evidence in the trial if McDougal had been an accomplice to murder, and their safest course was to find the libel not proven.

The Lord Justice-Clerk summed up at great length before sending the jury to consider its verdicts. It was half-past eight by this time. Burke sat calmly waiting, but Nelly was nervous and agitated, and Burke did his best to comfort her. The jury took fifty minutes to reach its conclusions. As the members filed back into court, their chairman, John McFie, gave their verdict to a momentarily hushed crowd of lawyers and clerks, reporters and spectators, 'The jury find the *pannel*, William Burke, guilty of the third charge in the indictment; and find the indictment not proven against the *pannel*, Helen McDougal.'

McDougal immediately broke down in tears and Burke said to her, 'Nelly, you're out of the scrape.' The jury had reached a majority verdict, not a unanimous one – two of its members had favoured a not proven verdict in Burke's case, too.

Lord Meadowbank went through the ritual of proposing the sentence of death by hanging, and having said that it would be unpardonable for him, after so many hours, to think of going over at length the appalling circumstances which had been revealed, he (already by far the most verbose of the judges) set off yet again. He delivered himself of the opinion that 'in the whole history of civilized society – there never has been exhibited such a system of barbarous and savage iniquity, or anything at all corresponding in atrocity, to what this trial has brought to light'. Warming to his task, his Lordship went on to say that they would, he believed, search in vain 'through both the real and fabulous histories of crime for anything at all approaching to this cold, hypocritical, calculating, and bloody murder'. He had not exhausted his superlatives yet, though all those in court, Presbyterian or otherwise, must have been gasping for their Christmas dinners. The case was, he concluded, 'one of the most terrific, and one of the most monstrous delineations of human depravity, that has ever been brought under your consideration'.

The Lord Justice-Clerk, with black cap perched on his wig, then made a few mercifully brief remarks, one of them expressing his doubt as to whether he should order Burke's body to be hung in chains as a deterrent to similar crimes in the future. He opted for the customary sentence of dissection after execution and added that 'if it is ever customary to preserve skeletons, yours will be preserved, in order that posterity may keep in remembrance your atrocious crimes'. He then formally sentenced Burke to be taken back to the Tolbooth of Edinburgh and fed on bread and water only, until Wednesday, 28 January, when he was to be taken to the common place of execution in the Lawnmarket and hanged by the neck until dead, after which his body was to be delivered to Professor Monro to be publicly dissected and anatomised.

After reminding Helen McDougal that she had not been declared not guilty, and that her own conscience must draw the proper conclusions, the Lord Justice-Clerk dismissed her and the Court rose. It was ten o'clock on Christmas morning. The trial had lasted twenty-four hours without any adjournment for refreshment or pause in concentration.

'No trial in the memory of any man now living,' the *Caledonian Mercury* said, 'has excited so deep, universal and (we may almost add) appalling an interest as that of Burke and his female associate.'[7]

Among those present in court during the trial had been a sixty-seven-year-old French sculptress, Marie Grozholtz, better known as Madame Tussaud, who made notes and sketches, and had a model of William Burke on show in Liverpool within a fortnight of his execution.

NOTES

[1] J.B. Atlay, *Famous Trials of the Century*, (London, Grant Richards, 1899), p. 24.

[2] William Roughead (ed.), *Burke and Hare*, part of *Notable British Trials* series, (Edinburgh, WM. Hodge, 1948 edn), p. 113.

[3] Ibid, p. 114.

[4] Ibid, p. 116.

[5] Ibid, p. 117.

[6] Ibid, p. 120.

[7] *Caledonian Mercury*, 25 December 1828.

8. BURKE

Probably the only leading figure in the trial who can have sat down to his Christmas dinner in complete satisfaction was Henry Cockburn. He had successfully challenged the Lord Advocate's intention of trying his client McDougal alongside Burke when he was being charged with three murders and she with only one, and won the right to discredit Hare's evidence by putting questions which the Lord Advocate and one of the judges thought inadmissible. How far Cockburn believed in his client's innocence is another matter. The story got around later that he had uttered an aside during his closing speech, 'Infernal hag! The gudgeons swallow it!' Of course, he denied that he had said any such thing. Nevertheless, he had saved his client from the gallows. Moncrieff could not save *his* client, and the Lord Advocate had secured the conviction of only one criminal when he must have hoped at one stage for four.

Burke and McDougal were kept in the safety of the Parliament House cells for the rest of the day. Hostile crowds filled the streets, besieging the newspapers' offices for reports of the trial and incensed at the news that only Burke was to receive his just desserts. In the early hours of Boxing Day, Burke and McDougal were removed to Calton jail, where Burke was put in the condemned cell. 'This is a bloody cold place you have brought me till!' he complained. *His* Christmas dinner consisted of bread and water.

Helen McDougal was released that evening and went home, lying low for most of Saturday. But that evening, she could not resist her need for whisky and went out to get some. She was recognised in no time and a threatening mob soon gathered. They may well have lynched her if police had not got to her first and taken her to the safety of the Wester Portsburgh watch-house, using their batons to get through the crowd, which then regrouped outside, crying for vengeance and smashing some windows. McDougal was smuggled out at the back of the building, dressed as a man, and taken to the police office in Liberton's Wynd for the night. Police calmed the mob a little by telling them that McDougal was being held to give evidence against Hare.

Next morning, she was escorted out of the town and went back to Falkirk, but was no more welcome there than in Edinburgh, to which she promptly returned. She called at the Calton jail with Constantine Burke and asked to see Burke, but was refused. Some time afterwards she was apparently in Newcastle, but being a liability to the police there as well, she was escorted to the Durham border, where she disappeared. We cannot place any reliance on a story that she died in Australia forty years later.

Hare and his wife were also kept in prison for their own safety. 'With unspeakable astonishment,' the *Caledonian Mercury* stated, 'we have learned that Hare is only detained in jail for his own personal protection until after New Year's Day.'[1] The paper expressed the popular opinion when it asserted that, 'This subtle fiend was Burke's master in the art of murder . . .' Sensational speculation ran riot. A broadsheet published in Glasgow purported to be Hare's confession to murdering 'between thirty and forty individuals in the City of Edinburgh'. We need not take too seriously the story Leighton tells of the hideous Hare dancing with glee at the success of his stratagem.

In a letter to his son Charles, Sir Walter Scott wrote:

> It is doubtless a sad thing this of R. Stephenson [a fraudulent banker] but I rather think not quite so anomalous as the Caledonian trade in dead bodies. Besides a banker's frolics only affect the rich whereas Mr Burke's occupation put an end to the *Cantabit vacuus* of the poor. Any person with the ordinary number of limbs was exposed to be kidnapd for Dr Knox's purposes – or indeed if he had more or less than the usual share his risque was only the greater.[2]

In the view of the public, the trial had fallen far short of achieving justice for the victims of Burke and Hare, and this perception fuelled a growing fury and a dangerous tendency for the mob to take the law into its own hands. At this point, just after the trial, the public had no idea of the extent of Burke's and Hare's crimes. But they knew that there was sufficient evidence of their murder of Mary Paterson and Jamie Wilson, and speculation ran wild about how many other murders they may have committed.

If Burke had been tried for the killing of Mary and Jamie, Dr Knox and his assistants would have been required to testify that bodies identifiable as theirs had been received at Surgeons' Square, in order to prove the fact of death. The bodies would have been destroyed by the time of the trial, and even if parts of them remained, Sir William Rae would have been well aware of the dangers of trying to prove they were parts of a particular person. Some years earlier, in Glasgow, the body of a Mrs McAlister had been dug up from Ramshorn churchyard, and police and her friends thought they had traced it to the College Street premises of a lecturer, Dr Granville Sharp Pattison. Parts of a female body found in a tub of water included a jawbone with false teeth, which Mrs McAlister's dentist identified, and a severed finger was recognised as her wedding-ring finger. Other body parts were found underneath floorboards. When Dr Pattison was charged with stealing the body and mangling it to prevent recognition, his counsel requested that the case be heard *in camera*, owing to the delicate nature of the evidence he was to present. This was refused, but newspaper editors were earnestly requested to give as little publicity as possible to the case, as the details would 'only tend to inflame the minds of the vulgar'. 'Our reporter was therefore told,' the *Glasgow Herald* said, 'that he could not be allowed to write down notes of the evidence; which prevents us from laying the case fully before our readers.'[3] The paper's report said simply that the medical witnesses had found it impossible to say whether the body was Mrs McAlister's or not. In fact, the defence had lost no time in playing its trump card. Mrs McAlister, it was pointed out, had been a mother, as several people had confirmed. But expert medical witnesses testified that a significant part of the body said to be hers was undoubtedly that of a virgin! The case against Dr Pattison was found Not Proven. And who appeared for the defence in this case, along with Mr John Clerk? Why, none other than Mr Henry Cockburn.

What else might have become public knowledge if Knox had gone into the witness box? A great many people considered that the doctor ought to have been in the dock alongside his suppliers, but he had not even been called as a witness, because, in the case of Mrs Docherty, he had never seen the body. The only person connected with Knox who gave evidence was David Paterson, and his revelations in the witness box made a bad impression on the largely unsuspecting public. He attempted to shift any blame from himself to Knox by writing a letter to the *Caledonian Mercury*, in which he adopted the classic stance of saying that he had only been obeying his employer's orders and had been made a scapegoat for Dr Knox. We shall return to this matter in due course.

Of the original fifty-five witnesses listed, only eighteen had been called to give evidence. If Sir William Rae had been allowed to proceed against Burke on all three counts in the indictment, then witnesses not called in the matter of Margery Docherty (or whatever her name was) would have been called in evidence relating to Mary Paterson and Jamie Wilson. Some of those omitted might have told very interesting stories, especially Janet Brown, Mary Paterson's friend. What might Elizabeth Main, an Irish servant in Hare's lodging-house, have told the court? In his *Courant* confession later, Burke said that 'Hare's servant girl could give information respecting the murders done in Hare's house, if she likes.' The girl had been in Hare's employment only since Whit Sunday that year (25 May), and after the Hares were arrested she sold some of their pigs and absconded with the money, but she had been at Tanner's Close during an active period in the sequence of murders and, according to Burke, had seen James Wilson's clothes in the house on the day he was killed.

Burke had given these clothes to his nephews, Richard and William, who were also listed as witnesses, along with their parents. If these two boys were grown up enough to make use of the eighteen-year-old Jamie's clothes, and old enough to give evidence in a court of law, their testimony might have been interesting. Where were they when Burke brought Janet Brown and Mary Paterson to their father's house, pretending he was a lodger there?

What had Isabella Paterson, the mother of David and his sister Elizabeth, to tell about these affairs, and what was William Pulteney Alison, Professor of Theory of Physic at the university, expected to say? Alas, the public was left in the dark by the Lord Advocate's decision to pursue the case of Mrs Docherty. Any testimony about Mary Paterson or James Wilson, particularly from David Paterson, would have been liable to damage the promising careers of Fergusson, and Knox's other assistants. And the Procurator-Fiscal, the Sheriff-substitute and their clerks would probably have had to reveal the contents of Hare's pre-trial statement as well as Burke's.

The press echoed the public mood in saying that the conviction of Burke would satisfy neither the law nor the country, and that Hare must be brought to justice. Public revulsion at this monster had the effect of producing some sympathy for Burke, who had now, it was felt, become 'another of Hare's victims'. Morbid curiosity began to attract a stream of visitors to Tanner's Close and Burke's house nearby to gape at the scenes of their crimes and take away such souvenirs as they could filch.[4] Sir Walter Scott wrote to a friend:

> In the mean time we have the horrors of the West-port to amuse us, and that we may appear wiser than our neighbours, we drive in our carriages filled with well dress'd females to see the wretched cellars in which these atrocities were perpetrated, and any one that can get a pair of shoes cobbled by Burke would preserve them with as much devotion as a Catholic would do the sandals of a saint which had pressd the holy soil of Palestine.[5]

Mr and Mrs Gray, who had blown the whistle on the murderers, were now lodging in the Grassmarket with a coal merchant named McDonald. A public subscription was raised to reward the couple, whose unswerving integrity had been instrumental in bringing the killing to an end. But less than £10 was collected for them, and their only reward was the satisfaction of a clear conscience.

In prison, Burke received the ministrations of both Catholic priests and Presbyterian clergy. He was visited by Father Reid and Father Stewart, as well as Rev. Porteous and Rev. Marshall. It was perhaps under their earnest exhortations that he volunteered to make a confession, and did so on 3 January after a week in the condemned cell, thus revealing to the authorities that he and Hare had become the most prolific serial-killing partnership in British judicial records. Burke naturally tried to shift much of the blame onto Hare.

Lord Cockburn (as he became) committed to print, many years later, a curious opinion of Burke:

> Except that he murdered, Burke was a sensible, and what might be called a respectable, man; not at all ferocious in his general manner, sober, correct in all his other habits, and kind to his relations.[6]

'Sensible' and 'respectable'? On this analogy, we might declare that Jack the Ripper was a gentleman! 'Sober'? Burke was a habitual drinker of spirits from early morning onward and had drunken squabbles with Hare both in public and in private. Heavy drinking accompanied each murder and gave him Dutch courage in going through with them. Indeed, Burke's mindless stupidity on the night of the Hallowe'en revels and the morning after (inviting the Grays in with a corpse lying on the floor, splashing whisky about and ordering people to keep away from the bed) can only lead to the conclusion that he was so drunk that he scarcely knew what he was doing, and the chances are that he was not only an alcoholic but was totally oblivious to reason and the consequences of his actions. 'Kind to his relations'? He had deserted his wife and children in Ireland, selected a relative of Nelly's as one of his victims, and must have been thought by Maggie Laird to be capable of murdering Nelly herself! What can have led Cockburn to make such an extraordinary judgement? Was it merely the effects of old age on his memory? Or did it have something to do with Burke's Irish charm and gift of the gab which enabled him to gain the trust of old women, teenage girls, gullible anatomists, police officers and, apparently, some lawyers?

It appears that Burke's mind in prison was subject to extreme mood swings. One day he might seem piously devoted to making his peace with God; another, he would rage against Hare's treachery. He is said to have complained one day that Dr Knox still owed him £5 for the body of Mrs Docherty, and that if he had it he could buy a decent coat and waistcoat for his final public appearance.

J.B. Atlay, among others, related the curious tale of Burke's embarrassing wound. 'When in the condemned cell Burke was treated surgically for a very severe wound, from which it was doubtful if he would ever have recovered. He told the minister of the Tolbooth Church, who was attending on him, that it arose from a bite given by "Daft Jamie" when he was being done to death.'[7] According to the 'Echo of Surgeons' Square', however, Burke had become a patient of Dr Knox as well as a supplier of subjects, 'and came to the Lecture Room to have his wound dressed', long before the murder of Daft Jamie.[8] This cannot have been earlier than December 1827, for if Burke had known Knox, he and Hare would not have had to make nervous enquiries for Dr Monro on the penultimate day of November when they wanted to sell old Donald's body. But it was before the murder of Mary Paterson in April, to judge from the pamphlet's wording. What appears to be the truth is that Burke was suffering from testicular cancer. It may well be that he was reluctant to admit this to a minister of religion, especially if it was associated with syphilis. Some writers appear to have felt (even in this gruesome litany of death and despoliation) that Burke's testicles were a taboo subject. But those – professional historians and amateur criminologists alike – who have referred to his scirrhous testicle, have been blissfully unanimous in misspelling the word as 'schirrous'. This disease might soon have killed him if the hangman had not got him first. The 'Echo' goes on to say that when Burke returned to Edinburgh after the harvest that summer, he 'called at the rooms to have the Doctor's opinion respecting his wound, which had assumed a dangerous appearance'.[9] His mental state must have been affected by this condition, and may even have helped him to become resigned to his fate, since he remained notably calm during the trial and in prison afterwards. It may also have contributed to his mode of careless abandon during the latter murders. But it also raises the question whether Burke was better known to Knox than anyone was prepared to admit. Did Knox really provide medical treatment to a man he assumed to be a body-snatcher and of whom he knew nothing except that he went by the name of 'John'?

One of the clergymen who visited Burke in Calton jail apparently told him that 'a dying man, covered with guilt, and without hope except in the infinite mercy of Almighty God . . . must prepare himself to seek it by forgiving from his heart all who had done him wrong', and advised him to speak the truth, and nothing but the truth, 'without any attempt to palliate his own iniquities, or to implicate Hare more deeply than the facts warranted'. He then asked the Irish labourer, 'By what means were these fearful atrocities perpetrated?'

A week or so before his execution, Burke made the statement known as the '*Courant* confession', which was more detailed than the one he had made to the Sheriff and the Procurator-Fiscal on 3 January. He completely ignored the advice of his spiritual adviser by implicating the Hares as deeply as he could. The emphasis on Hare's part in the murders is greater in the *Courant* confession than in the official one, although we should not be misled by the frequent references to 'Hare and Burke' into thinking that Burke was deliberately accentuating or exaggerating Hare's part or implying that Hare's was the leading role. We have become so accustomed to the familiar phrase 'Burke and Hare' that seeing the names the other way round is as strange as 'Spencer and Marks' or 'Hardy and Laurel'. But it was not a calculated ploy by Burke – merely the clerk's interpretation of his words.

It is not known who gained access to Burke in prison to obtain this statement. Several applications to see the prisoner had been refused, including one, apparently, from an Edinburgh solicitor calling himself 'J. Smith', who even wrote to the Home Office but, not surprisingly perhaps, without success. The new confession, made on the understanding that it would not be published until three months after Burke's death, came into the hands of the Edinburgh *Evening Courant*. Some of the details it contained were soon leaked, and for the first time the public got some intimation of the extent of the West Port murders.

When the *Courant* announced that it would publish the full confession the day after Burke's execution, Hare's counsel, Duncan McNeill, immediately applied for an injunction, or interdict, which was granted.

Meanwhile, Burke asked to see the Sheriff again as he wished to make a further statement, and on 22 January, in the presence of the Sheriff-substitute, Procurator-Fiscal, Assistant Sheriff-clerk and Father Reid, Burke clarified his former 'official' confession, though giving no further details, and declared that neither he nor Hare, as far as he knew, had supplied any subjects for dissection except those he had mentioned, and had never done so by raising dead bodies from the grave. He said they 'never allowed Dr Knox or any of his assistants, to know exactly where their houses were, but Paterson, Dr Knox's porter or door-keeper, knew. And this he declares to be the truth.'

The *Courant* confession, which Burke signed the day before this official supplement, contained a few general remarks in addition to the details we have already noted about the murders. But he said of the Docherty murder that 'Hare laid hold of her mouth and nose', and 'was not sitting on a chair at the time, as he said in the Court'. When he said that he 'did not know the days nor the months the different murders were committed', he added that 'he thinks Dr Knox will know by the dates of paying him the money for them'. Burke also declared that:

> It was God's providence that put a stop to their murdering career, or he does not know how far they might have gone with it, even to attack people on the streets, as they were so successful, and always met with a ready market, that when they delivered a body they were always told to get more.

He was never a resurrection man, he said, but they 'went under the name of resurrection men in the West Port'. Helen McDougal and Hare's wife were not present when the murders were committed, 'they might have a suspicion of what was doing, but did not see them done'. Later in the statement, he said that Hare's wife often helped them to pack the murdered bodies into the boxes. 'Helen McDougal never did, nor saw them done; Burke never durst let her know; he used to smuggle in drink, and get better victuals unknown to her; he told her he bought dead bodies, and sold them to the doctors, and that was the way they got the name of resurrection-men.'

Burke made some canting remarks for public consumption. Hare, he said, 'could sleep well at night after committing a murder'. But he himself 'repented often of the crime, and could not sleep without a bottle of whisky by his bedside, and a twopenny candle to burn all night beside him; when he awoke he would take a draught of the bottle – sometimes half a bottle at a draught – and that would make him sleep'. This does not appear consistent with his subsequent remark that if a stop had not been put to their murdering career, 'he does not know how far they might have gone with it . . .' Burke then wrote a final statement in his own hand:

> Burk deaclares that docter knox Never incoureged him Nither taught [word 'taught' written again and crossed out] or incoregd him to murder any person Neither any of his asistents that worthy gentleman Mr. fergeson was the only man that ever mentioned any thing about the bodies He inquired where we got that yong woman paterson
>
> Sined William Burk prisoner

So, on consecutive days, a week before his execution, Burke made statements exculpating Knox (whom he thought still owed him £5) from any suspicion of actually encouraging the murders. Clearly he had been got at in prison by someone with Dr Knox's interests at heart. In a letter Knox wrote to the *Caledonian Mercury* (see Appendix III), he mentioned that a Mr Ellis had been engaged by his (Knox's) friends to conduct a 'rigid and unsparing examination' of the facts. This was before a committee was set up around 7 February, and must have been before Burke's execution. It seems likely that Mr Ellis, among others perhaps, was allowed by the authorities to interview Burke in prison, and it may well have been as a result of this that Burke made his handwritten acquittal of Knox of any direct part in the murders.

For weeks before the execution, tenants of the tall 'lands' around the Lawnmarket had been offering their windows for hire, and every one with a good view of the traditional site of the scaffold was taken in advance by the fashionable of Edinburgh. Sir Walter Scott's daughter Anne wrote from Abbotsford on 28 December to Charles Kirkpatrick Sharpe saying that 'Papa . . . is much inclined to share a window with you on the day Mr Burke is hanged.'[10] A local bookbinder, Robert Seton, wrote on 14 January from 423 Lawnmarket to Sharpe, to say that, because of the demand, he was not able to reserve a window for Mr Sharpe and Sir Walter, as requested, but would be happy to accommodate them with a share of one.[11]

In the early hours of 27 January Burke, chained by the ankles, was taken by coach from Calton jail to the lock-up in Liberton's Wynd off the Lawnmarket. During that afternoon and evening, workmen were busy erecting barriers to keep spectators at a distance from the scaffold, which was in place by midnight. By eight o'clock next morning, Wednesday, 28 January, a vast crowd had gathered, in spite of pouring rain earlier. Some estimated the number of spectators at 25,000 – the largest crowd ever to have assembled in Edinburgh's streets. There was not a vacant window to be seen in any of the surrounding buildings, and people were even sitting on the high rooftops.

Burke had been allowed to sit by the fire in the lock-up and had been given a glass of wine, despite the mandatory diet of bread and water. Freed of his fetters, he met the executioner, Williams, and said 'I am not just ready for you yet.' At eight o'clock, he was led out into Liberton's Wynd and walked the few yards to the Lawnmarket with Father Reid at his side. As he emerged into the packed square, a tumultuous noise arose from the crowd, which visibly disconcerted the condemned man. He approached the scaffold and mounted the steps almost hurriedly, as if anxious to get the business over with, while cries of execration echoed through the streets. As the executioner prepared Burke for the drop, many shouts were heard, such as 'Burke him!', 'Bring out Hare!' and 'Hang Knox!' The only words uttered by Burke were to the executioner. 'The knot's behind,' he said, as Williams tried to loosen Burke's neckerchief in order to adjust the rope properly. A few seconds later, in the shadow of St Giles's Cathedral, the executioner launched Burke into eternity, as the common saying was. He died quickly, with only a couple of slight autonomic convulsions of his feet for the entertainment of the mob.

After hanging for the best part of an hour, Burke's corpse was taken down, put in a coffin and taken back to the lock-up, while the workmen who had erected the scaffold began to dismantle it, amid some scrambling for bits of the rope, which was bought, according to Sir Walter Scott, by one Sanders, who was 'ass enough to purchase the rope he was hanged with at half a crown an inch. Item the hangman became a sort of favourite was invited into a house and treated with liquor for having done his miserable duty on such a villain.'[12]

Scott also noted in his journal:

> The mob, which was immense, demanded Knox and Hare, but though greedy for more victims, received with shouts the solitary

wretch who found his way to the gallows out of five or six who seem not less guilty than he. But the story begins to be stale insomuch that I believe a doggerel ballad on it would be popular, how brutal soever the wit. This is the progress of human passion. We ejaculate, exclaim, hold up to heaven our hand, like the rustic Phidele – next morning the mood changes, and we dance a jig to the tune which moved us to tears.[13]

Before the morning was over, all signs of the execution had gone. But retribution for Burke's crimes was only half done. The 1752 'Act for Preventing the horrid Crime of Murder' (25 Geo II) had decreed that all executed murderers were to be either publicly dissected or hung in chains. 'It is become necessary,' the preamble said, 'that some further Terror and peculiar Mark of Infamy be added to the Punishment.' So now, on the morning of Thursday, 29 January, the naked corpse of William Burke was laid out on a slab in Professor Monro's lecture room at the university medical school, in accordance with the judge's sentence, and the murderer made his final contribution to medical research. Demand for admission to the lecture was so great that Dr Monro's regular students were issued with tickets to give them priority, then others were let in until the room was filled to capacity.

The lecture began at one o'clock. Burke's cranium was sawn off and his brain exposed. According to the author of the contemporary *West Port Murders*, 'the amount of blood that gushed out was enormous, and by the time the lecture was finished, which was not till three o'clock, the area of the class-room had the appearance of a butcher's slaughter-house, from its flowing down and being trodden upon'.[14] While Monro was delivering his lecture, students who had failed to get in were clamouring at the door, and police had to be called, but the officers were outnumbered by unruly students and a noisy affray broke out in which windows were broken and the police had to use their batons. Several men on both sides were injured. Order was only restored when Professor Christison negotiated an agreement whereby medical students were to be allowed into the lecture room, fifty at a time, to view the remains after Monro had finished with them.

Next day, the general public was also permitted to file past the corpse, which had by then been restored to a less gruesome condition, although the shaved head showed continuous stitching where the skull had been replaced, with signs of blood still on it. The procession began at ten o'clock in the morning, and by dusk it was estimated that 25,000 people had passed through. Seven women were among these spectators. The fact that women had been among the crowd watching the execution had drawn some comment in Edinburgh, but the news that seven members of the gentle sex had viewed the butchered corpse caused considerable shock.

Scott noted:

> The corpse of the Murderer Burke is now lying in state at the College, in the anatomical class, and all the world flock to see him. Who is he that says we are not ill to please in our objects of curiosity. The strange means by which the wretch made money are scarce more disgusting than the eager curiosity with which the publick have licked up all the carrion details of this business.[15]

But then, until the mid-twentieth century, British justice had an infallible instinct for increasing morbid curiosity and depravity by making the punishment even more gruesome and horrific than the original crime.

When all the gawping was over, the flesh was stripped from the bones and the skeleton was preserved as an exhibit in the Anatomical Museum of Edinburgh University, where it remains to this day, a mark of celebrity, like a marble statue in a public square or a wax effigy in Madame Tussaud's. But whereas they are mere likenesses of their subjects created by art, this *is* the subject, accorded the honour of perpetual visible corporality which neither saints nor emperors aspire to. Burke's ghost must have smiled with satisfaction.

Sensational pamphlets and broadsheets flooded the streets. One 'reported' the last words of Mrs Docherty as she was being suffocated, 'God abandoned! and thou, hideous carrion, your time is at hand – the wrath of Heaven, even now, is ready to fall on your heads. I – I – shall be the last.' Another imaginative piece of journalism gave Burke's last dying speech. It was on the streets of Newcastle before news of the execution could possibly have arrived there.

Phrenologists claimed to have measured the heads of Burke and Hare to find consistencies in the external variations in shape which could be identified as characteristic lesions of the brain in murderers. The leader of these pseudo-scientists was George Combe, a solicitor, who was among those who had been allowed to see Burke's corpse before Monro lectured on it. He had recently published *Essays on Phrenology* and founded *The Phrenological Journal*. Thomas Stone, President of the Royal Medical Society, poured scorn on this theory, which he described as a hypothesis 'which has been decidedly rejected by the most enlightened men in Europe, and which, from its earliest existence, has appealed rather to the credulity of the vulgar, than to the judgment of men of science'.[16]

In due course, the 'official' and *Courant* confessions were published simultaneously, in spite of a further temporary injunction against the *Courant* version, granted to the afore-mentioned solicitor Smith, who claimed that the so-called '*Courant* confession' had been intended by Burke for him, but had been given to the editor of the *Courant* by a turnkey named Wilson. On 27 January, the day before his execution, Burke had signed a paper authorising the demand of this confession from the *Courant* and its delivery to the Sheriff's Office. He referred to this document as the one 'which I signed for – Ewart', and said that although it was correct 'so far as I had time to examine it', the declaration made before the Sheriff was 'the only full statement that can be relied on'.

It seems clear that Burke was being pestered in the condemned cell by lawyers acting for various interested parties, some anxious to prevent premature publication of the full details, and the *Courant* eager to capitalise on what it saw as a major 'scoop'. Neither Smith nor the paper wanted their scoop to be upstaged by release of the 'official' confession, so they promptly came to some agreement, and both confessions were printed in the press on 7 February.

And so at last the full story of the Burke and Hare crimes was revealed to the public, and although the extent of the murders was established only on the basis of the criminals' own statements, there was no compelling reason to believe that they were lying or hiding the truth. Sixteen is the number of murders attributed to Burke and Hare ever since, although doubts remained for many years afterwards, even among those involved in bringing the pair to justice.

Lord Cockburn, whose memoirs were published twenty-seven years after the trial, recalled that 'it was nearly certain that, within a year or two, Burke and Hare had murdered about sixteen people, for the sale of their bodies to anatomists; and after his conviction Burke confessed this'.[17] Popular rumour naturally tended to put the figure much higher, but without the benefit of the slightest evidence. A Glasgow printer named Muir published a broadsheet purporting to be Hare's confession to murdering, with his accomplices, 'between 30 and 40 individuals in the City of Edinburgh'. But idle speculation and misinformation surrounded the whole affair. An anonymous American lawyer got the story so wildly wrong that he described the execution of both Burke and Helen McDougal on 22 January.[18]

Sir Robert Christison's characteristically cautious impression was quite different. In his autobiography, published after his death in 1882, he wrote that there was 'reason to suppose that this atrocious trade had been carried on during the whole winter of 1827–28. Burke, indeed, was said to have admitted after conviction, that sixteen victims had been murdered by his copartnery. But villains of his rare stamp are apt to indulge in the strange vainglory of exaggerating their actual wickedness.'[19]

Owen Dudley Edwards repeatedly ascribes seventeen murders to the pair. In the absence of hard evidence to the contrary, however, we may take it that Burke and Hare between them killed sixteen people in the course of nine months – an average of one every seventeen days.

NOTES

[1] *Caledonian Mercury*, 1 January 1829.

[2] Letter of 4 January 1829, Grierson, p. 89.

[3] *Glasgow Herald*, 10 June 1814.

[4] Tanner's Close and the slum area around it were demolished in 1902.

[5] Grierson, p. 102.

[6] Henry Cockburn, *Memorials of His Time*, (Edinburgh, A. & C. Black, 1856), p. 458.

[7] Atlay, p. 42(n).

[8] 'Echo of Surgeons' Square', *Letter to the Lord Advocate*.

[9] Ibid.

[10] Quoted in Roughead, p. 64.

[11] Ibid, p. 65.

[12] Grierson, p. 131.

[13] Sir Walter Scott, *Journal*, (Edinburgh, Oliver & Boyd, 1950 edn), p. 583.

[14] Ireland, *West Port Murders*, p. 254.

[15] Scott, *Journal*, p. 585.

[16] Thomas Stone, *Observations on the Phrenologial Development of Burke, Hare, and Other Atrocious Murderers*, (Edinburgh, 1829).

[17] Cockburn, p. 456.

18 Quoted in George Ryley Scott, *The History of Capital Punishment*, (London, Torchstream Books, 1950), pp. 49–50.

19 Robert Christison, *The Life of Sir Robert Christison, Bart,* (2 vols, Edinburgh, Wm Blackwood & Sons, 1885), Vol I, p. 308.

9. HARE

The Hares remained in prison all this time. They had been locked up for their own safety at first, but when it became clear that William Hare was soon to be released, as no further action was to be taken against him by the Crown, Daft Jamie's mother and sister, both named Janet Wilson, petitioned the Sheriff to have Hare detained in prison so that he could not cheat justice by fleeing to Ireland. It was their intention to bring a private prosecution for the murder of Jamie.

Press and public were at one in their fury that Hare seemed likely to get off scot-free. Many believed that the malevolent Hare was the worst of the evil pair. The general opinion was that Hare was not only the original instigator of the homicidal partnership, but also the one with most blood on his hands in the actual killing of their victims. Hare, 'the vilest of the two monsters', according to Lonsdale, 'suggested a fresh stroke of business, namely, to inveigle the old and infirm into his den and "*do for them*"'.[1] This slimy character, it was commonly maintained, had led Burke on throughout this grisly catalogue of crime, and had ended by treacherously sending his partner to the gallows, to save his own neck. He had not shown the slightest sign of remorse for his actions and, in fact, had given some appearance of being quite pleased at getting himself off the hook at Burke's expense.

Nevertheless, the Lord Advocate's position was clear, however much he and everyone else might regret it. If it had not been for Hare's testimony, Burke, as well as Nelly, would almost certainly have won a Not Proven verdict. Rae had used Hare to bring Burke to justice, and had guaranteed him immunity from prosecution if he testified against his erstwhile partner. If he now went back on his word, it would bring discredit on himself and the honour of his country.

We have already noticed Professor John Wilson's impressions of Hare in prison, and Sir Walter Scott was of a like mind as regards Hare:

This Hare is a most hideous wretch so much that I was induced to remark him from having observed his extremely odious countenance once or twice in the Street where in general I am no observer of faces but his is one which there is no passing without starting & I recognized him easily by the prints.[2]

Another character-sketch of him was provided by the afore-mentioned James Maclean, who told Charles Kirkpatrick Sharpe that Hare was a man of 'ferocious and tyrannical disposition, much inclined to quarrel, and very obstreperous when in liquor'. Maclean, a fellow-hawker as well as a fellow-Irishman, related how, during the summer of 1828, he was returning from the shearing[3] at Carnwath with Hare, Burke and others when they all went into a public house at Balerno, near Currie, for some refreshment:

The reckoning being clubbed, Hare snatched up the money from the table, and put it into his pocket; when Burke, fearing lest a disturbance should take place in the house, paid the whole amount. After they left the inn McLean observed to Hare it was a *scaly* trick to lift the money with an intention to affront them. On this Hare *knocked the feet from under* McLean, and when prostrate on the ground, gave him a tremendous kick on the face. His shoes being pointed with iron plates, commonly called *caulkers*, he wounded McLean severely, laying open his upper lip.[4]

When speculation was rife about the possible number of the pair's victims, Maclean himself was thought likely to be one of them, as he had gone missing. But he had been paying a visit to Glasgow and returned to Edinburgh in due course.

When a public subscription was announced to raise the costs of a private prosecution for the killing of the popular Jamie, the Edinburgh public, urged on by the *Caledonian Mercury*, responded at once, and by 16 January Mrs and Miss Wilson were able to retain Mr Francis Jeffrey as counsel and petition the Sheriff for Hare to be charged with the murder of James Wilson.

Three days later, while this new development was being considered by the law authorities, Margaret Laird was released, as the Crown could not proceed against her and she was not named in the private action against her husband. As she made her way back to the Old Town with her child in her arms, she was inevitably recognised, and a mob gathered to follow and pelt her with stones and mud. She, like McDougal earlier, had to be rescued by police and locked up again for her own safety. A few days later she was freed again, and after apparently wandering about the country in tatters, ended up a fortnight later in Glasgow, where she was again given refuge from the mob in a prison cell.

> She occasionally burst into tears while deploring her unhappy situation, which she ascribed to Hare's utter profligacy, and said all she wished was to get across the channel, and end her days in some remote spot in her own country in retirement and penitence.[5]

She remained in Glasgow for some time, nevertheless, trying to get aboard vessels bound for Ireland. Lucky at last, she was eventually assisted by the authorities in securing a passage on board the *Fingail* from Greenock to Belfast on 12 February.[6] Hearsay identified her with a woman called Mrs Hare, employed as a nursemaid in Paris thirty years later, but we may pass a verdict of Not Proven on this highly improbable story.

Hare, meanwhile, was taken into close confinement again and an examination of witnesses began. Burke, in the condemned cell at this time, might have hoped for a stay of execution if he was to provide evidence against Hare. On 20 January, Hare's legal representatives applied for the warrant to be withdrawn and for their client to be released. The Sheriff refused this on the grounds that there was nothing in a guarantee by the public prosecutor to prevent private proceedings. Hare's lawyers then took the case to the High Court, presenting a lengthy Bill of Advocation, Suspension and Liberation, in which they argued for Hare's immediate release. He had made a full disclosure of the murders, including James Wilson's, under assurance from the Lord Advocate of his personal protection, and he had given evidence at the trial under assurance from the judges that he would not be punished for any of the murders listed in the indictment.

The Wilsons were advised of this bill and their counsel was heard in reply to it. Hare was released from close confinement so that he could communicate freely with his advisers. The High Court then passed the bill to the Lord Advocate so that he could present *his* arguments on the matter. It was by now 26 January, and Burke was to be hanged in less than forty-eight hours.

The High Court of Justiciary, with the Lord Justice-Clerk, Lord Boyle, presiding, considered the submissions of all sides at great length. The Lord Advocate, Sir William Rae, told their lordships that in giving Hare immunity from prosecution he had intended to cover any case that might arise. His assurance was unqualified, and calculated to obtain Hare's cooperation by banishing from his mind any danger of future trial or punishment. Sir William considered that this freedom from prosecution, guaranteed in the public interest, included prosecution at the instance of any private party. He believed that he was now legally prevented from prosecuting Hare, and to do so would be dishonourable and unworthy of his office.

Mr Sandford, for the Wilsons, argued that Hare was not protected against private prosecution for Jamie's murder because such protection was given only in respect of the crime on which he gave evidence. During the trial, Hare was clearly warned that he need not answer any question relating to any other murder but Mrs Docherty's, because he could not claim the court's protection on other matters. Hare had refused to answer the one question put to him about the death of James Wilson.

Hare's representatives referred to 'Janet Wilson, alleged sister, and Janet Wilson, alleged mother of the said James Wilson, alias Daft Jamie; but who, the petitioner is informed, and has reason to believe, do not truly possess these characters, and have produced no evidence thereof.' Duncan McNeill argued that the Public Prosecutor alone had the right to punish criminals on the public's behalf, and relinquished the right to bring Hare to trial in order to obtain the conviction of Burke. Hare had kept his part of the bargain, and if the Crown was now to renege on its agreement, Hare would not have a fair trial, the ends of justice would not be served, and the public would lose faith in the absolute integrity of the law. This last point was perhaps of doubtful veracity. The public had little interest in the niceties of the law. It simply wanted Hare hanged.

The debate was too complicated for the judges to arrive at a quick decision, and they gave themselves a week in which to reach their final conclusions. It is significant, however, that there was no suggestion that the execution of Burke should be postponed.

On 2 February, their lordships met again to deliver their judgement. Lord Boyle was supported by Lords Gillies, Pitmilly, Mackenzie, Meadowbank and Alloway. By a majority of four to two, the High Court of Justiciary ruled that Hare could not be prosecuted for the murder of

James Wilson. They quashed the action of the Wilsons and ordered that Hare should be set free. The kernel of their decision was that, as Lord Mackenzie put it, 'the protection of a *socius criminis*, obtained by his appearance as a witness, in a prosecution by the Lord Advocate, operates also against the private prosecutor'. Otherwise, it would be possible in theory for Mrs Docherty's relations to prosecute Hare for a murder he had admitted, and he could be convicted without trial or jury on a charge on which he had been guaranteed immunity.

Hare was not out of the wood – or the prison cell – yet, however. The Wilson women immediately responded to the High Court judgement by notifying the Sheriff that they intended to bring a civil action against Hare for an 'assythment' of £500. This meant that they would sue him for damages, and they pleaded for him to be detained to prevent him from fleeing the country and avoiding this indemnity.

Hare was brought to court and questioned later that day, but refused to give any answers. He would not say if he was concerned in killing James Wilson, nor confirm where he was born, say where he intended to go if released from prison, or reply on any other matter, except that he admitted he could not write. But a fellow-prisoner named Lindsay said that Hare had told him that when he was liberated he would go back to Ireland. John Fisher, the chief warder at Calton jail, confirmed this. Hare then volunteered the information that he could not stay in Edinburgh as he had no home and no money, so he must go elsewhere to find work. He might remain in Scotland, or go to England or Ireland. The Sheriff therefore sent him back to prison until he could find £500. But there was no chance of him doing so, and the Wilsons withdrew the warrant after three days, resigning themselves to the inevitable. On 5 February 1829, Hare was freed from Calton jail at eight o'clock in the evening.

He was taken by hackney carriage in the company of Fisher, the turnkey, to meet the south-bound mail coach at Newington, a district he was not unfamiliar with. Hare, wearing a hat and well wrapped up in an old camlet coat against both cold and recognition, climbed up to an outside seat of the coach, and as it moved off, the considerate Fisher called out, 'Goodbye, Mr Black; I wish you well home.'

The first stage of the journey was completed at Noblehouse, a village twenty miles south of Edinburgh, where the passengers were set down at an inn for supper. There, according to the *Dumfries Courier*, Hare was recognised by one of the passengers who had been travelling inside the coach; none other than Mr Douglas Sandford, in fact, who had been junior counsel for the Wilsons![7] When the freezing Hare attempted to take an inside place for the next stage of the journey, Sandford ordered the guard to remove him and, to justify his action, revealed to his fellow-passengers the true identity of 'Mr Black'. When the coach reached Dumfries, news that Hare was on it travelled like wildfire and a large crowd gathered outside the King's Arms in the High Street. Soon the local police had something close to a riot on their hands, and Hare only escaped the fury of the mob by making it to the town jail. The crowd grew to an alarming 800-strong mob, and 100 special constables were hurriedly sworn in and armed with batons, while frenzied rioters hammered at the prison doors and smashed windows and lamps.

Hare was smuggled out in the early hours of the following morning and, escorted for some distance by local militia and one of the Sheriff's officers, he was left to his own devices on the road to Annan. He must have crossed the border into England and was reported to have been seen twice in the vicinity of Carlisle in the next few days. That is the last we know of Hare's fate or whereabouts.

Meanwhile, Burke's confessions appeared in the press, inflaming the public mind even more against the one who had got away. Wild speculation and rumour soon filled the vacuum left by the absence of fact. A broadsheet published by J. Johnstone & Co gave an account, 'copied', it said, 'from a Dublin Paper', of the lynching of Hare by a mob in Londonderry. Another, published by Neil & Co, purported to give an account of Hare's execution 'at New York in June, from an American Paper'.

J.B. Atlay, however, asserted that Hare 'certainly survived his confederate for over forty years'.[8] He produced no evidence for this statement other than the Victorian tale that a blind beggar who used to sit at a corner of London's Oxford Street was Hare. He had been disabled, it was said, by a workman who discovered who he was and blinded him with quicklime. 'His story was on the lips of every nursemaid, and he was pointed out to awestruck children as William Hare, one of the actors in the West Port murders.'[9] There is no good reason to believe that this really was Hare. It seems extremely unlikely, for his presence in London would not have been tolerated, and no one would have given him alms, when his vile career in Edinburgh had become known and led to copycat crimes in the capital, to say nothing of the widespread fear of 'burking' and urgent legislation to remove any incentive for similar crimes in the future.

It is more likely that Hare somehow made his way back to Ireland, probably from Liverpool, and ended his days there in obscurity with an assumed name, although it is only fair to mention that Lonsdale, writing in 1870, stated that Hare and his wife 'returned to their native country (Ireland), and were no more heard of except in the pages of fiction till a few months ago, when Hare was reported as being seen in London'.[10]

Now that we have followed the careers and fates of the homicidal quartet as far as we can, is it possible to apportion guilt with any confidence? To deal with the women first, was Burke telling the truth when he said they might have thought he and Hare were body-snatchers but had no suspicion of murder? This was his story in the 'official' confession, but he changed his tune somewhat in the *Courant* confession, eager to implicate both Hare and his wife. Although he repeated that 'Helen McDougal and Hare's wife were not present when those murders were committed', he said that it was Hare's wife who lured Daft Jamie into her house and, after signalling to Burke by stamping his foot in Rymer's shop, locked Jamie inside the room with Burke and Hare. It was also Hare's wife who urged Burke to murder Helen McDougal, if that story was true; and Hare's wife who often helped him and Hare to pack the murdered bodies into boxes. There cannot be a shadow of a doubt that Margaret Laird (or Hare) knew, at least at a later stage, what was going on and – willingly or otherwise – aided and abetted her husband and Burke in their crimes. Asked during the trial what she supposed had happened to Mrs Docherty when she (Hare) had come in from the passage and not seen the old woman, she replied, 'I had a supposition that she had been murdered. I have seen such tricks before.' The first sentence might have been part of the line she and Hare had agreed to take at the trial. The second sounds like a slip of the tongue, but no one in court pursued the point. This was presumably because she could not give evidence against her husband and there had been some prior agreement between the lawyers not to delve into any murders other than those in the indictment, in order not to inflame the volatile public even more. What astute advocate would have let pass her remark that she had 'seen such tricks before', without insisting on knowing what she meant by that?

Burke said that he 'had a good character with the police; or if they had known that there were four murderers living in one house they would have visited them oftener'. These are the words of a condemned Irishman retaining his macabre sense of humour, about ten days before his execution, with whoever interviewed him in prison and took down the *Courant* confession. It cannot, of course, be taken as evidence of Helen McDougal's guilt as an accessory.

However, one murder which points to guilt on McDougal's part is that of her distant relation, Ann McDougal. She was, according to Burke, a cousin of Nelly's 'first husband', and came to Edinburgh to visit Burke and Nelly, presumably at Nelly's invitation. She was murdered in Broggan's house when she had been in Edinburgh for a few days, and her corpse was in the house, where Nelly lived, for a few hours, packed in a trunk which Broggan saw, apparently open with a body in it. Now, if we give Nelly the benefit of the doubt and assume she was out all that time and saw neither the body nor the trunk, there is still the question of what she supposed had become of her friend and distant relation. Would she have believed Burke if he had told her that Ann had suddenly gone home to Falkirk without a parting word to Nelly? Maybe; but of all the murders, this is the one which most calls into question McDougal's ignorance of what was going on quite early in the proceedings.

The most powerful piece of evidence against Helen McDougal was the allegation by Mr and Mrs Gray that she had offered them money to keep quiet and not go to the police when the corpse of Mrs Docherty was found at the foot of her bed. Even if she had believed that Burke was acting within the law on previous occasions, she must have known that he was acting illegally this time, and therefore was an accessory during and after the fact. It is difficult to avoid the conclusion that, even if she had been entirely unaware of any murder before that of Mrs Docherty, she had tumbled to the truth by the night of Hallowe'en.

McDougal's attempted bribery of the Grays points to her guilty knowledge in more ways than one. How could she and Burke, even with the willing participation of Hare and his wife, possibly have afforded to pay the Grays hush-money of £10 a week? Clearly, if the Grays had accepted this offer, it would not have been long before they ended up on Knox's dissecting-table. It appears likely that McDougal made her ludicrous offer with this in mind. But she denied that she had offered any money to the Grays, and the other evidence against her was either based on the unreliable testimony of the Hares or was purely circumstantial, and consistent with a belief that Burke and Hare were body-snatchers.

Of course, if the Hares' evidence in the witness box had been believed, and McDougal indeed saw Burke on top of Mrs Docherty before running out of the room, that would have been conclusive. She cannot have thought the drunken Burke was about to rape the woman – she must have known that he was going to kill her. But the jury was right in deciding that the case against her as an accessory to murder had not been proven. In an English court, in these circumstances, a woman who was possibly innocent would quite probably have been sent to the gallows. We cannot say with certainty that she was not in on the whole series of murders right from the start, but she is entitled to the benefit of the doubt in our minds, as well as the jury's.

As to the actual perpetrators of the sixteen murders, it was widely believed at the time that the worst of the two fiends had got away with it. There was nothing to choose between them in moral terms, but it is worth keeping in mind that Burke was the one with such brains as the two possessed between them. He was the only one of the four who was literate, he had the wider experience, and he had the nous to be the chief motivator of a criminal partnership. It is difficult to believe that anyone with an ounce of sense would have followed Hare in a risky enterprise, although it may well have been Hare, who had lived in the squalid back streets of Edinburgh longer than Burke, who first thought of the idea of selling a body to the doctors. Sir William Rae, the Lord Advocate, was probably right in regarding Burke as the principal party in the affair. In which case, the man whom Lord Cockburn later called 'respectable' was the evil monster, and the one Professor Wilson called 'evil' was the cowardly dupe.

What if Rae had offered Burke immunity from prosecution instead of Hare? Since Nelly McDougal was not Burke's wife, the Lord Advocate could have had three defendants in the dock instead of two, and might have got two of them convicted, as Maggie Hare's guilt would probably have appeared rather less doubtful to the jury than McDougal's, and Burke would most probably have been more talkative in the dock than Hare was. Rae may have genuinely believed that Burke, as the more educated man, was the prime mover in the partnership, and that he should be the one to pay the supreme penalty; but he must also have been influenced in his choice by the probability that Hare would be the easier to frighten and coerce into turning King's Evidence.

Was there any way in which Hare might have been brought to justice *as well as* Burke? It was infinitely more desirable for the two men to be tried for murder than Burke and McDougal, for even if McDougal had been found guilty she was only an accessory and not a killer herself, as was also true of Maggie Hare. The only body in the case was that of Mrs Docherty, but the case of Mary Paterson was at least suspected before Hare made his statement and had been granted immunity from prosecution. Janet Brown (or 'Jess' as she was called in the 'Echo's' letter) had gone to the police with her story when she heard of the arrest of

Burke and Hare and their womenfolk. Perhaps more protracted and diligent enquiry after the discovery of Mrs Docherty's corpse might have led to a chink in the armour of silence that surrounded Knox and his students. Several people, according to David Paterson, had made sketches of Mary Paterson's corpse. If one of these had come to light it might have been accepted as sufficient evidence to subpoena Knox and his assistants to testify to the delivery of her body by 'John' and 'William' to 10 Surgeons' Square.

There would have been no proof that she had been murdered, but the fact that she had been in the company of Burke and Hare alive and well, and been delivered dead, on the same day, combined with the evidence about Mrs Docherty, should have been enough to persuade a jury of the guilt of both men. And if evidence had been given about the delivery of Daft Jamie as well – another young and relatively healthy person, some of whose property had been found in the possession of Burke and Hare, including the brass snuff-box and spoon – that would surely have proved conclusive, even by the admirable standards of cautious Scottish juries reluctant to take chances with the death penalty.

Another question arises about Jamie Wilson's corpse. If the order I have suggested for the murders is correct, and Burke and Hare got £8 for the body of Mrs Ostler and £10 for that of Ann McDougal, that would suggest that Mrs Ostler was murdered in September (Burke said it was 'September or October'), and Ann McDougal early in October. Knox advertised his new season's course of lectures in Practical Anatomy and Operative Surgery as commencing on 6 October, so we may take it that he paid winter rates for his subjects from about that date. So if Ann McDougal's corpse was the first that Burke and Hare sold to him after the summer recess, Jamie Wilson must have been murdered well into October, possibly halfway through the month.

Now, how long would Knox normally store a corpse before dissecting it? It could not be long, even in a cold cellar, in the days before refrigeration. But the body of Mary Paterson was apparently kept in spirits for three months before it was dissected. If the allegation was untrue that Jamie's corpse was mutilated and dissected at once to prevent recognition, it might well have been still whole in Knox's cellar when news reached him of the arrest of Burke and Hare, perhaps a fortnight, or at most three weeks, after he had bought Jamie's corpse from them.

If this were the case, what would Knox have done in such circumstances? He would either have destroyed the evidence at once, not wanting *another* recognisable corpse to be found on his premises; or he might have assumed with his customary arrogance that he could sweep aside any questions the police might put to him. But there appears to be a possibility, at least, that Jamie's corpse was intact on Knox's premises at the time of the arrest, and it could have been seized and subjected to a post-mortem examination which might have revealed more signs of a violent death than was the case with Mrs Docherty.

But thorough investigation of all the circumstances was not one of the hallmarks of this infamous case. Sir William Rae, of course, could not risk bringing four people to the dock and failing to get *any* of them convicted. He acted on the balance of probabilities, and the result was that the despicable Hare got away with multiple murder.

NOTES

[1] Lonsdale, p. 74.

[2] Grierson, p. 108.

[3] 'Shearing' meant reaping; i.e. the annual harvest when townsfolk traditionally went for a working holiday in the open air.

[4] Robert Buchanan et al, *Trial of William Burke and Helen McDougal*, p. xiv.

[5] *Glasgow Chronicle*, 10 February 1829.

[6] *Edinburgh Evening Courant*, 14 February 1829.

[7] *Dumfries Courier*, 10 February 1829.

[8] Atlay, p. 42.

[9] Ibid.

[10] Lonsdale, pp. 75–76(n).

10. ECHO

During the weeks since Christmas, while Burke was in the condemned cell awaiting execution and Hare was in prison waiting for legal arguments to end in his release, one other allegedly culpable associate of the foursome had kept what some regarded as a dignified silence.

Dr Knox was commonly perceived as a sinister ringmaster who got Burke and Hare dancing to his tune. Some believed he had actively encouraged sixteen murders, and most of those who would not go that far held him guilty of turning a blind eye, like Nelson, to a clear signal he chose not to see.

Near the end of January, a sixpenny pamphlet was published, entitled *Letter to the Lord Advocate, disclosing the accomplices, secrets, and other facts relative to the Late Murders; with a correct account of the manner in which the Anatomical Schools are supplied with subjects.* Its author hid behind the pseudonym 'The Echo of Surgeons' Square', but it has been attributed ever since to David Paterson, Knox's doorkeeper. This document has consistently been dismissed as the spiteful reaction of a man who had been sacked and was taking revenge on his employer, while at the same time clearing himself of any blame in the affair. No one in more than 100 years seems to have seriously questioned whether Paterson was really the author of this pamphlet. It is my belief not only that the pamphlet was not written by Paterson, but that it is more important than has been realised. The chief object of the Letter, it appears to me, was not to exonerate Paterson, but to urge the Lord Advocate to prosecute Hare as well as Burke and to bring Knox to justice for his part in the affair. What was meant, otherwise, by the title-page quote, 'What? Shall wealth screen thee from justice?' The pamphlet was written and printed in a very short time, before all hope of prosecuting Hare had gone, and by someone with prior knowledge of Burke's confessions, since they were referred to in the text. But he can only have seen the few leaked (and inaccurate) details of the *Courant* confession, for in *neither* of his confessions did Burke say, as the 'Echo' believed, that 'the first subject ever they sold to Dr K – was a female that died in Hare's house'. This at least proves that the author of the *Letter* was not the person who somehow gained access to Burke in prison and obtained the complete account.

Paterson lived with his mother and fifteen-year-old sister, Elizabeth, at 26 West Port. He described himself as 'keeper of the museum belonging to Dr Knox', and was referred to in court, during Burke's trial, as a 'medical person' by one lawyer and a 'surgeon' by another. But after Paterson's appearance in court and some damaging correspondence with the newspapers, Knox's senior students, keen to defend their mentor when he would do nothing to defend himself, denounced Paterson as a 'doorkeeper', a menial servant who had no responsibilities other than answering the door and keeping the premises clean, and was 'hired by the week at seven shillings'.

The truth, as is usually the case, seems to have been somewhere between the two extremes. Paterson had no medical qualifications but was rather more than a mere janitor. He was employed by Knox to keep his dissecting-room in good order, making it ready for demonstrations and cleaning it up afterwards, and he had some responsibility for accepting and storing the corpses ready for use when needed. He was authorised by Knox to receive bodies on his behalf when they were delivered, and was, at a later stage at least, Knox's go-between with the various suppliers.

There has been much confusion about the sequence of events in Paterson's brief appearance on the stage of judicial history. He did *not* reveal during Burke's trial, as some authors have said, that he had been attempting to sell to another anatomist, for a profit, a body intended for Dr Knox. Paterson wrote a letter to the *Caledonian Mercury*, published on 15 January, in which he claimed that he had been shamefully wronged as a result of his evidence during the trial, and denied that he had been dismissed from Dr Knox's service after absconding. He had a letter from Knox, in fact, asking him to go back. Addressed to 'Dear David', it acknowledged that 'the public clamour is of course much against you', but assured him that 'all such matters as these subside in a short period, provided the individuals themselves do not adopt false steps'. Paterson protested his innocence of any wrongdoing and challenged the authorities to bring him to trial if they could prove him guilty of any.

It was then that the *Mercury*, instead of offering him any crumbs of comfort, let it be known that the paper had information that Paterson had attempted to sell a body, intended for Dr Knox, to one of the doctor's rivals, and alleged that the body in question was that of Mrs Docherty, the last victim of Burke and Hare. Paterson admitted that he had attempted to profit from the sale of a body, and offered an explanation. James Syme, one of Knox's rival private lecturers in anatomy, was desperately short of subjects, and had asked Paterson if he had a surplus. On the same night that Burke and Hare had made it known to him that they had another subject for sale, a message dated 29 October had reached 10 Surgeons' Square from a well-known local body-snatcher named Andrew Merrilees, nicknamed 'Merry Andrew'. It read:

> Doctor am in the east, and has been doin little busnis, an short of siller [silver, or cash] send out abot aught and twenty shilins way the carer the thing will bee in abot 4 on Saturday mornin its a shusa [female corpse] hae the plase open. And. M-s.

Paterson, with two bodies due for delivery together, saw his opportunity for a little profit, and offered to Syme for £15 the one Merry Andrew was bringing in the early hours of the morning. Merrilees would not expect more than £10 or £12 from Knox. Paterson could pocket the difference. In the event, Merrilees failed to turn up with the corpse, but Paterson's admission got him into further trouble. It looked as if he could have been soliciting corpses in advance and inviting anatomists to bid against one another for them. He admitted that the coincidence of the two corpses looked 'rather suspicious', but maintained that these were the facts. The newspaper, however, stuck to its story, and in the end Paterson's letters to the editor had done him more harm than good. The general belief is that he then wrote the open letter in self-justification.

The open *Letter to the Lord Advocate* has been given short shrift by many previous writers on Burke and Hare, and Lonsdale, in his biography of Knox, only mentions Paterson in a brief and dismissive footnote. Isobel Rae, likewise, barely discusses the *Letter* at all. But the document raises some significant questions which have been largely ignored.

According to the author, 'when a just suspicion fell upon Burke about the beginning of October last, a policeman was stationed at his door, but even then, he eluded their vigilance, and the body was safely deposited in the Lecture Room'. Whose body was this? According to Burke's first confession, 'about the beginning of October' could have been before the murders of Mrs Ostler, Ann McDougal and Daft Jamie. But is it likely that Burke murdered four more victims (including Docherty) *after* he had come under suspicion and knew the police were watching him? And if someone had gone to the police with a suspicion about Burke, and Knox knew about it, would this not have alerted even the arrogant Knox to the danger he was in?

Later in the letter, the 'Echo' represents Paterson as saying that Burke had reported to him that he had a subject, but dare not bring it because a neighbour suspected that he had a body in his possession and a policeman 'seldom left the corner of the house'. On hearing of this, Knox said that 'John' was a coward and he (Knox) would write to the authorities and procure a protection for John to carry 'any packages safe to his Lecture Room'. Speaking later to Burke himself, Knox reportedly said that if he should be stopped on the street, he should go quietly to the police office until Knox could get him released and the package delivered. Burke allegedly replied that if he were once taken to the police office, he would not so easily get out again! This story, if true, suggests either that Knox really did believe that Burke was merely purchasing dead bodies or that, if he *did* have any suspicions, he was confident that no one could prove anything against him.

The body in question was not Daft Jamie's, because he was murdered at Hare's place in Tanner's Close. If it was Mrs Ostler's, Burke and Hare murdered two more people later, in the very house that the police were supposed to be watching. But it is more likely that the body was that of Ann McDougal, if it was during the early part of October, as they got £10 for her corpse, but only £8 for the washer-woman's. Nevertheless, Burke and Hare murdered at least two more people, and possibly three, *after* the police had been alerted by neighbours' suspicions and posted a man outside Burke's house. But these murders were not all committed there.

This part of the 'Echo's' argument tends, if anything, to absolve Knox of any knowledge or suspicion of murder, rather than implicate him, and thus does the opposite of what commentators have assumed to be the pamphlet's purpose – to achieve Paterson's revenge on Knox for sacking him.

If Paterson's claim that it was his own decision to leave Knox's employment is true, that would suggest that Paterson had some other employment lined up, so perhaps the rumour that he was about to go into partnership with Burke and Hare had some basis in fact. The idea (in Paterson's mind, at least) was not, presumably, to commit murder, but to obtain subjects from Ireland or elsewhere for the anatomy lecturers in Edinburgh. Paterson would have been aware of the possibilities of a lucrative living. He had already been approached by Syme, and knew well enough what prices corpses fetched.

Burke mentioned in the *Courant* confession that 'Hare and him had a plan made up, that Burke and a man were to go to Glasgow or Ireland, and try the same there, and to forward them to Hare, and he was to give them to Dr Knox.' Burke did not say who 'the man' was to be, but if it was Paterson, that would explain why he refused Knox's request for him to resume work as his doorkeeper. He could earn a lot more than seven shillings a week in partnership with Burke and Hare. In nine months they had earned about £150 between them – that is nearly £2 each a week on average.

The 'Echo' goes on to pose a pertinent question. If the police had been alerted to a suspicion that Burke had a corpse in his house, whether obtained by body-snatching or any other means, why did they not obtain a warrant to search the premises, rather than merely posting an officer outside to keep watch? The probable reason is that the local police had instructions to look the other way, to some extent, when faced with body-snatching, which is what they thought they were dealing with. The officer outside was merely a token show of law and order to pacify the neighbours because one of them had voiced a suspicion. If the police had raided every house where body-snatchers lived, the reputation of the Edinburgh medical school would have evaporated in no time at all and the training of surgeons there would have come to a complete stop.

It was a common practice for the authorities to turn a blind eye on the purchase of corpses for anatomical study, whether bought from body-snatchers or persons who had corpses in their possession legally. In London, Sir Astley Cooper felt morally bound to intercede on behalf of any of his regular suppliers who fell foul of the law. When Joshua Naples, then a gravedigger, was sentenced to imprisonment in 1802, Cooper had gone directly to the Home Secretary and got him released. And Sir Astley's accounts for May 1828 include this item:

> 6th. Paid Vaughan's wife 6s.
> 29th. Paid Vaughan for 26 weeks confinement, at 10s per week,
>   £13.

Tom Vaughan was a member of a gang of body-snatchers operating from Southwark, and one of Cooper's regular suppliers. Sir Robert Peel also quietly acquiesced, largely at Cooper's urging, in the importation of bodies from France and Ireland.[1]

Knox himself had been in the act of drafting a letter to the Home Secretary to complain about the difficulties in which teachers like himself were having to work in the present state of the law. He explained how shipments of corpses from Ireland were obstructed by Irish anatomists jealous of Scotland's reputation, and how packages intended for him had been seized and opened in places such as Liverpool and Carlisle by zealous Customs men, who only succeeded in occasioning pointless inquests and provoking local disturbances. 'There is one subject in particular,' Knox's letter continued, 'on which I beg most respectfully your attention.'

> Anatomists generally are most anxious to avoid public scenes such as these, and for this purpose they are careful to select subjects which are claimed by no relative or friend, and thus often avoid the painful necessity of violating the burial grounds and by doing so inflicting a shock on the most sacred feelings of human nature. Now, when anatomical subjects procured under such circumstances are nevertheless seized on their way to the schools, very alarming reprisals are made in the burying grounds of the place where the seizure has been made, often without the smallest regard to risk or circumstances . . .
>
> Permit me most respectfully to remark to you, that I have ever been an advocate for the making of these matters as little public as possible, but now that the anatomical enquiry is patent to all, I therefore thought it my duty to state to you the obstacles which impede the progress of anatomy in Great Britain.[2]

Just as Knox was about to despatch this letter to London, however, Burke and Hare and their women were arrested, and Knox wisely thought better of it.

What is clear in all this is that there was a conspiracy of silence among Edinburgh's elite. The chief reasons were almost certainly that, first, they wanted to hide the truth about the extent of body-snatching and the practices of the anatomists from the public, and, second, they were anxious to protect the reputation of Edinburgh as the leading medical school in Europe.

The author of the *Letter to the Lord Advocate*, whoever he was, was a man of education and had some formal literary style and sophistication. He adopted a high moral tone, betraying a Calvinistic severity, quoted Shakespeare and, if it *was* Paterson trying to disguise his own authorship, switched very skilfully from first to third person throughout the thirty-six-page document in reporting his own words as if they were being quoted in support of a carefully argued case.

We are asked to believe that this was the work of a mere janitor, earning seven shillings a week and living in a poor lodging with his mother and sister. One, moreover, who bore his former employer a grudge and had tried to cheat him. The same man who was believed to be about to go into a lucrative enterprise with Burke and Hare to supply the Edinburgh anatomists with corpses shipped over from Ireland. And was this anonymous author, posing persuasively as a man of conscience and integrity, the same irresponsible young man who had sent his fifteen-year-old sister, alone, to a gloomy back-alley to call on a man he already suspected of being a murderer of women, or at the very least, a drunken body-snatcher? I, for one, do not think so!

If Paterson had a sister who was fifteen years old, it is not very likely that he was more than, say, nineteen. He was a single young man, still living with his mother and uncertain of his direction in life. He had joined the army, but returned to Knox's employment after a couple of years. Is it conceivable that he would have possessed the self-assurance to address the Lord Advocate of Scotland in such confident formal tones?

And even if Paterson *did* write the pamphlet, who financed its printing? Was this low-paid whippersnapper so altruistic as to dig deep into his own pockets to publish an exhortation to the experienced Lord Advocate to 'strain every nerve, and sift this dreadful plot to its very core'? I think not!

The pamphlet was printed by Menzies and advertised as being for sale at 132 High Street on 29 January. The only clue to occupancy of property in Edinburgh at that time is the record of the local property tax, called the 'extent'. It appears probable from the extent roll in the Edinburgh City Archives that the ground-floor tenant of 132 High Street was James Stillie, a bookseller, stationer and proprietor of a circulating library. But there is no suggestion that he was a publisher – merely a retailer – and the person who paid for the printing and publishing of the pamphlet was most likely the man who wrote it.

The text of this obscure pamphlet is given as Appendix V, and reproduced in its entirety for the first time in any book about the Burke and Hare case, so that readers may judge its contents for themselves. My own impression is that the letter has something of the self-righteousness of a Puritan about it. But it is most likely the work of another medical man, probably one of Knox's jealous rivals. There is more than a hint that he frequented Surgeons' Square. Could the author have been Liston, who had good reason to hold a grudge against Knox? Or Syme, who was forced to give up lecturing on anatomy because he could not compete with Knox in keeping up a regular supply of subjects for his students to work on? Syme is known to have been an ill-tempered man who had good reason to want revenge on Knox, having suffered from his acid tongue. Syme became as eminent in the field of clinical surgery as Knox in anatomy, but jealous rivalry was ever-present in the relations of the medical men, as we have already noticed. That between Knox, Syme and Liston – all native Scotsmen – is particularly relevant to our present enquiry.

Robert Liston, born at Ecclesmachan, was three years younger than Knox, but like him, had gone to Barclay after failing anatomy under Monro. Liston was a tall, well-built man and a noted athlete of formidable strength. He was involved in almost legendary exploits as a body-snatcher before the advent of the professionals, and is reputed on one occasion to have carried two bodies away together, one under each arm. He was Barclay's assistant for five years, and subsequently taught anatomy in partnership with Syme, gaining a reputation as both a fine teacher and a great pioneering surgeon. He was particularly noted for the speed of his operations when speed was of the essence, in the days before anaesthetics. He could amputate a leg at the thigh, without assistance, in half a minute, including sutures.

Liston was also arrogant and quarrelsome, however, and he had good reason to dislike Knox, as we have seen. He was expelled from the Edinburgh Royal Infirmary in 1822, after a dispute with the authorities, and some years later, when the Professorship of Clinical Surgery became vacant at the university, Syme, a younger man, got the post in preference to Liston, who then left Edinburgh for London, where he died in 1847 aged fifty-three.

James Syme, born in Edinburgh, was Liston's junior by five years. He was a demonstrator in Liston's dissecting-room until 1823, when Liston decided to concentrate more on his practice, and Syme then took over the teaching role. Syme lectured on anatomy for five years, but gave up at the beginning of the 1828–29 season, abandoning anatomy for surgery because he could not compete with Knox in maintaining a large class. Syme had approached David Paterson at one point to ask where Knox's suppliers lived. Paterson is said to have replied that he did not know, but would mention Syme's interest when he saw them again, provided Dr Knox's supply was maintained.

Syme became Knox's implacable enemy. He first became a thorn in Knox's side by seconding a motion in May 1826 to defer electing Knox as Conservator of the new museum of the Edinburgh College of Surgeons. Then in September 1829 he was elected a Curator of the museum. He was a signatory to a proposal to institute a minute examination of all preparations in the museum to ascertain their condition, which was something of an insult to Knox, who had already declared them to be in good order. Syme crossed swords with Knox over one preparation, and complained formally to the College Committee, which admonished Knox for his 'incivility' to Syme.

Syme was by this time running his own surgical hospital, having been refused a post as surgeon at the Royal Infirmary, lest he should quarrel openly with Liston. Syme's enmity towards Knox continued when he seconded a Royal College motion which forbade Knox to hold teaching courses anywhere, informing twenty-two licensing boards throughout Britain of this decision.

Liston was not noted for the clarity of his literary style. He might have realised that he could do himself more harm than good by any public attack on Knox, if his authorship were to be discovered. Syme seems to have been more reckless and impulsive.

Whoever did write the *Letter to the Lord Advocate* scored a palpable hit. The publication incensed the Edinburgh public even more against a man whom they already held to be the patron and criminal accomplice of Burke and Hare. The execution of Burke and the escape of Hare and the two women from justice focused the attention of the populace on the one remaining participant, and Knox was eventually forced to heed the advice of his friends and take action to clear his name.

NOTES

[1] For this and other aspects of the partnership between anatomists and their suppliers, see Bailey, *The Resurrection Men*, (London, Macdonald, 1991).

[2] Quoted in Isobel Rae, *Knox the Anatomist*, (Edinburgh, Oliver and Boyd, 1964), p. 63.

11. KNOX

If Knox had been called as a witness at the trial, what would he have said? He *could* have volunteered information to the Lord Advocate *before* the trial which would have prevented Hare from escaping justice. But he was obviously not going to implicate himself by admitting in court that he knew or even suspected that any one of the three persons listed in the indictment had died by violence. He *might* have testified that the bodies delivered to his premises had not been laid out or buried. As he was not called, he was able to maintain a ruthless silence about the whole matter which was not dignified, but arrogant, as subsequent events were to prove. Knox did not consider himself accountable to public opinion, which he held in contempt. 'I will do just as I have done heretofore,' he told his students after the trial.

On 14 January, while three of the homicidal quartet were still in prison, Sir Walter Scott had felt obliged to arrange for a meeting of the Royal Society of Edinburgh:

> . . . as Mr Knox proposes to read an essay on some dissections. A bold proposal truly from one who has had so lately the boldness of trading so deep in human flesh. I will oppose his reading in the present circumstances if I should stand alone, but I hope he will be wrought upon to withdraw his essay or postpone it at least. It is very bad taste to push himself forward just now.[1]

Scott was at the meeting next day, and found that some members thought that:

> . . . declining to receive the paper would be a declaration unfavourable to Dr Knox. I think hearing it before Mr Knox has made any defence (as he is stated to have in view) would be an

intimation of our preference of the cause of Science to those of Morality and Common Humanity.[2]

Scott noted on 16 January that Knox had consented to withdraw his paper, 'or rather suffers the reading to be postponed'. But on the twenty-third Sir Walter's senses were again offended. He received a visit from George Sinclair, son of Sir John Sinclair, First Baronet of Ulbster:

> Young hopeful's business with me was to invite me to be one of a committee who were to sit as Mr Knox's friends in a Committee of enquiry on his late traffick with the West port. In other words to lend a hand to whitewash this much to be suspected individual. But he shall ride off on no back of mine, & I feel no call to mix myself in the business at all. The rest of the committee are to be doctors & surgeons (ask my fellow &c) and I suppose the doughty Sir John at the head of them all and this young boar pig to swell the cry. I will travell in no such boat.[3]

On 11 February, the intensity of feeling against Knox was increased to fever pitch by the announcement that a committee of gentlemen, to be headed by the Marquis of Queensberry, had undertaken to investigate, in the public interest, Dr Knox's dealings with Burke and Hare. *The Scotsman*, in welcoming this development, said that the enquiry must be 'full and fair, the evidence must be taken impartially, and none of any value refused; and what is still more important, the whole evidence, as well as the opinions of the examinators, must be laid before the public'.[4]

Next day, a mob assembled on Calton Hill, bearing aloft a life-size effigy of the obnoxious anatomist, labelled with his name on the back for fear anyone should be in any doubt as to whom it was meant to represent. The crowd set off for Newington, gathering reinforcements en route, and stopped outside 4 Newington Place, where, amid hysterical shrieking and cries for Knox's blood, the figure was hanged from the branches of a tree. An attempt was then made to set fire to it, but it would not burn, so it was torn to pieces instead. Knox himself, meanwhile, had escaped by the back door, and the police, having gained entry there, rushed out at the front and drove some of the rioters from the doctor's garden, but the mob remained in the street and took to throwing stones, which broke windows in the house and caused minor injuries to police officers.

There were more riots elsewhere in the city. Noisy crowds gathered in the High Street and Canongate, and damage was done to Knox's premises in Surgeons' Square. Another effigy was carried to Portobello, whence it was suspected that Knox had retreated, and there it was hanged from an ancient gibbet at the top of Tower Street and burnt. After dark, further damage was done to Knox's house at Newington. Some twenty rioters, mostly youths, were arrested that night, but were dealt with leniently (and wisely) by the magistrates. The handful convicted were bound over and ordered to pay fines, but the fines were met from a fund which had been set up, apparently, for that very purpose. The Edinburgh *Weekly Chronicle* repeated a warning it had issued before, that 'the agitation of public feeling will never subside till the city be released of this man's presence, or until his innocence be manifested. In justice to himself, if he is innocent, in justice to the public if he is guilty, he ought to be put upon trial.'

The press continued to stoke the fires of public fury against Knox. One paper considered his relation to Burke the same as that of Banquo's murderers to Macbeth.[5] Another accused him of recklessness bordering on guilty knowledge, and continued:

> With regard to Dr Knox, too much delicacy and reserve have been maintained by a part of the press. When the atrocities in question first transpired, it was stated that Knox conducted himself with the utmost civility towards the police officers who went to his house in search of the body, when the fact is, he swore at them from his window, and threatened to blow their brains out; and it was only upon their proceeding to force the door of his lecture-room, that it was opened by one of the keepers.[6]

Professor Wilson attacked Knox in *Blackwood's Edinburgh Magazine*, challenging him to 'prove to the conviction of all reasonable men that it was impossible he could suspect any evil . . .' 'The whole world,' he said, 'shudders at the transactions, and none but a base, blind, brutal beast can at this moment dare to declare, *"Dr Knox stands free from all suspicion of being accessory to murder"*.'[7]

Wilson (Christopher North) has been severely criticised in some quarters for his attacks on Knox. 'Literary ruffianism,' Lonsdale wrote, 'is too mild a term to apply to the foul words used by Wilson . . .' But Lonsdale himself seems to have absorbed some of his mentor's immunity or indifference to the genuine fears and objections of the poor:

> There was a clamour against the anatomists, emanating, it is true, from a frothy, democratic class, blind to their own interests, and ungrateful for the many benefits they had received from the medical profession.[8]

The fact is that both Professor Wilson and Sir Walter Scott gave literate voice to popular sentiment, which was not ignorant, but angry and apprehensive. Had Knox once expressed his shock and regret at the revelations of multiple murder, and taken some part in the prosecution of the murderers, the public anger against him may not have been so vociferous. But not only did he fail to express a word of remorse for his failure to suspect murder, he repudiated any suggestion of responsibility for it. Added to which, the paradox that a science which was intended to benefit the poor had encouraged their victimisation and murder was seen by the public as unspeakable hypocrisy.

Meanwhile, Knox continued his lectures as before, never missing a session, and when his students were distracted by the noise of hostile crowds outside, he told them not to be alarmed. 'It is my life, not yours, they seek. The assailants of our peace may be big in menace, but they are too cowardly in act to confront such a phalanxed body of gentlemen as I see before me.'[9] This drew cheers from his audience, but it could easily have become another of Knox's fatal misjudgements. The public hostility to all anatomists and dissection had already led to attacks on medical students as well as their teachers, in both England and Scotland. As long ago as 1730, before professional body-snatchers had appeared on the scene, students who had dug up corpses from the churchyards of Cambridge and neighbouring villages for dissection in the medical colleges had given rise to 'disturbances between the scholars and the inhabitants'.[10] A medical student had nearly been lynched by an angry mob in Glasgow in August 1828. This recent incident was passed over by the national press as a little local disturbance. At Carlisle, a surgeon-anatomist had been shot in the face and his colleague thrown to his death over the parapet of a bridge.

On 23 February, it was announced that Lord Queensberry, chairman of the committee 'investigating' Knox's dealings, had withdrawn from it. No reason was given and none has ever been produced.[11] Could Queensberry (Charles Douglas, the 6th Marquis) have been got at by someone such as Scott or Wilson, one wonders? The chairmanship was taken over by John Robinson, Secretary of the Royal Society of Edinburgh. The other members were not all doctors and surgeons closing ranks, as Sir Walter had feared, but they were all carefully chosen citizens who met with Knox's approval. They were William Pulteney Alison, Professor of the Theory of Physic (who had been listed as a trial witness but was not called); Sir George Ballingall, Professor of Military Surgery; Dr James Russell, Professor of Clinical Surgery; Sir William Hamilton, Professor of Universal History; George Sinclair of Ulbster (who had sought Scott's participation); Thomas Allan, a banker; and M.P. Brown and J. Shaw Stewart, both lawyers.

The committee's report was published in the Edinburgh papers on 21 March. It fell a long way short of the standards proposed by *The Scotsman*. The enquiry took place in private and none of the evidence it gathered was made public. The committee's report is given as Appendix IV. Briefly, the committee exonerated Knox, clearing him of either knowing or suspecting that Burke and Hare were murdering the people whose corpses he paid for. It had been 'proved' to the committee's satisfaction that no mutilation or disfigurement was practised to conceal the identity of the subjects. The committee mildly reproved Knox for what it called 'laxity of the regulations under which bodies were received'. The circumstances in which his seven assistants and his doorkeeper received fresh subjects from suppliers whom they thought were body-snatchers, with instructions from Knox not to enquire where the bodies had come from, were incautious and demanded greater vigilance. That was the extent of the committee's censure. It had found no evidence of any suspicion having been aroused either in the mind of Dr Knox, '*or of any other of the individuals who saw the bodies of these unfortunate persons prior to the apprehension of Burke*'. The italics are mine, and it is clear that this assertion does not agree with the impression given in the 'Echo's' open letter to the Lord Advocate.

The committee's satisfactory conclusions (from Knox's point of view, at least) led him to forward the report to the *Caledonian Mercury* for publication with a covering letter from himself – the only word of self-defence he ever committed to print on the subject. He clearly resented criticism of himself, though he handed it out readily to others. He appeared indifferent to the fact that some of his subjects had met violent deaths, and expressed no word of regret. He implied that the committee had been set up by his friends after he had been dissuaded from bringing libel actions against some of his critics. Although there were sufficient grounds for such actions, 'disclosures of the most innocent proceedings even in the best-conducted dissecting-room must always shock the public and be hurtful to science'. Knox considered himself the unfortunate victim of circumstance which could have befallen anyone else in his situation.

A fortnight after the report was published, Sir Walter Scott noted in his journal that he had received a letter:

> from one David Paterson, who was Dr Knox's jackall for buying murderd bodies, suggesting that I should write on the subject of Burke and Hare, and offering me his invaluable collection of anecdotes. '*Curse him's imperance and him's damn insurance,*' as Mungo says in the farce. 'Did one ever hear the like?' The scoundrel has been the companion and patron of such atrocious murderers and kidnappers, and he has the impudence to write to any decent man.[12]

This is the last we hear of Paterson, although Alexander Leighton noted in 1860 that Paterson was still a 'respected citizen' of Edinburgh.

Knox carried on as before and weathered the storm for a time, but he was *persona non grata* in Edinburgh society, and his classes diminished in size as students began to migrate to Glasgow or Dublin. Sometimes people would recognise him in the streets and point him out to their friends as the notorious anatomist Knox. He finally gave up teaching anatomy. In 1837 he applied for the recently vacated Chair of Pathology at the university. The day after his application was received, a proposal that the Chair should be abolished was signed by Sir Charles Bell and Professors Alison, Christison and, needless to say, perhaps, Syme. In the end, the Chair was not abolished, but Knox did not get it. Quite apart from his association with Burke and Hare, he was considered a dangerous radical as well as untrustworthy.

In the *Medical Gazette* of 30 October 1840, Knox published what he claimed was a discovery of his own concerning the placenta. But it had been brought to his notice by Dr John Reid. When censured by Reid for this discourtesy, Knox said that he had told his students about it in 1839. It became evident that Knox's honesty, or his memory, could not be relied upon.

Knox obtained an appointment as lecturer in anatomy at the extra-mural medical school in Argyle Square, but found that he could no longer attract sufficient students. When he left Edinburgh for London, he disposed of his school in Surgeons' Square to his former pupil, Henry Lonsdale.

Cold-shouldered by his colleagues, he was hounded out of Edinburgh's medical hierarchy and struck off the Roll of Fellows of the Royal Society. Professor Christison wrote later that Knox:

> ... never recovered in Edinburgh society from the stigma which thus attached to him ... after various vicissitudes, and successive descents, he sank, before his death in London, to a state not much above destitution. One of his last occupations was that of lecturer, demonstrator, or showman, to a travelling party of Ojibbeway Indians.[13]

This was wildly misleading. The native Americans Christison referred to had attracted great interest when they came to England, and Knox, one of whose subsequent publications was *Ethnology, or the Races of Men*, naturally took a scientific interest in them. Knox's wife died in 1841, after giving birth to their sixth child, and soon afterwards, their four-year-old son died. Knox wrote several books on a variety of subjects while trying in vain to get another permanent position.

His literary works were far from being restricted to scientific manuals on anatomy and surgery. He published a book on fishing in Scotland, a *Manual of Artistic Anatomy for the Use of Painters, Sculptors, and Amateurs*, and what was commonly regarded as his best work, *Ethnology, or the Races of Men*. He also translated works from the French.

Syme continued to hound Knox. In November 1856, he wrote to *The Lancet* criticising Fergusson, who had published an article describing Liston's surgical techniques. Syme pointed out that Fergusson had never been a pupil of Liston's, but had always been loyal to Knox, 'of whose dissecting-room he had the principal charge during a very eventful period'. This allusion, raising the spectre of the Burke and Hare scandal, was made by Syme, in Fergusson's opinion, from despicable motives. The letter appeared shortly after Knox, after many trials and tribulations, had at last obtained an appointment, at the age of sixty-three, as pathological anatomist at the Cancer Hospital in London. Syme was a master at kicking a man when he was down. Nevertheless, Knox held that post until his death from apoplexy at his home in Hackney on 20 December 1862.

Henry Cockburn wrote in his memoirs:

> All our anatomists incurred a most unjust, and a very alarming, though not an unnatural odium; Dr Knox in particular, against

whom not only the anger of the populace, but the condemnation of more intelligent persons, was specially directed. But tried in reference to the invariable, and the necessary practice of the profession, our anatomists were spotlessly correct, and Knox the most correct of them all.[14]

Lord Cockburn wrote and published these words while Knox was still alive, and was thus one of very few who were prepared to be seen defending him.

The *Medical Times and Gazette* printed a long and generous obituary in which there was no mention at all of Burke and Hare, nor any hint of the difficulties Knox had experienced after the exposure of their crimes, though it did comment on 'the bitterness with which Dr Knox inveighed against all authority, political, civil, and religious'. It noted only that in 1845 he 'left Edinburgh and came to London', and that 'during a part of his career he was not free from all blemish . . .' Nevertheless:

> In gifts of speech he was unequalled. His voice bland and harmonious; his manner earnest and persuasive; his *facundia*, or by whatever other name we may call that seemingly inexhaustible flow of the choicest and most apposite language, his clearness, his logical precision in speaking, and the enormous amount of information on all subjects connected with natural history and fine art, which flowed without effort from his lips – all conspired to make him justly a favourite with all who formed his acquaintance.[15]

The article dwelt almost entirely on Knox's intellect and his literary works, and sought to explain the 'savage radicalism' of a man who was, in his private life, 'pre-eminently tender, friendly, and affectionate':

> First of all, there was the blood of the Knox family. Make allowance for the difference between a preacher-politician and a philosophical anatomist. The Doctor was but the reformer 'in a higher power'; and carried out against all 'kingcraft and priestcraft' the same revolt which his predecessor had instituted against 'the monstrous regiment of women', and the religious authorities of his day.[16]

The obituary also revealed something which neither of Knox's biographers pursued.

> Radical as he was, he yet felt the honest pride of a Scotsman at his own ancestry, and longed to get possession of Ranfurly, an ancient domain where his family had been lairds, and the occupation of which place and title by his Irish kinsman, Knox, Earl of Ranfurly, he complained of.[17]

It was Thomas Knox who had been created 1st Earl of Ranfurly. It may be that a gnawing resentment of what he perceived as an injustice was also part of the make-up of Robert Knox's character, and perhaps contributed to the impatience and intolerance of which he was so often guilty. The Ranfurly estate is near Bridge of Weir, west of Glasgow, and is still the seat of that branch of the Knox family which holds the title today.

A number of authors, mostly in the medical profession, have tried to restore Knox's reputation since his death. He was, it is said, made a scapegoat by his fellow-surgeons and anatomists in the intolerant Edinburgh of the time. He was a victim of professional jealousy. He was a prophet without honour in his own country. His friend, biographer and former pupil, Henry Lonsdale, described him as a man of genius, gifted with 'rare intellect' and 'commanding eloquence', and insisted that he was 'humane, compassionate, and kind-hearted', and 'tender to a degree, wherever humanity was concerned'.[18] Lonsdale told an affecting little story which would nowadays, sadly but inevitably, raise suspicions of paedophilia. Knox was walking in the meadows with his friend Dr Adams when a pretty little girl, aged about six, caught his notice while she was playing:

> He gave her a penny, and said, 'Now, my dear, you and I will be friends. Would you come and live with me if you got a whole penny every day?' 'No,' said the child; 'you would, may be, sell me to Dr Knox.' The anatomist started back with a painfully stunned expression; his features began to twitch convulsively, and tears appeared in his eyes.[19]

Of course, we can think of several human monsters who were kind to children and animals. Another medical author stated that Knox was a 'great, strong, outstanding, and valiant character; the most versatile, and the most thorough teacher of anatomy that Scotland, a country which has long been noted for the excellence of its anatomical instruction, ever has produced . . .'[20]

So should Knox be accorded 'benefit of clergy'? Consider one more of his biographer's apologias for his former teacher and colleague:

> It was by the merest accident . . . that Knox was brought in relation with Burke at all; and his contemporaries should have remembered that *his* misfortune might have been *theirs*, and was within an ace of being Monro's.[21]

That is not necessarily so. It was undoubtedly Knox's bad luck that one of his eager students, thinking to do him a service, directed Burke and Hare to his premises when they were looking for Monro's. If they had found Monro, he – or any other teacher of anatomy – would have acted, some say, in the same way as Knox did. This, however, is a debatable conclusion, and we can point to at least one man who did *not* act as Knox did. Furthermore, other anatomists did not pay as much for subjects as Knox did, and did not pay as promptly. Nor did they leave students to deal with body-snatchers, with instructions not to ask awkward questions. It is possible that Burke and Hare might not have been greeted elsewhere with such encouragement, and might soon have come to the conclusion that the business was too risky.

The question is, was Knox guilty of criminal negligence in not suspecting foul play or, at the very least, not enquiring how Burke and Hare had come by their fresh, unburied corpses, which included those of a twelve-year-old boy and two or three other young people who were, to all appearance, healthy? (Mary Paterson, Jamie Wilson and Ann McDougal, who was described as a young, married woman.) If it was true that Knox had taken Jamie Wilson's corpse for dissection out of turn and had it disfigured to prevent recognition, why had he preserved another young and recognisable body, that of Mary Paterson, for longer than usual, on account of its beauty? Could it have been because she was a prostitute, beyond redemption, whose demise he assumed no one would care about? And if Knox believed that the bodies brought by Burke and Hare were generally those of derelicts or old people who had died of drink or other diseases and been sold by their friends or relations, what did he think about the twelve-year-old boy who was brought in *at the same time as his grandmother*, both of them packed tightly into a herring-barrel?

According to Isobel Rae, a later biographer of Knox, he 'had no reason, then, to believe that the body of Mrs Docherty was other than that of one of the many unclaimed strangers who died natural deaths in the city'.[22] But she fails to point out that this was the last in a long series of unburied corpses.

The committee of enquiry's assertion that *no one* entertained any suspicion about the bodies delivered to Knox clearly contradicts Paterson's evidence during Burke's trial, and what the 'Echo of Surgeons' Square' said in his open letter, as well as other medical opinions which came to light afterwards. Sir Robert Christison wrote, many years later:

> My own opinion at the time was, that Dr Knox, then the most popular lecturer on anatomy in Edinburgh . . . had rather wilfully shut his eyes to incidents which ought to have excited the grave suspicions of a man of his intelligence. In a conversation I had with him before the information obtained from Hare and his wife had been communicated to me, I observed that the body taken by the police from his rooms must have been delivered there while warm and flexible, and consequently never had been buried. He made very light of this suggestion, and told me that he had ten or eleven bodies brought the previous winter to his rooms in as recent a state; and that they were got by his providers watching the low lodging-houses in the Cowgate, Grassmarket, and West Port, and, when a death occurred, purchasing the body from the tenant before any one could claim it for interment . . . Knox, a man of undoubted talent, but notoriously deficient in principle and in heart, was exactly the person to blind himself against suspicion, and fall into blameable carelessness. But it was absurd to charge him with anything worse.[23]

Dr Thomas Wakley, founder and editor of the medical journal *The Lancet*, wrote that if the receiver of the sixteen bodies had 'been punishable as well as the murderer, the crimes which have cast a stain on the character of the nation and of human nature, would not have been committed'.[24]

It was impossible to tell with certainty that a person who had died from suffocation had been murdered, unless there was other external evidence of violence. The Royal College of Surgeons of England, submitting to the government a petition for a change in the law in 1831, stated, 'It is vain to imagine it is always possible to distinguish the body of a person who has been murdered from that of any one who has died a natural death.'[25] But the petition also said, 'The large prices which have of late been given for anatomical subjects have operated as a premium for murder.' This comment was made in the light of copycat murders occurring in London, and perhaps seems like being wise after the event. But in the spring of 1828, *before* the crimes of Burke and Hare had been discovered, Sir Benjamin Brodie, of St George's Hospital in London, certainly had murder in mind when he told a Select Committee of the House of Commons that he considered it 'a dangerous thing to society that body-snatchers should be able to get ten guineas for a body'.[26] And Sir Henry Halford, President of the Royal College of Physicians, told the same committee that 'when there is difficulty in obtaining bodies, and their value is so great, you absolutely throw a temptation in the way of these men to commit murder for the purpose of selling the bodies of their victims'.[27] The philosopher Jeremy Bentham had foreseen the danger in 1826, and other eminent medical men were aware of it before anyone had heard of Burke and Hare.[28] And, of course, there was the old Scottish precedent of Torrence and Waldie.

Knox purchased from Burke and Hare, in the course of nine months, seventeen bodies which had clearly not been buried. They were fresh and still supple. The orifices had not been plugged and the bodies were unwashed. One or two were still warm. Mary Paterson's hair still had paper curlers in it and she, like Mrs Docherty, had traces of blood about the mouth and nose. The faces of some, if not all the subjects, had a livid colour.

It appears that there are but two possible explanations for Dr Knox's failure to raise any suspicions about the origins of these subjects. Both were clearly expressed by the author of the *Letter to the Lord Advocate*:

> . . . I have always been led to consider that suffocation or strangulation causes the blood to flow to the head, consequently makes the face of a strong livid colour, with a small discharge of blood from the mouth, nose, and ears. Now, as most of the subjects produced by Burke and Hare had suffered death by suffocation, and as these bodies were generally disposed of to Dr K–, I think it but natural to infer, that if the Doctor saw these bodies, he is either horribly ignorant of his profession, or he wilfully withheld that information he ought to have given.[29]

Since it is universally acknowledged, even by his enemies, that Robert Knox, so far from being ignorant of his subject, was a master of it, the only possible conclusion is that if he did not *know* that he was dealing with murderers, he must have *suspected* that he could be, but chose to remain silent, because *he did not care where the subjects came from so long as they suited his purposes.*

The late Dr Betty Bostetter, who was working at the time of her death on a major biography of Thomas Wakley, claimed to have found a fragment of a letter to Wakley from Robert Liston, who wrote in May 1828 that he had seen the corpse of Mary Paterson in Knox's premises, and suspected foul play at once. The idea of her body being dissected by students (such as Fergusson) who had probably slept with her offended his sense of decency, and a quarrel ensued between Liston and Knox during which Knox was knocked down in front of his students. Liston said that he then took away Mary Paterson's body for burial. Unfortunately, Dr Bostetter's papers are not available for confirmation, but if this is all true, it proves beyond doubt not only that other doctors had suspicions about the sources of Knox's subjects as early as the spring of 1828, but that Knox himself was well aware of such doubts, and chose to ignore them.[30] Of course, it also shows that Liston could have given important evidence to the Lord Advocate. As he was not listed as a trial witness, he must either have chosen or been persuaded to remain silent.

At what point should Knox have had sufficient suspicion to raise the alarm? After the second corpse, or the third, or the sixth, or the tenth? Burke was clearly an accomplished liar, and if my proposed order of the murders is correct, there is no reason why Knox or anyone else should have had any strong suspicions about the first two, or perhaps three, bodies sold to him by Burke and Hare. After all, the poor who appeared to have died in workhouses and other such places with no friends or relatives to claim the bodies were just what the doctors ordered. But it seems reasonable, in all the circumstances, to suggest that, even without Liston's intervention, Mary Paterson's corpse ought to have been the one to alert him to the possibility of murder, and make him speak out. If he had done so, Knox could have saved the lives of perhaps a dozen people and Hare could have been brought to justice as well as Burke. Dr Knox's silence was a costly evasion, and may be seen in retrospect as part of a tacit conspiracy.

Sir Robert Peel said after the trial that he doubted whether uncertainty as to the extent and history of the murders was not as great an evil as any exposure of the facts could be. But that was clearly not the view of the Edinburgh elite. Knox's remark in his letter to the *Caledonian Mercury*, that as he had not been charged, it proved that the authorities had nothing to charge him with, was patently absurd. But the intellectual leadership produced by the Scottish Enlightenment would have been irreparably damaged by public arraignment of one of its most celebrated members.

NOTES

[1] Scott, *Journal*, p. 574.

[2] Ibid, p. 575.

[3] Ibid, p. 580.

[4] *The Scotsman*, 11 February 1829.

[5] *Caledonian Mercury*, 29 December 1828.

[6] *Edinburgh Weekly Chronicle*, quoted in George MacGregor, *The History of Burke and Hare*, (Glasgow, Thos. D. Morison, 1884), p. 157.

[7] *Blackwood's Edinburgh Magazine*, March 1829.

[8] Lonsdale, p. 108.

[9] Ibid, p. 111.

[10] Sir Humphrey Rolleston, 'Provincial Medical Schools a Hundred Years Ago', Cambridge University Medical Society magazine, 1932, p. 8.

[11] I am told by the present Marquis that he has no family papers relating to the matter.

[12] Scott, *Journal*, p. 618.

[13] Christison, p. 311.

[14] Cockburn, pp. 457–58.

[15] *Medical Times and Gazette*, 27 December 1862. (The editor of the journal and author of this notice was Dr Robert Druitt, an uncle of Montague Druitt, who committed suicide in 1888 and remains one of the chief suspects in the 'Jack the Ripper' murders.)

[16] Ibid.

[17] Ibid.

[18] Lonsdale, pp. 149, 236, 363, 394.

[19] Ibid, p. 115.

[20] Ball, p. 96.

[21] Lonsdale, p. 89.

[22] Rae, p. 61.

[23] Christison, pp. 310–11.

[24] *The Lancet*, 21 March 1829.

[25] *Petition of the Royal College of Surgeons in London to the Viscount Melbourne*, 1831.

[26] *Report and Evidence of the Select Committee on Anatomy*, House of Commons, 1828.

[27] Ibid.

[28] Dr Ruth Richardson cites a draft letter of April 1826 from Bentham to the Home Secretary, Sir Robert Peel, in her *Death, Dissection and the Destitute* (London, Routledge & Kegan Paul, 1987), p. 112.

[29] 'Echo of Surgeons' Square', *Letter to the Lord Advocate.*

[30] Richardson, p. 327.

12. AFTERMATH

It is one of the inescapable paradoxes of human existence that out of what we regard as evil can come goodness. Body-snatching itself was a necessary evil. Burke and Hare and their unfortunate victims contributed to medical science and helped to educate much-needed surgeons. They were also about to expedite changes in the law which had been long overdue. Events in Edinburgh blasted the government's apathy with an explosion of outrage.

Burke also made a contribution to the English language. He gave it a new verb which is still in the dictionaries. Within months of his execution, the anatomical theatre of Dr Andrew Moir in Aberdeen had been nicknamed 'the burkin' hoose'. To 'burke' was used originally as a synonym for 'kill' or 'murder', but soon came to mean, more specifically, to smother or suffocate someone. For a time afterwards, moronic youths in Scottish and some English towns thought it a great joke to leap out at women and girls in the streets and slap sticking-plaster over their mouths, delighting in the shock and terror they caused in the aftermath of such fearful revelations. A confusion of ideas seems to have linked Burke and Hare with sticking pitch-plasters over their victims' faces. But in the few *serious* cases of 'burking' recorded, the evidence appears to suggest that this method was being used to facilitate sexual assault. 'Burkophobia', as it was called, among other names, certainly caused genuine and widespread fear and distress, and some actual injury, but it never resulted in murder.

On the same day that the Knox committee's report was published in Edinburgh, 21 March 1829, the House of Commons in London was presented with a Bill by Henry Warburton, MP for Bridport and Commons spokesman for the medical profession, who had headed a Select Committee appointed to enquire into the subject of teaching anatomy. The Bill was intended to bring some control to the study of anatomy by licensing qualified teachers, providing a legal supply of subjects, making grave-robbing a felony, and repealing the Act which gave judges the power to order dissection after execution, thus removing the widely felt stigma resulting from the association of anatomy with crime. The Bill was supported by Sir William Rae, the Lord Advocate for Scotland. The Home Secretary, Sir Robert Peel, said the measure was necessary to put a stop to the various atrocities caused by the difficulties of obtaining dead bodies. It was painful, he said, to allude to the recent Edinburgh murders, but he hardly dared to think that those were the only crimes that had sprung out of the system.

Sir C. Forbes, the Member for Malmesbury, observed that the sick in hospitals could only be visited once a week, on Tuesdays. He feared that if this Bill became law, 'a husband might enquire after his wife's health on one Tuesday and be told that she was getting well, and on the following Tuesday, he might be told that she was dead and dissected'. Another MP expressed his fear that 'in a moment of excitement or intoxication', some men might engage to 'sell their bodies to the Jews'. Nevertheless, the Bill was passed by the Commons on 20 May, but thrown out by the House of Lords on 5 June, opposition to it there being led by the Archbishop of Canterbury.

There was a great deal of nervousness in government circles about legalising the dissection of unclaimed corpses from hospitals and workhouses, as the Bill proposed, and it was considered unsatisfactory in its present form, notwithstanding that one member of the Select Committee, Ralph Leycester, delivered himself of the opinion that paupers would welcome dissection after their deaths in poorhouses because they would thus be able to repay the debt they owed to those who had cared for them! The truth, of course, was as Edward Gibbon Wakefield explained it:

> The thought of being dissected after death, or of having the body of a relative dissected, is quite horrible to the great majority of people of all conditions. This prejudice, against the conversion of inanimate flesh to the only useful purpose of which it is susceptible, has been fostered in various ways; and in particular by the law, which directs that the bodies of murderers shall be 'anatomised'.[1]

Thomas Wakley took the opportunity to attack the government's timid approach to the problem, writing in *The Lancet* that, had it not been for Burke and Hare, there would be no debate, and:

. . . that which would never have been sanctioned by the deliberate wisdom of parliament, is about to be extorted from its fears . . . It would have been well if this fear had been manifested and acted upon before sixteen human beings had fallen victim to the supineness of the Government and the Legislature. It required no extraordinary sagacity to foresee, that the worst consequences must inevitably result from the system of traffic between resurrectionists and anatomists, which the executive government has so long suffered to exist. Government is already in a great degree, responsible for the crime which it has fostered by its negligence, and even encouraged by a system of forbearance.[2]

During the Lords debate the Earl of Harewood considered that it was a national disgrace that the recent affairs in Edinburgh had not been investigated more fully and the public properly informed of the facts, but he was answered by the Earl of Haddington, who assured their lordships that the dreadful atrocities which had taken place in Edinburgh had in fact been probed as deeply as possible. Lord Tenterden thought that greater vigilance by doctors in discovering whether subjects were victims of barbarity, or persons who had died a natural death, would prevent any recurrence of such crimes as had lately been committed in Edinburgh.

The Scottish press was full of fresh revelations about body-snatching and accompanying riots, but as far as the London papers were concerned, Scotland was a long way off and most of the trouble there was put down by *The Times* to Scottish hooliganism and the magistrates' lack of wisdom. The English, however, were soon to get a shock of their own.

Meanwhile, in July, John Broggan, the man who had absconded with his wife and the rent money from the basement flat which Burke and McDougal had lived in, was arrested in Glasgow and accused, along with one Bernard Docherty, of the attempted murder, in the course of robbery, of Andrew Naismith, a tailor, by means of laudanum. In September, James Gray, the homeless labourer who had blown the whistle on the homicidal careers of Burke and Hare, died penniless. His widow wrote to Charles Kirkpatrick Sharpe, 'the only friend that I have in this place', begging for financial help to bury him.[3] Mr Gray's honesty and selfless action had undoubtedly saved lives. If it had not been for his incorruptible character, Burke and Hare would have continued undetected for who knows how long.

On Saturday, 5 November 1831, two London body-snatchers, John

Bishop and James May, called on William Hill, porter at the King's College medical school, and offered him a subject for twelve guineas. It was, they said, a male of about fourteen years, very fresh, and they could deliver it that afternoon. The porter knocked the price down to nine guineas. The two men came back later, while it was still daylight, with another body-snatcher, Thomas Williams, and a street porter carrying a hamper. They tipped a corpse out on to the floor and asked for their money. But Mr Hill was immediately suspicious. It was obvious that the boy's body had not been buried. Rigor mortis was still present and there was a deep cut on the forehead with blood round it. The lips and jaw were swollen and there was blood about the mouth and neck. Hill asked what the boy had died of, but May, who was drunk, told him that was neither his business nor theirs. The anatomy demonstrator, Richard Partridge, then came in to look at the body.

Mr Partridge did immediately what Dr Knox had never done at all. He detained the men, on the pretext of having no cash ready to hand, while someone went for the police. All four men were arrested on suspicion of murder. Enquiries revealed that the same body had previously been offered to Guy's Hospital and Grainger's Anatomical Theatre, but both had declined to purchase it. The outcome was that at the Old Bailey on 1 December 1831 – almost two years after the trial of Burke – Bishop and Williams were found guilty of murder and sentenced to death. In the condemned cell, Bishop admitted that they had got the idea of murdering the boy, and two other victims, from the Burke and Hare case. He thought that all the body-snatchers in London had tried 'burking'. Bishop and Williams had rendered their victims insensible with rum laced with laudanum, then drowned them by lowering them head-first into a well in Bishop's garden, apparently in the belief that the contents of the stomach would run out at the mouth, leaving no trace of foul play. Bishop and Williams were hanged outside Newgate Gaol and their bodies dissected, Bishop's at King's College and Williams's at St Bartholomew's Hospital.

Horace Bleackley wrote in *The Hangmen of England*:

> The case of Bishop and Williams caused a great sensation in England, coming as it did so soon after the similar crimes of Burke and Hare, 'the Scottish resurrection men', who had murdered more than a dozen victims in West Port, Edinburgh, by suffocating them with pitch-plasters in order to sell the corpses to the surgeons.[4]

An anonymous letter to the Home Secretary, signed 'Anatomicus' and dated 29 November 1831, suggested that all dissection should be suspended until other arrangements were made to supply subjects for teaching anatomy. There was not the shadow of a doubt, the writer claimed, 'but that the practice of Burkeing (horrible to relate!) was adopted at Edinburgh by members of the fraternity of Resurrectionists', and similar outrages 'transpire here daily'.[5]

A few days later, Henry Warburton presented a revised Bill to the House of Commons. A much improved version of the proposal to license anatomists and provide them with a legal supply of subjects, it also proposed abolition of the practice of dissecting executed murderers, and its provisions obviated the need for new laws against grave-robbing. It thus successfully dissociated the study of anatomy from crime. By this time, the country had a new government, and Sir Robert Peel had been replaced as Home Secretary by William Lamb, Viscount Melbourne.

Even if we go back no further than the beginning of the nineteenth century, the successive governments of Pitt, Addington, Grenville, Portland, Perceval, Liverpool, Canning, Goderich and Wellington, all of them Tory except one (Lord Grenville's), had failed to respond to constant calls from the medical profession to change the law on dissection. To the gentleman politicians, the subject was sordid and unseemly, affecting the poor and ignorant rather than the wealthy and privileged, and they preferred to pass by on the other side. Even now, when the Whig government of Earl Grey was intent on getting the Anatomy Bill through Parliament, few turned up for the debates.

Less than forty Members were present in the House for the revised Bill's second reading – a clear sign of continuing reluctance to tackle a distasteful subject and reach difficult decisions. Alexander Perceval, the Member for County Sligo, thought that dissection of animals would provide nearly all the advantages which could result from the mutilation of human bodies, while John Cresset Pelham, the Member for Shropshire, considered that the field of battle in time of war should furnish enough subjects for surgeons to obtain a competent knowledge of anatomy. The Member for Preston, Henry Hunt (the radical agitator known as 'Orator Hunt') had recommended elsewhere that 'in the first place . . . the bodies of all our kings be dissected, instead of expending £700,000 or £800,000 of the public money for their interment'.

In the House of Lords, the Duke of Sussex, who became President of the Royal Society, said that he had made provision for his own body to be dissected, 'for I have some reason to think that there is a peculiarity in my conformation, the knowledge of which may possibly serve the interests of science'.

> I cannot sit down without expressing my full conviction, that if some arrangements be not speedily made, you will drive the study of anatomy altogether from this country, and compel our medical men to resort to foreign countries for that information which they ought to be able to obtain at home.

(It is perhaps worth noting that, in the event, the Duke, who died in 1843, was not dissected. No doubt the royal family had something to say about that. The sixth son of George III, Augustus had suffered all his life from painful and sometimes dangerous paroxysms which mystified his physicians, but are now thought to have been symptoms of a hereditary disease of the royal family, porphyria.)[6]

Among the Bill's supporters was Lord Macaulay, who said:

> If the education of a surgeon should become very expensive, if the fees of surgeons should rise, if the supply of surgeons should diminish, the sufferers would be, not the rich, but the poor in our country villages, who would be left again to mountebanks, and barbers, and old women; to charms and quack medicines . . . I think this is a Bill which tends to the good of the people, and which tends especially to the good of the poor.

While the new Bill was being debated in Parliament, another resurrectionist murder hit the London headlines. A couple named Edward Cook and Eliza Ross (aka Cook or Reardon) were tried at the Old Bailey for the murder of an old woman named Caroline Walsh or Welsh. There was no body in the case, but the chief witness against Ross was her twelve-year-old son, who had heard his mother tell his father that she had sold the body to the London Hospital. Both defendants were known as drink-sodden body-snatchers. There was insufficient evidence against Cook, but Eliza Ross was found guilty and hanged in January 1832. Her body was delivered to the London Hospital for dissection.

Warburton's Anatomy Bill was approved in both Houses of Parliament. It received the Royal Assent on 1 August 1832 and became law as an Act for regulating Schools of Anatomy. The preamble acknowledged that 'in order further to supply Human Bodies for such

Purposes, divers great and grievous Crimes have been committed, and lately Murder, for the single Object of selling for such Purposes the Bodies of the Persons so murdered'.[7] The Act provided for executors and other persons legally in charge of dead bodies to give them to licensed surgeons and teachers of anatomy unless the deceased had expressed conscientious objection to being dissected.

We have no knowledge of how professional body-snatchers felt about those – principally Burke and Hare – who were responsible for bringing the curtain down on their lucrative proceedings. It is virtually certain that if murder had not made an entrance on the scene, the show would have gone on for several more years at least, since the government had no reason or appetite for alienating its supporters for the sake of a few stolen corpses which were no one's legal property. Nevertheless, the Anatomy Act put a decisive end to the trade in dead bodies, and without the huge public outcry that many had feared. It ended the careers of body-snatchers as appendages of the medical profession, and they vanished into the underworld shadows from which they had emerged with the advent of this long-flourishing and peculiarly British black market, while the names of Burke and Hare were used, especially in Scotland, to frighten naughty children.

What remains are some important gaps in our knowledge of Burke and Hare which, if it were possible to fill them, would perhaps give us one or two surprising facts about the most notorious serial-killing partnership in the annals of crime in Britain. What happened to Hare's statement? It was never published and neither the original nor any copy is to be found in Edinburgh or in Home Office papers in the Public Record Office. It seems clear that it was destroyed as part of a conspiracy of silence regarding the teaching of anatomy in general, and Hare's part in the murders in particular. If Hare admitted murder in it, any leak would have called into question the Lord Advocate's judgement and inflamed the populace even more about Hare's escape from justice. The Sheriff of Edinburgh told the Lord Provost that:

> Hare disclosed nearly the same crimes in point of number, of time, and of the descriptions of persons murdered, which Burke has thus confessed; and in the few particulars in which they differed, no collateral evidence could be obtained calculated to show which of them was in the right.[8]

Note that '*nearly*'! How instructive it would be to discover the points on which they differed. It is only because Sir Walter Scott saw Hare's statement, and said that he gave the *same* account of the number and the same description of the victims, that we accept – because we have no alternative – that there were sixteen murders.

If we had Hare's statement and the testimony of potential witnesses who were never called – not only Knox himself but also Fergusson and others – we might know with certainty what we can only surmise. But Knox and his associates were kept out of the witness box because that, too, presumably, would have implicated Hare more deeply in the murders as well as publicising unpalatable facts about the everyday practices of the anatomists. What happened to Dr Knox's account books? Why did the Marquis of Queensberry resign from the committee at an early stage? What evidence was given to the committee – and what *not* given – that enabled the members to reach their unanimous conclusions? Who was allowed to visit Burke in the condemned cell, and what was the true identity of the 'Echo of Surgeons' Square'?

It seems probable that such questions will remain unanswered, unless some dusty and forgotten old file is one day discovered in some secret vault. We assert in our books of criminal records that Burke and Hare murdered sixteen people, but only one murder was proved beyond doubt in a court of law, and there is independent circumstantial evidence of only two others. Of the thirteen citizens (and possibly more) who were deprived of their lives by these hideous killers, we know nothing more than what Burke told us, and that was very little. Worth more dead than alive, their only humble claim on our memories is that they happened to be in the wrong place at the wrong time, and fell foul of an evil pair unrivalled in infamy and of an arrogant and amoral lecturer.

We prefer our images of famous men to be simple and straightforward. We do not easily embrace opposing characteristics in one individual, and would prefer to be told that Knox was either a great man or a wicked scoundrel. But the facts deny us such black-and-white simplicity, and we have to come to terms with the paradox of a man deserving our respect and our contempt at the same time. There can be no doubt at all that Knox's knowledge and teaching of anatomy were of the highest calibre, maintaining the reputation of Edinburgh as the leading medical school and, more importantly, advancing the progress of surgery at a time of great need. But he was also a man of low moral principle, arrogantly indifferent to decent common human feelings and caring nothing about where his 'subjects' came from as long as they served his purposes. Leaving aside the question of the two women, there were three ghouls at work in Edinburgh in the year 1828 – and one of them was Robert Knox.

NOTES

[1] Edward Gibbon Wakefield, *Facts Relating to the Punishment of Death in the Metropolis*, (London, Ridgway, 1832 edn), pp. 207–8.

[2] *The Lancet*, 28 March 1829.

[3] Roughead, p. 39.

[4] Horace Bleackley, *The Hangmen of England*, (London, Chapman and Hall, 1929), p. 216.

[5] Home Office papers in Public Record Office, HO 44/24.

[6] Ida Macalpine and Richard Hunter, *George III and the Mad-Business*, (London, Allen Lane, the Penguin Press, 1969), pp. 258–61.

[7] 'An Act for Regulating Schools of Anatomy', 1832.

[8] Letter to the Lord Provost, 5 February 1829.

APPENDICES

I Burke's Official Confession
II Burke's *Courant* Confession
III Knox's Letter to the *Caledonian Mercury*
IV Report of Knox's Committee of Enquiry
V Open Letter to the Lord Advocate by 'The Echo of Surgeons' Square'

Note: The appendices are all reproduced verbatim.
No corrections have been made to grammar, spelling,
punctuation or printers' apparent errors.

APPENDIX I

BURKE'S OFFICIAL CONFESSION

Statement made in Calton jail on 3 January 1829 in the presence of George Tait, Sheriff-substitute; Archibald Scott, Procurator-fiscal; and Richard Moxey, Assistant Sheriff-clerk.

Compeared William Burke, at present under sentence of death in the jail of Edinburgh, states that he never saw Hare till the Hallow-fair before last (November, 1827), when he and Helen M'Dougal met Hare's wife, with whom he was previously acquainted, on the street; they had a dram, and he mentioned he had an intention to go to the west country to endeavour to get employment as a cobbler; but Hare's wife suggested that they had a small room in their house which might suit him and M'Dougal, and that he might follow his trade of a cobbler in Edinburgh; and he went to Hare's house, and continued to live there, and got employment as a cobbler.

An old pensioner, named Donald, lived in the house about Christmas, 1827; he was in bad health, and died a short time before his quarter's pension was due, that he owed Hare £4; and a day or two after the pensioner's death, Hare proposed that his body should be sold to the doctors, and that the declarant should get a share of the price. Declarant said it would be impossible to do it, because the man would be coming in with the coffin immediately; but after the body was put into the coffin and the lid was nailed down, Hare started the lid with a chisel, and he and declarant took out the corpse and concealed it in the bed, and put tanner's bark from behind the house into the coffin, and covered it with a sheet, and nailed down the lid of the coffin, and the coffin was then carried away for interment. That Hare did not appear to have been concerned in any thing of the kind before, and seemed to be at a loss how to get the body disposed of; and he and Hare went in the evening to the yard of the College, and saw a person like a student there, and the declarant asked him if there were any of Dr Monro's men about, because he did not know there was any other way of disposing of a dead body – nor did Hare. The young man asked what they wanted with Dr Monro, and the declarant told him that he had a body to dispose of, and the young man referred him to Dr Knox, No 10 Surgeon Square; and they went there, and saw young gentlemen, whom he now knows to be Jones, Miller, and Ferguson, and told them that they had a subject to dispose of, but they did not ask how they had obtained it; and they told the declarant and Hare to come back when it was dark, and that they themselves would find a porter to carry it. Declarant and Hare went home and put the body into a sack, and carried it to Surgeon Square, and not knowing how to dispose of it, laid it down at the door of the cellar, and went up to the room, where the three young men saw them, and told them to bring up the body to the room, which they did; and they took the body out of the sack, and laid it on the dissecting-table. That the shirt was on the body, but the young men asked no questions as to that; and the declarant and Hare, at their desire, took off the shirt, and got £7 10s. Dr Knox came in after the shirt was taken off, and looked at the body, and proposed they should get £7 10s, and authorised Jones to settle with them; and he asked no questions as to how the body had been obtained. Hare got £4. 5s and the declarant got £3. 5s. Jones, &c, said that they would be glad to see them again when they had any other body to dispose of.

Early last spring, 1828, a woman from Gilmerton came to Hare's house as a nightly lodger, – Hare keeping seven beds for lodgers: That she was a stranger, and she and Hare became merry, and drank together; and next morning she was very ill in consequence of what she had got, and she sent for more drink, and she and Hare drank together, and she became very sick and vomited; and at that time she had not risen from bed, and Hare then said that they would try and smother her in order to dispose of her body to the doctors. That she was lying on her back in the bed, and quite insensible from drink, and Hare clapped his hand on her mouth and nose, and the declarant laid himself across her body, in order to prevent her making any disturbance – and she never stirred; and they took her out of bed and undressed her, and put her into a chest; and they mentioned to Dr Knox's young men that they had another subject, and Mr Miller sent a porter to meet them in the evening at the back of the Castle; and declarant and Hare carried the chest till they met the porter, and they accompanied the porter with the chest to Dr Knox's class-room, and Dr Knox came in when they were there: the body was cold and stiff. Dr Knox approved of its being so fresh, but did not ask any questions.

The next was a man named Joseph, a miller who had been lying badly in the house: That he got some drink from declarant and Hare, but was not tipsy: he was very ill, lying in bed, and could not speak sometimes, and there was a report on that account that there was fever in the house, which made Hare and his wife uneasy in case it should keep away lodgers, and they (declarant and Hare) agreed that they should suffocate him for the same purpose, and the declarant got a small pillow and laid it across Joseph's mouth, and Hare lay across the body to keep down the arms and legs; and he was disposed of in the same manner, to the same persons, and the body was carried by the porter who carried the last body.

In May, 1828, as he thinks, an old woman came to the house as a lodger, and she was the worse of drink, and she got more drink of her own accord, and she became very drunk, and declarant suffocated her; and Hare was not in the house at the time; and she was disposed of in the same manner.

Soon afterwards an Englishman lodged there for some nights, and was ill of the jaundice: that he was in bed very unwell, and Hare and declarant got above him and held him down, and by holding his mouth suffocated him, and disposed of him in the same manner.

Shortly afterwards an old woman named Haldane, (but he knows nothing farther of her) lodged in the house, and she had got some drink at the time, and got more to intoxicate her, and he and Hare suffocated her, and disposed of her in the same manner.

Soon afterwards a cinder woman came to the house as a lodger, as he believes, and she got drink from Hare and the declarant, and became tipsy, and she was half asleep, and he and Hare suffocated her, and disposed of her in the same manner.

About Midsummer 1828, a woman, with her son or grandson, about twelve years of age, and who seemed to be weak in his mind, came to the house as lodgers; the woman got a dram, and when in bed asleep, he and Hare suffocated her, and the boy was sitting in the fire at the kitchen, and he and Hare took hold of him, and carried him into the room, and suffocated him. They were put into a herring barrel the same night, and carried to Dr Knox's rooms.

That, soon afterwards, the declarant brought a woman to the house as a lodger; and after some days, she got drunk, and was disposed of in the same manner: That declarant and Hare generally tried if lodgers would drink, and if they would drink, they were disposed of in that manner.

The declarant then went for a few days to the house of Helen M'Dougal's father, and when he returned he learned from Hare that he had disposed of a woman in the declarant's absence, in the same manner, in his house; but the declarant does not know the woman's name, or any farther particulars of the case, or whether any other person was present or knew of it.

That about this time he went to live in Broggan's house, and a woman, named Margaret Haldane, daughter of the woman Haldane before mentioned, and whose sister is married to Clark, a tinsmith in the High Street, came into the house, but the declarant does not remember for what purpose; and she got drink, and was disposed of in the same manner: That Hare was not present, and neither Broggan nor his son knew the least thing about that or any other case of the same kind.

That in April, 1828, he fell in with the girl Paterson and her companion in Constantine Burke's house, and they had breakfast together, and he sent for Hare, and he and Hare disposed of her in the same manner; and Mr Ferguson and a tall lad, who seemed to have known the woman by sight, asked where they had got the body; and the declarant said he had purchased it from an old woman at the back of the Canongate. The body was disposed of five or six hours after the girl was killed, and it was cold, but not very stiff, but he does not recollect of any remarks being made about the body being warm.

One day in September or October 1828, a washer-woman had been washing in the house for some time, and he and Hare suffocated her, and disposed of her in the same manner.

Soon afterwards, a woman named M'Dougal, who was a distant relation of Helen M'Dougal's first husband, came to Broggan's house to see M'Dougal; and after she had been coming and going to the house for a few days, she got drunk, and was served in the same way by the declarant and Hare.

That 'Daft Jamie' was then disposed of in the manner mentioned in the indictment, except that Hare was concerned in it. That Hare was lying alongside of Jamie in the bed, and Hare suddenly turned on him, and put his hand on his mouth and nose; and Jamie, who had got drink, but was not drunk, made a terrible resistance, and he and Hare fell from the bed together, Hare still keeping hold of Jamie's mouth and nose; and as they lay on the floor together, declarant lay across Jamie, to prevent him from resisting, and they held him in that state till he was dead, and he was disposed of in the same manner, and Hare took a brass snuff-box and a spoon from Jamie's pocket; and kept the box to himself, and never gave it to the declarant – but he gave him the spoon.

And the last was the old woman Docherty, for whose murder he has been convicted. That she was not put to death in the manner deponed to by Hare on the trial. That during the scuffle between him and Hare, in the course of which he was nearly strangled by Hare, Docherty had crept among the straw, and after the scuffle was over, they had some drink, and after that they both went forward to where the woman was lying sleeping, and Hare went forward first, and seized her by the mouth and nose, as on former occasions; and at the same time the declarant lay across her, and she had no opportunity of making any noise; and before she was dead, one or other of them, he does not recollect which, took hold of her by the throat. That while he and Hare were struggling, which was a real scuffle, M'Dougal opened the door of the apartment, and went into the inner passage and knocked at the door, and called out police and murder, but soon came back; and at the same time Hare's wife called out never to mind, because the declarant and Hare would not hurt one another. That whenever he and Hare rose and went towards the straw where Docherty was lying, M'Dougal and Hare's wife, who, he thinks, were lying in bed at the time, or, perhaps, were at the fire, immediately rose and left the house, but did not make any noise, so far as he heard, and he was surprised at their going out at that time, because he did not see how they could have any suspicion of what they (the declarant and Hare) intended doing. That he cannot say whether he and Hare would have killed Docherty or not, if the women had remained, because they were so determined to kill the woman, the drink being in their head; – and he has no knowledge or suspicion of Docherty's body having been offered to any person besides Dr Knox; and he does not suspect that Paterson would offer the body to any other person than Dr Knox.

Declares, That suffocation was not suggested to them by any person as a mode of killing, but occurred to Hare on the first occasion before mentioned, and was continued afterwards because it was effectual, and showed no marks; and when they lay across the body at the same time, that was not suggested to them by any person, for they never spoke to any person on such a subject; and it was not done for the purpose of preventing the person from breathing, but was only done for the purpose of keeping down the person's arms and thighs, to prevent the person struggling.

Declares, That with the exception of the body of Docherty, they never took the person by the throat, and they never leapt upon them; and declares that there were no marks of violence on any of the subjects, and they were sufficiently cold to prevent any suspicion on the part of the Doctors; and, at all events, they might be cold and stiff enough before the box was opened up, and he and Hare always told some story of their having purchased the subjects from some relation or other person who had the means of disposing of them, about different parts of the town, and the statements which they made were such as to prevent the Doctors having any suspicions; and no suspicions were expressed by Dr Knox or any of his assistants, and no questions asked tending to show that they had suspicion.

Declares, that Helen M'Dougal and Hare's wife were no way concerned in any of the murders, and neither of them knew of any thing of the kind being intended, even in the case of Docherty; and although these two women may latterly have had some suspicion in their own minds that the declarant and Hare were concerned in lifting dead bodies, he does not think that they could have any suspicion that he and Hare were concerned in committing murders.

Declares, That none of the subjects which they had procured, as before mentioned, were offered to any other person than Dr Knox's assistants, and he and Hare had very little communication with Dr Knox himself; and declares, that he has not the smallest suspicion of any other person in this, or in any other country, except Hare and himself, being concerned in killing persons and offering their bodies for dissection; and he never knew or heard of such a thing having been done before.

Wm Burke.
G. Tait.

On 22 January, Burke made a further statement. The same three officials were present, as well as Rev William Reid, a Catholic priest.

Compeared William Burke, at present under sentence of death in the gaol of Edinburgh, and his declaration, of date the 3d current, being read over to him, he adheres thereto. Declares further, that he does not know the names and descriptions of any of the persons who were destroyed except as mentioned in his former declaration. Declares that he never was concerned in any other act of the same kind, nor made any attempt or preparation to commit such, and all reports of a contrary tendency, some of which he has heard, are groundless. And he does not know of Hare being concerned in any such, except as mentioned in his former declaration; and he does not know of any persons being murdered for the purpose of dissection by any other persons than himself and Hare, and if any persons have disappeared any where in Scotland, England, or Ireland, he knows nothing whatever about it, and never heard of such a thing till he was apprehended. Declares, that he never had any instrument in his house except a common table knife, or a knife used by him in his trade as a shoemaker, or a small pocket knife, and he never used any of those instruments, or attempted to do so, on any of the persons who were destroyed. Declares, that neither he nor Hare, so far as he knows, ever were concerned in supplying any subjects for dissection except those before mentioned; and, in particular, never did so by raising dead bodies from the grave. Declares, that they never allowed Dr Knox or any of his assistants, to know exactly where their houses were, but Paterson, Dr Knox's porter or door-keeper, knew. And this he declares to be truth.

APPENDIX II

BURKE'S '*COURANT*' CONFESSION

Statement published in the Edinburgh *Evening Courant* on 7 February 1829.

Abigail Simpson was murdered on the 12th February, 1828, on the forenoon of the day. She resided in Gilmerton, near Edinburgh; has a daughter living there. She used to sell salt and camstone. She was decoyed in by Hare and his wife on the afternoon of the 11th February, and he gave her some whisky to drink. She had one shilling and sixpence, and a can of kitchen-fee. Hare's wife gave her one shilling and sixpence for it; she drank it all with them. She then said she had a daughter. Hare said he was a single man, and would marry her, and get all the money amongst them. They then proposed to her to stay all night, which she did, as she was so drunk she could not go home; and in the morning was vomiting. They then gave her some porter and whisky, and made her so drunk that she fell asleep on the bed. Hare then laid hold of her mouth and nose, and prevented her from breathing. Burke held her hands and feet till she was dead. She made very little resistance, and when it was convenient they carried her to Dr Knox's dissecting-rooms in Surgeon Square, and got £10 for her. She had on a drab mantle, a white-grounded cotton shawl and small blue spots on it. Hare took all her clothes and went out with them; said he was going to put them into the canal. She said she was a pensioner of Sir John Hay's. [Perhaps this should be Sir John Hope.]

The next was an Englishman, a native of Cheshire, and a lodger of Hare's. They murdered him in the same manner as the other. He was ill with the jaundice at the same time. He was very tall; had black hair, brown whiskers, mixed with grey hairs. He used to sell spunks in Edinburgh; was about forty years of age. Did not know his name. Sold to Dr Knox for £10.

The next was an old woman who lodged with Hare for one night, but does not know her name. She was murdered in the same manner as above. Sold to Dr Knox for £10. The old woman was decoyed into the house by Mrs Hare in the forenoon from the street when Hare was working at the boats at the canal. She gave her whisky, and put her to bed three times. At last she was so drunk that she fell asleep; and when Hare came home to his dinner, he put part of the bed-tick on her mouth and nose, and when he came home at night she was dead. Burke at this time was mending shoes; and Hare and Burke took the clothes off her, and put her body into a tea-box. Took her to Knox's that night.

The next was Mary Paterson, who was murdered in Burke's brother's house in the Canongate, in the month of April last, by Burke and Hare, in the forenoon. She was put into a tea-box, and carried to Dr Knox's dissecting-rooms in the afternoon of the same day; and got £8 for her body. She had twopence halfpenny, which she held fast in her hand. Declares that the girl Paterson was only four hours dead till she was in Knox's dissecting-rooms; but she was not dissected at that time, for she was three months in whisky before she was dissected. She was warm when Burke cut the hair off her head; and Knox brought a Mr —, a painter, to look at her, she was so handsome a figure, and well shaped in body and limbs. One of the students said she was like a girl he had seen in the Canongate as one pea is like to another. They desired Burke to cut off her hair; one of the students gave a pair of scissors for that purpose.

In June last, an old woman and a dumb boy, her grandson, from Glasgow, came to Hare's, and were both murdered at the dead hour of night, when the woman was in bed. Burke and Hare murdered her the same way as they did the others. They took off the bed-clothes and tick, stripped off her clothes, and laid her on the bottom of the bed, and then put on the bed-tick, and bed-clothes on the top of her; and they then came and took the boy in their arms and carried him ben to the room, and murdered him in the same manner, and laid him alongside of his grandmother. They lay for the space of an hour; they then put them into a herring barrel. The barrel was perfectly dry; there was no brine in it. They carried them to the stable till next day; they put the barrel into Hare's cart, and Hare's horse was yoked in it; but the horse would not drag the cart one foot past the Meal-Market; and they got a porter with a hurley, and put the barrel on it. Hare and the porter went to Surgeon Square with it. Burke went before them, as he was afraid something would happen, as the horse would not draw them. When they came to Dr Knox's dissecting-rooms, Burke carried the barrel in his arms. The students and them had hard work to get them out, being so stiff and cold. They received £16 for them both. Hare was taken in by the horse he bought that refused drawing the corpse to Surgeon Square, and they shot it in the tan-yard. He had two large holes in his shoulder stuffed with cotton, and covered over with a piece of another horse's skin to prevent them being discovered.

Joseph, the miller by trade, and a lodger of Hare's. He had once been possessed of a good deal of money. He was connected by marriage with some of the Carron Company. Burke and Hare murdered him by pressing a pillow on his mouth and nose till he was dead. He was then carried to Dr Knox's in Surgeon Square. They got £10 for him.

Burke and Helen M'Dougal were on a visit seeing their friends near Falkirk. This was at the time a procession was made round a stone in that neighbourhood; thinks it was the anniversary of the battle of Bannockburn. When he was away, Hare fell in with a woman drunk in the street at the West Port. He took her into his house and murdered her himself, and sold her to Dr Knox's assistants for £8. When Burke went away he knew Hare was in want of money; his things were all in pawn; but when he came back, found him have plenty of money. Burke asked him if he had been doing any business, he said he had been doing nothing. Burke did not believe him, and went to Dr Knox, who told him that Hare had brought a subject. Hare then confessed what he had done.

A cinder-gatherer; Burke thinks her name was Effy. She was in the habit of selling small pieces of leather to him (as he was a cobbler), she gathered about the coach-works. He took her into Hare's stable, and gave her whisky to drink till she was drunk; she then lay down among some straw and fell asleep. They then laid a cloth over her. Burke and Hare murdered her as they did the others. She was then carried to Dr Knox's, Surgeon Square, and sold for £10.

Andrew Williamson, a policeman, and his neighbour, were dragging a drunk woman to the West Port watch-house. They found her sitting on a stair. Burke said, 'Let the woman go to her lodgings.' They said they did not know where she lodged. Burke then said he would take her to lodgings. They then gave her to his charge. He then took her to Hare's house. Burke and Hare murdered her that night the same way as they did the others. They carried her to Dr Knox's in Surgeon Square, and got £10.

Burke being asked, did the policeman know him when they gave him this drunk woman into his charge? He said he had a good character with the police; or if they had known that there were four murderers living in one house they would have visited them oftener.

James Wilson, commonly called Daft Jamie. Hare's wife brought him in from the street into her house. Burke was at the time getting a dram in Rymer's shop. He saw her take Jamie off the street, bare-headed and bare-footed. After she got him into her house, and left him with Hare, she came to Rymer's shop for a pennyworth of butter, and Burke was standing at the counter. She asked him for a dram; and in drinking it she stamped him on the foot. He knew immediately what she wanted him for, and he then went after her. When in the house, she said, you have come too late, for the drink is all done; and Jamie had the cup in his hand. He had never seen him before to his knowledge. They then proposed to send for another half mutchkin, which they did, and urged him to drink; she took a little with them. They then invited him ben to the little room, and advised him to sit down upon the bed. Hare's wife then went out, and locked the outer door, and put the key below the door. There were none in the room but themselves three. Jamie sat down upon the bed. He then lay down upon the bed, and Hare lay down at his back, his head raised up and resting upon his left hand. Burke was standing at the foreside of the bed. When they had lain there for some time, Hare threw his body on the top of Jamie, pressed his hand on his mouth, and held his nose with his other. Hare and him fell off the bed and struggled. Burke then held his hands and feet. They never quitted their gripe till he was dead. He never got up nor cried any. When he was dead, Hare felt his pockets, and took out a brass snuff-box and a copper snuff-spoon. He gave the spoon to Burke, and kept the box to himself. Sometime after, he said he threw the box away in the tan-yard; and the brass-box that was libelled against Burke in the Sheriff's-office was Burke's own box. It was after breakfast Jamie was enticed in, and he was murdered by twelve o'clock in the day. Burke declares that Mrs Hare led poor Jamie in as a dumb lamb to the slaughter, and as a sheep to the shearers; and he was always very anxious making inquiries for his mother, and was told she would be there immediately. He does not think he drank above one glass of whisky all the time. He was then put into a chest that Hare kept clothes in, and they carried him to Dr Knox's, in Surgeon Square, that afternoon, and got £10 for him. Burke gave Daft Jamie's clothes to his brother's children; they were almost naked; and when he untied the bundle they were like to quarrel about them. The clothes of the other murdered persons were generally destroyed, to prevent detection.

Ann M'Dougal, a cousin of Helen M'Dougal's former husband. She was a young woman, and married, and had come on a visit to see them. Hare and Burke gave her whisky till she was drunk, and when in bed and asleep, Burke told Hare that he would have most to do to her, as she being a distant friend, he did not like to begin first on her. Hare murdered her by stopping her breath, and Burke assisted him the same way as the others. One of Dr Knox's assistants, Paterson, gave them a fine trunk to put her into. It was in the afternoon when she was done. It was in John Broggan's house; and when Broggan came home from his work he saw the trunk, and made inquiries about it, as he knew they had no trunks there. Burke then gave him two or three drams, as there was always plenty of whisky going at these times, to make him quiet. Hare and Burke then gave him £1 10s each, as he was back in his rent, for to pay it, and he left Edinburgh a few days after. They then carried her to Surgeon Square as soon as Broggan went out of the house, and got £10 for her. Hare was cautioner for Broggan's rent, being £3, and Hare and Burke gave him that sum. Broggan went off in a few days, and the rent is not yet paid. They gave him the money that he might not come against them for the murder of Ann M'Dougal, that he saw in the trunk, that was murdered in his house. Hare thought that the rent would fall upon him, and if he could get Burke to pay the half of it, it would be so much the better; and proposed this to Burke, and he agreed to it, as they were glad to get him out of the way. Broggan's wife is a cousin of Burke's. They thought he went to Glasgow, but are not sure.

Mrs Haldane, a stout old woman, who had a daughter transported last summer from the Calton jail for fourteen years, and has another daughter married to –, in the High Street. She was a lodger of Hare's. She went into Hare's stable; the door was left open, and she being drunk, and falling asleep among some straw, Hare and Burke murdered her the same way as they did the others, and kept the body all night in the stable, and took her to Dr Knox's next day. She had but one tooth in her mouth, and that was a very large one in front.

A young woman, a daughter of Mrs Haldane, of the name of Peggy Haldane, was drunk, and sleeping in Broggan's house, was murdered by Burke himself, in the forenoon. Hare had no hand in it. She was taken to Dr Knox's in the afternoon in a tea-box, and £8 got for her. She was so drunk at the time that he thinks she was not sensible of her death, as she made no resistance whatever. She and her mother were both lodgers of Hare's, and they were both of idle habits, and much given to drinking. This was the only murder that Burke committed by himself, but what

Hare was connected with. She was laid with her face downwards, and he pressed her down, and she was soon suffocated.

There was a Mrs Hostler washing in John Broggan's, and she came back next day to finish up the clothes, and when done, Hare and Burke gave her some whisky to drink, which made her drunk. This was in the day-time. She then went to bed. Mrs Broggan was out at the time. Hare and Burke murdered her the same way they did the others, and put her in a box, and set her in the coalhouse in the passage, and carried her off to Dr Knox's in the afternoon of the same day, and got £8 for her. Broggan's wife was out of the house at the time the murder was committed. Mrs Hostler had ninepence halfpenny in her hand, which they could scarcely get out of it after she was dead, so firmly was it grasped.

The woman Campbell or Docherty was murdered on the 31st October last, and she was the last one. Burke declares that Hare perjured himself on his trial, when giving his evidence against him, as the woman Campbell or Docherty lay down among some straw at the bedside, and Hare laid hold of her mouth and nose, and pressed her throat, and Burke assisted him in it, till she was dead. Hare was not sitting on a chair at the time, as he said in the Court. There were seven shillings in the woman's pocket, which were divided between Hare and Burke.

That was the whole of them – sixteen in whole: nine were murdered in Hare's house, and four in John Broggan's; two in Hare's stable, and one in Burke's brother's house in the Canongate. Burke declares that five of them were murdered in Hare's room that has the iron bolt in the inside of it. Burke did not know the days nor the months the different murders were committed, nor all their names. They were generally in a state of intoxication at those times, and paid little attention to them; but they were all from 12th February till 1st November, 1828; but he thinks Dr Knox will know by the dates of paying him the money for them. He never was concerned with any other person than Hare in those matters, and was never a resurrection man, and never dealt in dead bodies but what he murdered. He was urged by Hare's wife to murder Helen M'Dougal, the woman he lived with. The plan was, that he was to go to the country for a few weeks, and then write to Hare that she had died and was buried, and he was to tell this to deceive the neighbours; but he would not agree to it. The reason was, they could not trust to her, as she was a Scotch woman. Helen M'Dougal and Hare's wife were not present when those murders were committed, they might have a suspicion of what was doing, but did not see them done. Hare was always the most anxious about them, and could sleep well at night after committing a murder; but Burke repented often of the crime, and could not sleep without a bottle of whisky by his bedside, and a twopenny candle to burn all night beside him; when he awoke he would take a draught of the bottle – sometimes half a bottle at a draught – and that would make him sleep. They had a great many pointed out for murder, but were disappointed of them by some means or other; they were always in a drunken state when they committed those murders, and when they got the money for them while it lasted. When done, they would pawn their clothes, and would take them out as soon as they got a subject. When they first began this murdering system, they always took them to Knox's after dark; but being so successful, they went in the day-time, and grew more bold. When they carried the girl Paterson to Knox's, there were a great many boys in the High School Yards, who followed Burke and the man that carried her, crying, 'They are carrying a corpse'; but they got her safe delivered. They often said to one another that no person could find them out, no one being present at the murders but themselves two; and that they might as well be hanged for a sheep as a lamb. They made it their business to look out for persons to decoy into their houses to murder them. Burke declares, when they kept the mouth and nose shut a very few minutes, they could make no resistance, but would convulse and make a rumbling noise in their bellies for some time; after they ceased crying and making resistance, they left them to die of themselves; but their bodies would often move afterwards, and for some time they would have long breathings before life went away. Burke declares that it was God's providence that put a stop to their murdering career, or he does not know how far they might have gone with it, even to attack people on the streets, as they were so successful, and always met with a ready market, that when they delivered a body they were always told to get more. Hare was always with him when he went with a subject, and also when he got the money. Burke declares, that Hare and him had a plan made up, that Burke and a man were to go to Glasgow or Ireland, and try the same there, and to forward them to Hare, and he was to give them to Dr Knox. Hare's wife always got £1 of Burke's share, for the use of the house, of all that were murdered in their house; for if the price received was £10, Hare got £6, and Burke got only £4; but Burke did not give her the £1 for Daft Jamie, for which Hare's wife would not speak to him for three weeks. They could get nothing done during the harvest-time, and also after harvest, as Hare's house was so full of lodgers. In Hare's house were eight beds for lodgers; they paid 3d. each;

and two, and sometimes three, slept in a bed; and during harvest they gave up their own bed when throng. Burke declares they went under the name of resurrection men in the West Port, where they lived, but not murderers. When they wanted money, they would say they would go and look for a shot; that was the name they gave them when they wanted to murder any person. They entered into a contract with Dr Knox and his assistants that they were to get £10 in winter, and £8 in summer for as many subjects as they could bring to them.

Old Donald, a pensioner, who lodged in Hare's house, and died of a dropsy, was the first subject they sold. After he was put into the coffin and the lid put on, Hare unscrewed the nails and Burke lifted the body out. Hare filled the coffin with bark from the tan-yard, and put a sheet over the bark, and it was buried in the West Church Yard. The coffin was furnished by the parish. Hare and Burke took him to the College first; they saw a man there, and asked for Dr Monro, or any of his men; the man asked what they wanted, or had they a subject; they said they had. He then ordered them to call at 10, Dr Knox's, in Surgeon Square, and he would take it from them, which they did. They got £7 10s for him. That was the only subject they sold that they did not murder; and getting that high price made them try the murdering for subjects.

Burke is thirty-six years of age, was born in the parish of Orrey, county Tyrone; served seven years in the army, most of that time as an officer's servant in the Donegal militia; he was married at Ballinha, in the county of Mayo, when in the army, but left his wife and two children in Ireland. She would not come to Scotland with them. He had often wrote to her, but got no answer; he came to Scotland to work at the Union Canal, and wrought there while it lasted; he resided for about two years in Peebles, and worked as a labourer. He wrought as weaver for eighteen months, and as a baker for five months; he learned to mend shoes, as a cobbler, with a man he lodged with in Leith; and he has lived with Helen M'Dougal about ten years, until he and she were confined in the Calton Jail, on the charge of murdering the woman of the name of Docherty or Campbell, and both were tried before the High Court of Justiciary in December last. Helen M'Dougal's charge was found not proven, and Burke found guilty, and sentenced to suffer death on the 28th January.

Declares, that Hare's servant girl could give information respecting the murders done in Hare's house, if she likes. She came to him at Whitsunday last, went to harvest, and returned back to him when the harvest was over. She remained until he was confined along with his wife in the Calton Jail. She then sold twenty-one of his swine for £3, and absconded. She was gathering potatoes in a field that day Daft Jamie was murdered; she saw his clothes in the house when she came home at night. Her name is Elizabeth M'Guier or Mair. Their wives saw that people came into their houses at night, and went to bed as lodgers, but did not see them in the morning, nor did they make any inquiries about them. They certainly knew what became of them, although Burke and Hare pretended to the contrary. Hare's wife often helped Burke and Hare to pack the murdered bodies into the boxes. Helen M'Dougal never did, nor saw them done; Burke never durst let her know; he used to smuggle in drink, and get better victuals unknown to her; he told her he bought dead bodies, and sold them to doctors, and that was the way they got the name of resurrection-men.

Burke declares that docter Knox never incoreged him, nither taught him or incoregd him to murder any person, nether any of his asistents, that worthy gentleman Mr. Fergeson was the only man that ever mentioned any thing about the bodies. He inquired where we got that yong woman Paterson.

(*Signed*) WILLIAM BURK, *prisoner.*
Condemned Cell, January 21, 1819.

APPENDIX III

DR KNOX'S LETTER, DATED 17 MARCH 1829, TO THE
CALEDONIAN MERCURY, ACCOMPANYING
THE COMMITTEE'S REPORT

Sir,

I regret troubling either you or the public with anything personal, but I cannot be insensible of the feelings of my friends, or of the character of the profession to which I have the honour of belonging. Had I alone been concerned, I should never have thought of obtruding on the public by this communication.

I have a class of above 400 pupils. No person can be at the head of such an establishment without necessarily running the risk of being imposed upon by those who furnish the material of their science to anatomical teachers; and, accordingly, there is hardly any such person who has not occasionally incurred odium or suspicion from his supposed accession to those violations of the law, without which anatomy can scarcely now be practised. That I should have become an object of popular prejudice, therefore, since mine happened to be the establishment with which Burke and Hare chiefly dealt, was nothing more than what I had to expect. But if means had not been purposely taken, and most keenly persevered in, to misrepresent facts and to inflame the public mind, that prejudice would at least have stood on right ground, and would ultimately have passed away, by its being seen that I had been exposed to a mere misfortune which would almost certainly have occurred to anybody else who had been in my situation.

But every effort has been employed to convert my misfortune into positive and intended personal guilt of the most dreadful character. Scarcely any individual has ever been the object of more systematic or atrocious attacks than I have been. Nobody acquainted with this place requires to be told from what quarter these have proceeded.

I allowed them to go on for months without taking the slightest notice of them; and I was inclined to adhere to this system, especially as the public authorities by never charging me with any offence, gave the whole attestation they could that they had nothing to charge me with. But my friends interfered for me. Without consulting me, they directed an agent to institute the most rigid and unsparing examination into the facts. I was totally unacquainted with this gentleman, but I understood that in naming Mr Ellis they named a person whose character is a sufficient pledge for the propriety of his proceedings.

The result of his inquiries was laid before the Dean of Faculty and another Counsel, who were asked what ought to be done. These gentlemen gave it as their opinion that the evidence was completely satisfactory, and that there was no want of actionable matter, but that there was one ground on which it was my duty to resist the temptation of going into a Court of law. This was, that the disclosures of the most innocent proceedings even of the best-conducted dissecting-room must always shock the public and be hurtful to science. But they recommended that a few persons of undoubted weight and character should be asked to investigate the matter, in order that, if I deserved it, an attestation might be given to me which would be more satisfactory to my friends than any mere statements of mine could be expected to be. This led to the formation of a Committee, which was never meant by me to be anything but private. But the fact of its sitting soon got into the newspapers, and hence the necessity under which I am placed of explaining how that proceeding, in which the public has been made to take an interest, has terminated.

I have been on habits of friendship with some of the Committee, with others of them I have been acquainted, and some of them I don't even know by sight. I took no charge whatever of their proceedings. In order that there might be no pretence for saying the truth was obstructed from fear, I gave a written protection to every person to say what he chose about or against me. The extent to which this was in some instances taken advantage of will probably not be soon forgotten by those who witnessed it.

After a severe and laborious investigation of about six weeks, the result is contained in the following report, which was put into my hands last night. It is signed by every member of the Committee except one, who ceased to act long before the evidence was completed.

I cannot be supposed to be a candid judge of my own case, and therefore it is extremely probable that any opinion of mine on the last view adopted by the Committee is incorrect and theirs [*sic*] right. If it be so, I most willingly submit to the censure they have inflicted, and shall hold it my duty to profit from it by due care hereafter. My consolation is, that I have at least not been obstinate in my errors, and that no sanction has ever been given in any fair quarter to the more serious imputations by which it has been the interest of certain persons to assail me. Candid men will judge of me according to the situation in which I was placed at the time, and not according to the wisdom which has unexpectedly been acquired since.

This is the very first time that I have ever made any statement to the public in my own vindication, and it shall be the last. It would be unjust to the authors of the former calumnies to suppose that they would not renew them now. I can only assure them that, in so far as I am concerned, they will renew them in vain.

I have the honour to be, etc,

R. KNOX.

APPENDIX IV

REPORT OF THE COMMITTEE APPOINTED TO INVESTIGATE DR KNOX'S ROLE IN THE MURDERS

The Committee who, at the request of Dr Knox, undertook to investigate the truth or falsehood of the rumours in circulation regarding him, have gone into an extensive examination of evidence, in the course of which they have courted information from every quarter. They have been readily furnished with all which they required from Dr Knox himself, and though they have failed in some attempts to procure evidence, they have in most quarters succeeded in obtaining it, and especially from those persons who have been represented to them as having spoken the most confidently in support of these rumours, and they have unanimously agreed on the following report.

1. The Committee have seen no evidence that Dr Knox or his assistants knew that murder was committed in procuring any of the subjects brought to his rooms, and the Committee firmly believe that they did not.

2. On the question whether any suspicion of murder at any time existed in Dr Knox's mind, the Committee would observe that there were certainly several circumstances (already known to the public), regarding some of the subjects brought by Burke and Hare, which, now that the truth has come out, appear calculated to excite suspicion, particularly the very early period after death at which they were brought to the rooms, and the absence of external marks of disease, together with the opinion previously expressed by Dr Knox, in common with most other anatomists, of the generally abandoned character of persons engaged in this traffic. But, on the other hand, the Committee, after much anxious inquiry, have found no evidence

195

of their actually having excited it in the mind of Dr Knox, or of any other of the individuals who saw the bodies of these unfortunate persons prior to the apprehension of Burke.

The bodies do not appear in any instance to have borne any external marks by which it could have been known whether they had died by violence or suddenly from natural causes, or from disease of short duration, and the mode of protracted anatomical dissection practised in this and other similar establishments is such as would have made it very difficult to ascertain the causes of death, even if special inquiry had been instituted with that intention.

No evidence whatever has come before the Committee that any suspicion of murder was expressed to Dr Knox by any one, whether of his assistants or of his very numerous class (amounting to upwards of 400 students), or other persons who were in the practice of frequently visiting his rooms, and there are several circumstances in his conduct, particularly the complete publicity with which his establishment was managed, and his anxiety to lay each subject before the students as soon as possible after its reception, which seem to the Committee strongly to indicate that he had no suspicion of the atrocious means by which they had been procured.

It has also been proved to the satisfaction of the Committee, that no mutilation or disfigurement of any kind was ever practised with a view to conceal the features, or abstract unseasonably any part of the body, the presence of which might have facilitated detection, and it appears clearly that the subjects brought by Burke and Hare were dissected in the same protracted manner as those procured from any other quarter.

3. The Committee have thought it proper to inquire further, whether there was anything faulty or negligent in the regulations under which subjects were received into Dr Knox's rooms, which gave, or might give, a peculiar facility to the disposal of the bodies obtained by these crimes, and on this point they think it their duty to state their opinion fully.

It appears in evidence that Dr Knox had formed and expressed the opinion, long prior to any dealings with Burke and Hare, that a considerable supply of subjects for anatomical purposes might be procured by purchase, and without any crime, from the relations or connections of deceased persons in the lowest ranks of society. In forming this opinion, whether mistaken or not, the Committee cannot consider Dr Knox to have been culpable. They believe there is nothing contrary to the law of the land in procuring subjects for dissection in that way, and they know that the opinion which Dr Knox had formed on this point, though never acted on to any extent in the profession, has been avowed by others of the highest character in the profession. But they think that Dr Knox acted on this opinion in a very incautious manner.

This preconceived opinion seems to have led him to give a ready ear to the plausible stories of Burke, who appears from all the evidence before the Committee to have conducted himself with great address and appearance of honesty, as well as in his conversations with Dr Knox as in his more frequent intercourse with his assistants, and always to have represented himself as engaged in negotiations of that description, and occasionally to have asked and obtained money in advance to enable him and his associate to conclude bargains.

Unfortunately also Dr Knox had been led, apparently in consequence of the extent and variety of his avocations, to entrust the dealings with persons supplying subjects and the reception of the subjects brought to his assistants (seven in number) and to his doorkeeper indiscriminately. It appears also that he directed or allowed these dealings to be conducted on the understanding (common to him with some other anatomists) that it would only tend to diminish or divert the supply of subjects to make any particular inquiry of the person bringing them as to the place and mode of obtaining them.

In these respects, the Committee consider the practice which was then adopted in Dr Knox's rooms (whatever be the usage in this or other establishments in regard to subjects obtained in the ordinary way) to have been very improper in the case of persons bringing bodies which had not been interred. They think that the notoriously bad character of persons who generally engage in any such traffic in addition to the novelty and particular nature of the system on which these men professed to be acting, undoubtedly demanded greater vigilance.

The extent, therefore, to which (judging from the evidence which they have been able to procure) the Committee think that Dr Knox can be blamed on account of transactions with Burke and Hare is, that by this laxity of the regulations under which bodies were received into his rooms, he unintentionally gave a degree of facility to the disposal of the victims of their crimes, which under better regulations would not have existed, and which is doubtless a matter of deep and lasting regret, not only to himself but to all who have reflected on the importance and are therefore interested in the prosecution of the study of anatomy. But while they point out this circumstance as the only ground of censure which they can discover in the conduct of Dr Knox, it is fair to observe, that perhaps the recent disclosures have made it appear reprehensible to many who would not otherwise have adverted to its possible consequences.

John Robinson, *Chairman* W.P. Allison
M.P. Brown Geo. Ballingall
James Russell George Sinclair
J. Shaw Stewart W. Hamilton
  Thomas Allan

13th March, 1829

APPENDIX V

LETTER TO THE LORD ADVOCATE, DISCLOSING THE
ACCOMPLICES, SECRETS, AND OTHER
FACTS RELATIVE TO THE LATE MURDERS;
WITH A CORRECT ACCOUNT OF THE MANNER
IN WHICH THE ANATOMICAL SCHOOLS ARE SUPPLIED WITH
SUBJECTS. BY THE ECHO
OF SURGEONS' SQUARE.

'What? Shall wealth screen thee from justice.'

'Good friends! let me not stir you up
To any sudden flood of mutiny.'

Mark Antony.

To Sir William Rae, Baronet, His Majesty's Advocate for Scotland.

My Lord,

You are aware that, at this moment, the public feeling is strongly excited against the perpetrators of the late foul and cold blooded murders that have taken place in the very centre of a populous and civilized city. The exact extent to which this traffic in blood has been carried on, and by whom, is yet a secret. Part of the gang have been brought to light, and by a strict investigation, I have no doubt but the remainder may also be brought to condign punishment. Your Lordship is aware, that in all civilized nations, blood calls for blood. The holy religion to which we subscribe, and the God of all nature hath expressly said, 'That he who sheddeth man's blood, by man shall his blood be shed.' The late horrible traffic has chilled every breast against the individuals, and it only surprises the public that such a traffic should be carried on in the heart of a populous city, and in so open a manner, without coming to the knowledge of the men in power; in carefully perusing this letter, your Lordship will perceive, that at one period, when a just suspicion fell upon Burke about the beginning of October last, a policeman was stationed at his door, but even then, he eluded their vigilance, and the body was safely deposited in the Lecture Room. Your Lordship will pardon me for not making farther remarks, until I give verbatim the words of some of the parties said to have acted a conspicuous part in the tragedy. My motives for setting the inquiry on foot were these, viz:– To have a candid statement from the individuals in the service of Dr Knox, who must have known when and how they became acquainted with Burke and Hare, – by what means the bodies were procured; from whence, – and by whom are the Anatomical Schools supplied, – who are the parties that examine the bodies before dissection, – and if there is any register of opinion kept respecting them.

Your Lordship must be aware that the public eye is fixed upon you, as public prosecutor, and as the greater portion of that public is ignorant of the regular routine and evidence required, before your Lordship can file a Bill of Indictment, with any degree of certainty as to its issue, and as it is a known trait in your Lordship's character, to lean to the side of mercy, yet, in this case, we trust you will strain every nerve, and sift this dreadful plot to its very core. I will now proceed to detail P—n's own words, which appears to me, (especially as it is supported by other proofs) to carry a considerable share of plausibility along with it.

David P—n was first in the employment of Dr K— in the year 1824 or 1825, for about one year, and on his return from the army at the close of 1827, did apply to Dr K— for his former situation, and was engaged in the beginning of February 1828, as the Museum keeper; his salary was very small, but from the fees paid him by the students, he contrived to make a very comfortable livelihood. He had nothing whatever to do with the subjects (or bodies) brought to the Lecture Room, his sole charge was to keep the Museum, and be answerable for articles therein; at that time he did not know how the Doctor obtained subjects. But shortly after saw Burke and Hare, (Burke was called *John*, and Hare *William*) who had brought a subject, and delivered it to Mr M—r, an assistant, who had the management of that traffic, and from the conversation that then passed, understood that they, (Burke and Hare) had been in the habit of supplying Dr K— with subjects previous to that time.

During the Lectures, Burke or Hare, and sometimes both, frequently called towards evening, and informed Mr M——r that they had a subject for the Doctor, when Mr M——r would accompany them, and return in the course of an hour and a half, or thereabout, the Doctor always desiring P——n to be in the way with the keys, as it would not do to keep the parties waiting on their return, and that the rooms should be kept open until they did return. In this manner did they continue to supply, or rather assist in supplying the Lecture Room during the season, nothing particularly occuring to his notice, until they had brought a female subject. Now, my Lord, mark his own words, "Not being in the room when the body was brought, – I found Mr M——r in close conversation with Burke and Hare, and a female subject stretched upon the floor, the beautiful symmetry and freshness of the body attracted my attention; soon after I heard Mr F——, another assistant of Dr K——, say that he was acquainted with the deceased, and named her as Mary Mitchell, (this was the girl Paterson,) my curiosity being roused, I was determined to enquire at the first opportunity where they had got the subject in question; accordingly, at their next appearance, which was a few days after, either informing Mr M——r that they had another subject, or requesting payment for the last, but not having heard their general conversation, could not say which, I then took the oportunity of enquiring at Burke where he had procured the last subject; when he answered, that he had purchased it from the friends of the deceased; it was rather a new thing for me to hear of the relatives selling the corpse of their friends, and I enquired where the relatives lived; at this, Burke looked very suspiciously at me, and at length said, as nearly as I can recollect, If I am to be catechised by you, where and how I get subjects, I will inform the Doctor of it, and if he allows you to do so, I will bring no more to him, mind that. Now, as I remembered that I had positive orders from the Doctor not to interfere at all with these men, I was content to be silent." To a question put to P——n, whether he had any suspicion of Burke and Hare, as to the manner they had obtained the body of the female, or if he heard any of the students or assistants making any remarks upon it. Answered, that he had not the slightest suspicion as to the deceased having met with a premature death, but did think that it really was sold by the relatives, or by some one who kept a brothel or lodging house for paupers, from whom the resurrectionists purchase subjects; the only remark he ever heard made by either the assistants or students was, that it was a fine proportioned body, and that she must have been a very handsome woman, so much so indeed, that many of the students took sketches of it, one of which is in his possession.

About this time it appears that Burke and Hare became rather troublesome at the Doctor's house, and he not being altogether over anxious of such visitors, requested to know where they lived, and finding that they resided in Portsburgh, requested P—n, as his lodgings was in Portsburgh also, to take any message for him they might have, which he was to convey to Newington, and return an answer, this he absolutely refused, saying that he did not wish resurrectionists to be coming about his lodgings, but they ought to call at the Lecture Room; this did not suffice, for either the Doctor, or some one for him, had given P—'s address, and in a few days they called at his lodgings, requesting a small sum, which they said the Doctor was due. He accordingly went to the Doctor and received the money for them, not at all pleased with the mission.

Previous to this period, Burke became a patient of Dr K—'s, and came to the Lecture Room to have his wound dressed. He disappeared for some time during harvest. P—n being also from home during the vacation, the rooms were under the care of Mr Angus M—n. On his (P—n's) return, he learned from (M—n) that Hare, or William as he was called, had been there a short time before with a subject, unattended by Burke, but P—n could not say whether it was male or female, as he did not see it, and although he firmly believes it to be the case – cannot vouch any father than M—n's own words. When he again received the keys from M—n, and when the Lectures were about to commence, the Doctor made frequent enquiries at his assistants if any of them had seen John, (meaning Burke,) going about, and requested P—n to find him out, and desire him to call upon the Doctor. P—n's enquiries were fruitless; some time after Burke called at the rooms to have the Doctor's opinion respecting his wound, which had assumed a dangerous appearance. He said he had been either at the country or at the harvest. The Doctor and his assistants seemed glad of Burke's visit, and he was earnestly requested by them to resume his supplies of subjects as formerly.

Burke's confession, as stated in the Caledonian Mercury, sets forth, that P—n had frequently urged Burke and Hare to procure as many subjects as possible. P—n admits that, on one occasion, he was requested by the Doctor to desire John to get as many subjects as possible, as he would require all he could get; but denies that he ever received any fee or reward above his regular salary and students fees; and that he had nothing to do with the procuring of subjects, that being entirely the assistants' duty, which another part of Burke's confession fully corroborates, when he says, that he never sold a subject to any other person but the Doctor or his assistants; and that he had no more to do than leave the body at the Rooms and go to the Doctor for the money. Another proof that others were equally, if not more culpable, than P—n, is as follows:– At the commencement of the Lectures in October last, P—n overheard a conversation, rather in high words, between Mr F—n, one of the assistants, and Messrs Burke and Hare, the import of which was, that Burke and Hare were insisting on raising the price of subjects, whereas F— insisted upon £8 being a fair price. The sum demanded he did not hear, nor knows how the dispute was settled. Now, my Lord, you will observe, they did not apply to P—n as to the individual they considered authorized to make a bargain; but here is a more important point, and one to which I trust your Lordship will pay particular attention. He says, "That about this time Burke called at the Lecture Room and informed some of the assistants that he had a subject for the Doctor, and requested a box and a little money, he got a trunk and a few shillings and went away. He, however, did not fulfil his promise that evening, but called on the following day, and requested me to inform the Doctor that his neighbours, or the neighbours, suspected he had a subject in the house, and that as a policeman was watching their motions, and seldom left the corner of the house, he was afraid to bring it. I went and informed the Doctor what Burke had said, when he desired me to make minute inquiry into the truth of Burke's statement; but not knowing where he (Burke) lived, and it being rather a delicate point to inquire after, I obtained no information; that day also elapsed without any appearance of the subject, and the following day the Doctor got rather enraged, he remarked that John was a coward, and said, that he would write to the authorities and procure a protection for him to carry any packages safe to his Lecture Room. Burke having called at the nick of time, I told him what the Doctor had said, and in a few minutes he saw the Doctor himself. The conversation was nearly as follows: after Burke requesting the protection, the Doctor said he had not got it yet; but that he (Burke) should bring the box, and that if he, or those employed by him, were stopt upon the street, they were for their own personal safety to suffer themselves to be taken to the Police Office along with the package. In a short time they would be relieved, and the package would assuredly be sent to him from the Office; Burke's reply was, that if he was once taken to the Police Office he would not so easily get out again."

Did your Lordship ever hear this before? – Did such a statement come out upon Burke's trial? or, were such questions ever put to P—n? If this statement therefore is correct, and information given to the Police that a corpse supposed to be disinterred, or otherwise, was actually in the possession of Burke or Hare, why not instead of placing a policeman as a watch over their motions? I say, why should not a warrant have been granted to search the premises? If this had been done, it might have been the means of saving many victims that afterwards fell into the hands of these blood-thirsty miscreants. It may be asked, how could the authorities prove that the individuals were murdered? seeing that even our professors of anatomy could not perceive any thing like external marks of violence, or symptoms of an internal nature, to lead them for a moment to suppose that the subjects heretofore brought by Burke and Hare had met with a premature death. I am inclined to think that this part of the mystery has been overlooked, not by any means imputing any blame to Dr K— or his assistants. But, Tyro, as I am on matters of anatomy, I have always been led to consider that suffocation or strangulation causes the blood to flow to the head, consequently makes the face of a strong livid colour, with a small discharge of blood from the mouth, nose, and ears. Now, as most of the subjects produced by Burke and Hare had suffered death by suffocation, and as these bodies were generally disposed of to Dr K—, I think it but natural to infer, that if the Doctor saw these bodies, he is either horribly ignorant of his profession, or he wilfully withheld that information he ought to have given. I will ask any of the professors of anatomy, candidly and honestly, that if two men, of the appearance of Burke and Hare, had brought them ten or a dozen bodies, with the same appearance as those brought by B. and H. must have had, what would be their opinion? I am certain of one thing, that it would, at least, have a great tendency to rouse their suspicions, and make minute inquiries as to the manner they obtained such subjects. But we are told that Dr K— did not know, nor had he the most distant idea, that these subjects were any thing but disinterred bodies; all the subjects brought to him by Burke and Hare, and that were examined by him, he could not even guess at the cause of their death. On these grounds we are bound to believe that no blame can be attached to the Doctor, seeing *he himself is equally as ignorant as his Students*. In respect to the words said to have been spoken by the Doctor with regard to the protection, and that if they were stopt, to suffer themselves to be taken into custody, when they would soon be released, and the package assuredly sent to him. If such really was the case, does it not stigmatize [*sic*] the Police establishment in the eyes of the public. – An establishment which we with confidence look to for protection, and pay a heavy tax for its support. I am inclined to think that there must be some mistake in this part of the story, for I feel pretty confident, that if the body had been taken to the Police Office and examined, a thousand to one but the surgeon of that establishment would at once say that it had come by a premature death, and Burke seems to have been pretty much of the same opinion, as he knew that if once there, the body would be examined, and consequently an investigation would take place that might lead to a discovery of his nefarious traffic. But to proceed with P—n's narrative. "One day they (Burke and Hare) called upon Mr M—n formerly mentioned, who resides in Surgeons' Square, and told him, that they had a subject for the Doctor, and requested him to be in readiness; that evening about seven o'clock I called upon Mr M – n and found him waiting in the Square, he then told me that a subject was expected for the Doctor. In a short time three men (Burke, Hare, and M'Culloch) made their appearance with a large box, or chest, which was deposited in one of the rooms; and as they insisted upon having money, we thought proper to look into the box previous to reporting to the Doctor. When we did so we found it contained the corpse of a stout young man, but did not examine it; I immediately went and informed the Doctor that the parties before mentioned had brought a subject, and were anxious for some money. The sum given to me by the Doctor I delivered to them, and they called the following day for the remainder, making in all L.10. When the body was examined in the morning, one of the assistants remarked, that it was very like DAFT JAMIE, in which opinion all present agreed. I myself remarked, that I did not think Jamie either so stout or robust as the subject before me, and that I did not think he was dead, as I had seen him a day or two before; but did say that there was a strong resemblance. Some discourse then took place amongst the students respecting the manner the body had been obtained, when it was generally supposed, that if it really was JAMIE, his friends must have sold him to the procurers. Dr K— all along persisting that it was not Jamie; nothing more of consequence occurred until a report that Jamie was amissing reached Surgeons' Square, when the dissection of the body was ordered. It may be necessary to remark, that the usual method adopted by the students in dissecting, is to make a transverse section of the cranium, or to separate the superior portion from the base, in order to enable the student to dissect the brain. In dissecting this body the head was kept entire at the express request of

one of the Doctor's assistants, but for what purpose I cannot say; Mr F—n, another assistant, seemed doubly anxious to have the feet of this subject, which he received from the students that dissected the body. It is a common practice amongst the students that when they wish to preserve the bones of any limb entire, to immerse it in a jar of water until decomposition takes place, when the soft is cleaned from the bone; but in this case, however, Mr F—n deviated considerably from the usual method, for he immediately was at the no small trouble of detaching bone from bone PREVIOUS to their being immersed in water. I do not pretend to offer any opinion upon his doing so, I merely state facts."

Now, my Lord, I will again call your attention to the above statement. It is well known that James Wilson, or Daft Jamie, had a very peculiar physiognomy, he was also partially deprived of the use of his right side. One of his feet was very much contracted; in short, any individual that ever saw him in life would know his corpse. Again, it is usual to make use of the oldest subjects first, that is those subjects that have been the longest in the possession of the lecturer. Now, my Lord, it will be observed, that on the rumour of Jamie being amissing, or thereabouts, his body was ordered for dissection, although it was the last and freshest subject in the Doctor's possession. His head was kept entire and not suffered to be lectured upon; his feet were requested of the students, and when given, instead of going through the usual preparation of immersing them in water, they were instantly separated bone from bone, although this manner of procedure was infinitely more laborious than the other. What is your Lordship's opinion? does it not look very like a concealment? In such a case I should be very apt to consider that the parties had discovered that the body actually was *Jamie's*, and that in order to destroy every trace of detection, they made away with those parts most likely to be recognized. Or did the Doctor wish to prepare the skull, knowing it to be the head of an idiot, and along with other venerable relics of the same kind, commence a course of lectures on phrenology, and supersede Dr Combe. Be this as it may, I am certain your Lordship will agree with me, that if the Doctor is not highly culpable, and, in the true sense of the law, GUILTY art and part, he is at least deserving of public censure for his negligence in not giving that information which must have been in his power to communicate.

Paterson goes on to state, "That when the rumour of Jamie's absence was generally known, many and singular were the remarks made by the students. For his part, he then, and not till then, began to form a very different opinion of the individuals Burke and Hare, and had determined in his own mind, at all hazards, to watch the motions of these villains more minutely, and examine the next subject they brought to the rooms. He says, I did not wait long in suspense, for a few evenings after, to wit, 31st October, 1828, being invited to partake of a beef-steak supper with a friend; on my return home about 12 o'clock, and on going up stairs, I heard a knocking at the door of my lodgings. I enquired who was there twice, before receiving any answer, at length a voice answered, John, and asked if I was Dr K——'s man; having answered in the affirmative, he said he wanted to see me at his own house, but on my informing him that I did not know where his house was, he offered to accompany me. I knew by this time that it was *Burke*, and as I perceived him a little intoxicated, I thought it would be a good opportunity to commence my inquiries. We went down stairs in solemn silence, and conducted by Burke, got to his house, remarking to him, that he lived in a very strange and intricate situation, his answer was, that it suited his purpose. On entering the house, I observed a man, *Hare*, and two women, all more or less intoxicated. The motive for his wishing to see me at his own house, I did not then know. Just as he had got in, he tapped me on the shoulder, and pointing to a quantity of straw, said, "*there lies something for the Doctor to-morrow*", at that instant, I fixed my eyes stedfastly upon Burke; and, from the suspicions I entertained in my own mind, I in a moment glanced at the other individuals; but seeing nothing to raise my suspicions, I merely answered at the time, (to the best of my recollection,) that they might send it any time tomorrow. Burke asked if I would give him some blunt, my answer was, that I had nothing to do with these matters, and that the Doctor would pay him when he brought the subject. I did not see the body, but immediately left the house. On my return home, I found that a man answering to Burke's description, had called for me at the early part of the evening. When I retired to bed, I took a retrospective view of the conduct of Burke and Hare, I remarked their shyness in answering the questions I formerly put to them respecting the body of the girl Paterson. The subjects generally brought by them, seemed always fresher than those from other quarters. The circumstance of *Jamie* being still amissing, and no accounts whatever concerning him, rushed on my mind, the conduct of the individuals that very night, while a corpse was lying in one corner of the hovel, in the same place, the parties seemed to have been carousing in the height of jollity; another circumstance of greater moment, now passed before me, the subjects generally brought by them to the Lecture Room, were uniformly packed in a box or chest; now, thought I, if these men actually disinterred the body said to be among the straw, it is more than probable, that they would have packed it up before sending it to their own house, and not at all likely that they would have unpacked it again. However, the circumstances of Jamie alone, prompted me to determine, that if the subject was brought in time next day, I would satisfy myself as to any external marks of violence. Next day I impatiently waited for the package, and towards evening I began to suspect that it was a trick, in order to get money. About seven o'clock on the Saturday evening, Burke, Hare, and M'Culloch brought a package, and delivered it in the presence of Mr Jones; as they insisted for money, Mr Jones accompanied me to the Doctor's house. We told the Doctor that the men had brought the package they had promised him, and that they were clamorous for money. The Doctor gave me £5, desiring me to give it them, and they would receive the remainder on Monday. It being now late, I had no opportunity of examining the body that night, but resolved to go on the morrow, (Sunday,) and satisfy my curiosity, for which purpose I took the keys of the Lecture Room with me.

Early on the Sunday morning I was awakened by Lieutenant Paterson and Serjeant-major Fisher of the Police establishment, who informed me that they had brought an order from Dr K— for me to accompany them with the keys of the lecture rooms, and allow them to search for the body of a woman said to have been murdered and sold to the Doctor. My former surmises now rushed upon me, and I inquired of Lieutenant Paterson if he really thought there was any truth in it, when he informed me, that there were some persons in custody upon suspicion; I went with them, and on opening the rooms said, that to prevent all unnecessary trouble, I would show them the package left on Saturday evening untouched, and did so. Lieutenant Paterson then requested me to assist in opening the package, which I did accordingly, and stretched the body at full length upon a table in order to inspect it minutely. Lieutenant Paterson requested to know my opinion, but as I had no knowledge in surgery, could not give an opinion any farther than from the appearance of the face, and a little blood at the corners of the mouth, I should suppose, from what I have heard, that the person must have died by suffocation or poison; and not perceiving any external marks of violence, could not hazard any just opinion. I however had my own thoughts; the appearance of this body, (Campbell or Docherty,) coincided exactly with that of the girl Paterson; and combining these circumstances with that of Jamie, and of the individuals that brought those bodies to the Lecture Room being in custody, I delivered up the keys to Lieutenant Paterson, requesting him to take the body under his own charge; a person then arrived with a policeman who recognized the deceased, and said it was the same they were in search of.

Here Paterson remarked, that if the version of the Confession of Burke, as given in the public prints is correct, he has in many instances given the words of Dr K— as his (Paterson's). And to show your Lordship what confidence can be placed in Burke's Confession, Paterson relates the following anecdote, as told him by Mr A. M—n, on whose veracity he can depend, and who was in the employment of Dr K— long before Paterson was engaged: "The first time Mr M—n saw Burke or Hare was about the end of 1827, when one of them called at the Rooms during the day and inquired of him if the Doctor would purchase a subject, on being answered he would, they returned in the evening with the body of a very tall man in a sack. One carried the sack while the other assisted behind. One of the arms of the subject was hanging outside, at that time they seemed flurred and in a great hurry." Now it will be remembered, that in Burke's Confession, he says, that the first subject ever they sold to Dr K— was a female that died in Hare's house, this seems strange; but as they were in the habit of supplying the Doctor before my time, I cannot solve that mystery.

By reviewing the foregoing statement, and coupling it with circumstances that has since transpired, I think your Lordship will admit that there is strong circumstantial evidence existing against the parties, who have all along steered clear of this affair. I will commence my remarks as far back as February 1828; at that time, *Burke* and *Hare* had been supplying Dr K— with subjects for at least two or three months previous; at that time, Mr M—r, an assistant, if not always, frequently went with them, and again returned in about an hour and a half with a subject. Mr M—r ought to be examined on this point; he must know where these subjects came from, – who were the individuals he saw, – possibly can tell whether the subjects were male or female. It has been said that one murder was committed in Broggan's house. Did Broggan not see a third person in his house when he left it, and on his return, found only Burke and Hare, with a package in the room, this package, it is said, Broggan suspected to be a body, and was anxious that it should be removed. Now if Broggan saw three persons enter his house without a package, he knew the character of Burke and Hare too well, not to be acquainted with the motives that had brought them there; if, on his return, he found the third person amissing, and in his or her place a package, a package too that he suspected to contain a body, ought he not to have enquired after the party missing, and what that package contained. No, no, Mr Broggan was no novice to the trade; he was well aware that they had a *subject*, and consequently knowing, without giving information, is guilty art and part. – Probably Mr M——r, the assistant, can throw some light on this subject.

The story of the girl Paterson, or Mitchell, is still more glaring. Jess Brown states, that Paterson was in her company when they were accosted by two men, (Burke and Hare); the men would not accompany them to the house proposed by Brown, but insisted upon the girls going with them; they contrived to give Brown the slip, or Brown gave them the slip, and observed Burke, Hare, and the girl Paterson proceed towards the Canongate; they were admitted into Burke's brother's house in the Canongate; she was seen there by Burke's brother, who is a scaffenger, and he sat carousing with them until his avocations called him away early in the morning; after his departure the murder was committed; the body was taken the same evening to Surgeons Square, and sold for £10; the next day it was recognized by Mr F——, an assistant to Dr K——; the face was of a strong livid colour, and traces of blood were observable at the mouth, nose, and ears. Here is a chain of strong circumstantial evidence against Hare, so much so, that an English jury would not have the least hesitation in returning a verdict against him; still it may be said, that there is no proof as to these men being the perpetrators of the murder.

Your Lordship must be aware that the law does not always require eye witnesses to the fact, for it justly observes, that these acts are generally done in so secret a manner, that nine cases out of ten would go unpunished; but that a chain of circumstantial evidence, well supported, taking into consideration the previous character of the parties, will be sufficient to condemn. There is sufficient proof that Burke and Hare were seen last in Paterson's company; there is also sufficient proof, that Burke and Hare brought the body of Paterson to Surgeons Square, fifteen hours after she was seen by Burke's brother. One witness can swear it was her body he saw in the Lecture Room; combine this with the circumstance of her mysterious disappearance, and, as an honest man, ask your own conscience, if there is not sufficient proof to put HARE upon his trial for the murder. I will call your Lordship's attention to another circumstance. HARE brought a subject to Surgeons Square while Burke was absent in the country, and delivered it to Mr M——. I think it would be proper to examine Mr M—— upon this point, as it possibly might be the body of the person that was murdered in Broggan's house, and the evidence obtained from Dr K—, Mr M—, Broggan, and possibly others, might be of service in the prosecution. Another chain of circumstantial evidence against HARE is this, James Wilson, or DAFT JAMIE, was seen by many, the day of that evening the murder was committed; he was last seen in the West Port with *Burke* or *Hare*; the night after the murder he was carried to Surgeons Square by M'Culloch, accompanied by *Burke* and *Hare*; the observations of the students the next day, that they knew it to be JAMIE, and when the story of his disappearance became general, – the ordering of that body for dissection, instead of the uniform practice of making use of the body longest in possession of the lecturer, – and even then destroying all traces of such parts of the body as were most likely to lead to a discovery, this calls loudly upon the lecturer to give the public some satisfactory reason, why he deviated in this case from the usual mode of procedure. There is Mr M—l, a student, who on, lifting up the head of the subject, declared it at once to be Jamie, and many others coincided in his opinion. If these gentlemen will now come forward and state upon oath, to the best of their knowledge, that the body alluded to, was that of James Wilson, or *Daft Jamie*, and the parties that last saw him, – time and place; the party that carried the body to Surgeons Square, – from whom did he receive it, and from whence he carried it; the party that received the body, – from whom and by whom accompanied, with time and place; the party that paid the money for the body, and to whom did they pay it. If in this chain of circumstances there is no proof that HARE has acted a principal part, it is not to be supposed that your Lordship can file a bill against him; but, on the other hand, should your Lordship see the least ground of evidence that can be supported by circumstances, I trust you will, with your wonted alacrity, bring him forward to answer for those crimes of which he seems to be a principal accomplice. Public justice demands it, and the public feeling must be appeased.

In the foregoing statement, your Lordship and the public will perceive, that David P—n did not act the part assigned to him in the public prints; it will be observed that all along it was the assistants to the Doctor that bargained with Burke and Hare for the subjects, and P—n seems to have been made a kind of scape goat; it will also be observed, that long before P—n came into the Doctor's service, Mr M—r, an assistant, had been in the habit of going with Burke and Hare for the bodies, and it is not till very lately that P—n was employed as a go-between the Doctor and Burke and Hare; be this as it may, let the public judge for themselves. From the inquiries I have made respecting him, I find that he is friendless, has uniformly borne a good character, and has refused to return to his situation.

The public are aware that the lecturers on anatomy must be supplied with subjects; a meeting of that respectable body has already taken place on this topic, the result of which I am yet ignorant. But as the public must also be satisfied on this point, I will here detail to your Lordship what facts respecting the procuring of subjects are in my possession. It is next to impossible that any subjects can be got in or within twenty miles of Edinburgh, without the concurrence of the persons employed to watch the ground, which sometimes, but rarely, happens. But at great toil and eminent danger bodies are sometimes procured some thirty miles round, and the schemes and stratagems then employed to ensure a safe deliverance in Edinburgh are truly ingenious. From Newcastle there is generally a good supply, sent in trunks and hampers, either anonymously addressed, or without any address. But previous to this package being sent to the coach office, an invoice, or a letter of advice, is sent by post, stating, that by such a coach, and on such a day, a subject inclosed in a particular box or hamper, with a certain address, or marked soft goods, chrystal, or paper, to be kept dry, will be forwarded accordingly. A person is in waiting at the office to claim such package, pay the carriage, and it is safely deposited in Surgeons Square. Now, it must be very pleasant for an outside passenger to know, that probably he may be sitting cheek by jowl with his deceased grandmother, or perhaps covering the remains of an affectionate wife; nay, our Christmas presents are not exempt from bearing company with, and probably imbibing the effluvia of the deceased. I do not mean to say that the coach proprietors are always aware of the company they carry, but this I know, that at one time they must have been, which the following anecdote will illustrate: a porter, one day in February last, brought a box to a certain Lecture Room, and as this box was very similar to those in which subjects generally came, and without any address or mark; it was understood by the porter, and by those to whom it was delivered, that it contained a subject. Some little time after the porter was gone the box was opened, (as a subject was advised,) but to the utter astonishment of those present, instead of a dead body, there came forth a very fine bacon ham, a large cheese, a basket of eggs, and a huge clue of Hodden grey worsted, – a present, no doubt, from a country cousin, and intended to have reached a different destination. A body in a box without address had come by the same conveyance, and had, no doubt, been changed by mistake; but what the feelings of the party were who received it, judge ye!

I am told that sometimes the resurrection men procure bodies from the Royal Infirmary; the stratagem they make use of is nearly this, they hear by their spies that such a person has died without friends, one goes immediately and claims kindred with the deceased, a coffin is procured, and they are generally removed to some house adjacent for interment. The body, however, does not receive this last token of respect, for with all possible speed a box is procured into which the corpse is crammed and mediately disposed of.

On one occasion, I remember to have witnessed one of the most daring scenes I ever beheld. On turning the corner of Surgeons Square, I observed two men at the trot with a coffin on their shoulders, in open day, they instantly plunged into a certain Lecture Room, the corpse of a female was rolled out on the flour, and the coffin broke in a hundred pieces; they received very little for this body, as some person in the surgical department of the Royal Infirmary had, with an instrument, so mangled the body, as to render it almost useless to any Lecturer. I do not mean to say, that the gentleman who has the sole charge of the surgical department, and through whose hands all bodies ought to pass before their friends can receive them, was in any manner connected with the mangling of the body. But if it was suspected, that the persons claiming the deceased, intended it for dissection, why give it up to them, and if not, why should the body be mangled; possibly this is a new regulation of the Hospital, of which I have not yet heard. I am confident that no blame can be attached to Mr Marshall, his late conduct in tracing and recovering a body out of Mr M'K—'s Lecture Room, places him above the reach of suspicion – So much for home, I will now take a trip to Ireland, which is the grand mart for subjects. There are several agents who supply the Edinburgh Lecturers with subjects, at about £7 each, expences included, these come in lots of ten or twelve, sometimes addressed to one individual, and when such is the case, the other professors attend and cast lots; this is when a general cargo arrives, but the more frequent is for each professor to receive his own barrel, box, or hamper. A large hamper sometimes contains from three to four bodies, packed up with a motely assortment of Irish law papers, or liquid blacking in bottles, or as pickled beef or pork. The usual route of conveyance is by Greenock, Glasgow, and down the Union Canal; in all this, there is nothing dreadfully appalling; bodies must be had, come from where they will, and I think were an act passed, that all those who die upon the parishes or in Hospitals, without friends to inter the bodies, were to be forwarded to the Lecture Rooms, at the professor's expence, it would in a short time, supersede every other method now in use.

Your Lordship, I trust, will pardon me for any expressions in this letter you may consider harsh or improper. I solemnly assure you that such was not my intention. I have merely stated facts, which can be supported upon oath. If I have erred in giving these publicity, it is with a desire that the public should be made acquainted with that portion of this mysterious affair they seemed so anxiously to wish for. Something ought to be done, nay must be done, to appease the public feeling; and I am confident that your Lordship will, to the utmost of your power, endeavour to do so, for which you will not only have the thanks of a wise and discerning public, but all the information that lies in the power of

THE ECHO.

SELECT BIBLIOGRAPHY

OFFICIAL DOCUMENTS
Evidence and Report of the Select Committee on Anatomy, House of
Commons, 1828
'An Act for Regulating Schools of Anatomy', 2 and 3 Will. IV, c. 75, 1832
Hansard, Parliamentary Debates, 1829–32
Home Office Papers in Public Record Office

OTHER PRIMARY SOURCES
Robert Buchanan et al, *Trial of William Burke and Helen McDougal
before the High Court of Justiciary at Edinburgh on Wednesday,
December 24, 1828, for the murder of Margery Campbell, or Docherty*,
(Edinburgh), 1829
'Echo of Surgeons' Square', *Letter to the Lord Advocate, Disclosing the
Accomplices, Secrets, and Other Facts Relative to the Late Murders, etc.*,
Menzies (Edinburgh) 1829
Manuscript diary of a body-snatcher in the Library of the Royal College
of Surgeons, London

ARTICLES, PAMPHLETS, ETC.
Sir Humphrey Rolleston, 'Provincial Medical Schools a Hundred Years
Ago', Cambridge University Medical Society magazine, 1932
*A Laconic Narrative of the Life and Death of James Wilson, known by the
name of Daft Jamie*, W. Smith (publisher), (Edinburgh), 1829

BOOKS
J.B. Atlay, *Famous Trials of the Century*, Grant Richards (London), 1899
Brian Bailey, *The Resurrection Men*, Macdonald (London), 1991
James Blake Bailey (ed.), *The Diary of a Resurrectionist*, Swan
Sonnenschein (London), 1896

James Moores Ball, *The Body-Snatchers*, Dorset Press (New York), 1989

Horace Bleackley, *The Hangmen of England*, Chapman and Hall (London), 1929

Pauline Chapman, *Madame Tussaud's Chamber of Horrors*, Constable (London), 1984

Kellow Chesney, *The Victorian Underworld*, Penguin Books (London) 1982 edn.

Robert Christison, *The Life of Sir Robert Christison, Bart*, (2 vols), Wm Blackwood & Sons (Edinburgh), 1885

Henry Cockburn, *Memorials of his Time*, A. & C. Black (Edinburgh), 1856

C.H. Creswell, *Royal College of Surgeons of Edinburgh* (Edinburgh), 1926.

V. Mary Crosse, *A Surgeon in the Early Nineteenth Century*, E. & S. Livingstone (Edinburgh), 1968

H.C. Darby (ed.), *A New Historical Geography of England after 1600*, Cambridge University Press (Cambridge), 1976

Daniel Defoe, *A Tour Through the Whole Island of Great Britain*, Penguin Books (London), 1971 edn.

Dictionary of National Biography

Hugh Douglas, *Burke and Hare*, Robert Hale (London), 1973

Owen Dudley Edwards, *Burke and Hare*, Polygon Books (Edinburgh), 1980

M. Dorothy George, *London Life in the Eighteenth Century*, Penguin Books (London), 1985

H.J.C. Grierson (ed.), *The Letters of Sir Walter Scott*, Vol XI, 1828–31, Constable (London), 1936

Thomas Ireland (publisher), *West Port Murders*, (Edinburgh), 1829

Alexander Leighton, *The Court of Cacus*, Houlston & Wright (Edinburgh), 1861

J.G. Lockhart, *Memoirs of Sir Walter Scott*, Vol IX, A. & C. Black (Edinburgh), 1869

Henry Lonsdale, *A Sketch of the Life and Writings of Robert Knox the Anatomist*, Macmillan (London), 1870

Ida Macalpine & Richard Hunter, *George III and the Mad-Business*, Allen Lane, the Penguin Press (London), 1969

George MacGregor, *The History of Burke and Hare and of the Resurrectionist Times*, Thos D. Morison (Glasgow), 1884

Peter Mackenzie, *Old Reminiscences of Glasgow and the West of Scotland* (2 vols), J.P. Forrester (Glasgow), 1890

C.S. Parker, *Sir Robert Peel*, Vol II, John Murray (London), 1899

Isobel Rae, *Knox the Anatomist*, Oliver & Boyd (Edinburgh), 1964

Ruth Richardson, *Death, Dissection and the Destitute*, Routledge & Kegan Paul (London), 1987

William Roughead (ed.), *Burke and Hare*, part of *Notable British Trials* series, Wm Hodge (Edinburgh), 1948

George Ryley Scott, *The History of Capital Punishment*, Torchstream Books (London), 1950

Sir Walter Scott, *Journal*, Oliver & Boyd (Edinburgh), 1950

Thomas Stone, *Observations on the Phrenological Development of Burke, Hare, and Other Atrocious Murderers*, (Edinburgh), 1829

John Struthers, *Historical Sketch of the Edinburgh Anatomical School*, Maclachlen and Stewart (Edinburgh), 1867

Cecil Howard Turner, *The Inhumanists*, Alexander Ouseley (London), 1932

Edward Gibbon Wakefield, *Facts Relating to the Punishment of Death in the Metropolis*, Ridgway (London), 1831

West Port Murders, Thos Ireland (Edinburgh), 1829

Sir Llewellyn Woodward, *The Age of Reform, 1815–70*, Oxford University Press (Oxford), 1997

NEWSPAPERS AND JOURNALS
Aberdeen University Review
Blackwood's Edinburgh Magazine
Caledonian Mercury
Dumfries Courier
Edinburgh Evening Courant
Edinburgh Weekly Chronicle
Glasgow Chronicle
Glasgow Herald
Lancaster Gazette
Liverpool Mercury
Medical Times & Gazette
Scots Magazine
The Kaleidoscope
The Lancet
The Quarterly Review
The Scotsman
The Times
Westminster Review

INDEX